Praise for *San Francisco & Beyond:* *101 Affordable Excursions*

"Even natives will be surprised
at the many out-of-the-way,
yet high-quality adventures located by Hegarty,
from experiencing harvest season on a Victorian farm
to visiting the Snoopy Gallery."
—The Bookwatch

"Gives backgrounders on museums,
gardens, children's attractions,
businesses that offer tours, parks, towns,
and seasonal attractions in the Bay Area."
—Motorland Magazine

"The sheer range of Hegarty's choices...
can prove pretty inspiring. A useful resource
for parents who are tired of the local playground."
—Parents' Press

"You'll find that the city's financial district is built
on hundreds of sunken ships abandoned by
gold-seekers. When you visit Portsmouth Square,
you'll be where Robert Louis Stevenson
wrote much of *Treasure Island* and *Kidnapped*."
—Senior Magazine

"Hegarty has spent a good deal of her time combing San Francisco and surrounding areas to discover new, out-of-the-ordinary and fun day trips for visitors with a yen for exploring."
—Inn Room Magazine

"Useful for locals and tourists. Covers outings and activities as far north as Mendocino, south to Carmel and east to Yosemite."
—Oakland Tribune

"These gems aren't your standard, charter bus tour stops. This book should keep us busy on weekends for a few years."
—Peninsula Times Tribune

"Presents the in-depth story behind each excursion, enriched with intriguing histories and fun trivia."
—Contra Costa Times

"Liked being able to visit, enjoy affordable areas within a few hours drive from my home— <u>great book</u>!"
"Gave me ideas to share with overseas visitors."
"Large selection of ideas. Many places I've never heard of."
"Love your text and all the wonderful information it holds. My granddaughter and I loved the Barbie Museum—what a trip!"
"I would buy the next book."
—Satisfied Readers

San Francisco & Beyond

101
Affordable
Excursions

Second Edition

Fun, Historic, Cultural
and Outdoor things to do...

All for $7 or less per person!

by Pamela P. Hegarty

Travel for Less Press

On the Cover: Children get up close and personal with dolphins at the California Academy of Sciences' Steinhart Aquarium. See story in For Kids of All Ages chapter.

San Francisco & Beyond: 101 Affordable Excursions

Copyright © 1992, 1994 by Travel for Less Press
Photo Copyright © 1992 by Pamela P. Hegarty

First edition: January 1992
Second edition: July 1994

Although the author and publishers have made every effort to ensure all information contained herein is accurate and complete, we assume no responsibility for omissions, inconsistencies, inaccuracies, or any other errors. We would appreciate any comments or suggestions for future editions.

ISBN 0-9630791-2-3

Published by   Travel for Less Press
                    209 Apollo Dr., # 5
                    Hercules, CA 94547
                    (510) 741-8440

Printed and Bound in the United States of America

Special Sales: This book is available at special discounts for quantity purchases for promotions or premiums. For more information, contact the publisher.

This book is dedicated to Brian,
to my family
and to the enthusiastic volunteers
who keep these wonderful sites affordable
for all of us.

Table of Contents

WELCOME   1

BEHIND THE SCENES   3

Levi Strauss   *San Francisco*   4
Walking Tours   *San Francisco*   6
Acres of Orchids   *Peninsula*   8
Sunset Magazine   *Peninsula*   10
Long Marine Laboratory   *Monterey Area*   12
Dreyer's Ice Cream   *East Bay*   14
Glass Blowers of Benicia   *East Bay*   16
Takara Sake   *East Bay*   18
California Cooperative Creamery *Sonoma*   20
Anheuser Busch Brewery   *Delta*   22
Jelly Belly Factory   *Delta*   24
Hershey Chocolate Factory   *High Sierra*   26

FOR KIDS OF ALL AGES   29

Academy of Sciences   *San Francisco*   30
Cable Car Barn Museum   *San Francisco*   32
Hyde Street Pier   *San Francisco*   34
Musée Mécanique
  and Cliff House   *San Francisco*   36
Barbie Doll Hall of Fame   *Peninsula*   38
The Tech Museum of Innovation   *Peninsula*   40
Mystery Spot   *Monterey Area*   42
Lawrence Hall of Science   *East Bay*   44
Lindsay Museum   *East Bay*   46
Tilden Regional Park   *East Bay*   48
Snoopy and Skating   *Sonoma*   50
California State
  Railroad Museum   *Sacramento*   52
Travis Air Force Museum   *Delta*   54
Western Railway Museum   *Delta*   56
Mercer Caverns   *Gold Country*   58

WE GOT CULTURE   61

Asian Art Museum	*San Francisco*	62
Chinese Historical Society	*San Francisco*	64
Coit Tower	*San Francisco*	66
de Young Museum	*San Francisco*	68
Fort Mason Ethnic Museums	*San Francisco*	70
Haas-Lilienthal House	*San Francisco*	72
North Beach	*San Francisco*	74
Old Mint and Ansel Adams Center	*San Francisco*	76
Rodin Sculpture Garden	*Peninsula*	78
Rosicrucian Egyptian Museum	*Peninsula*	80
Behring Auto & UC Berkeley Museums at Blackhawk	*East Bay*	82
Judah L. Magnes Museum	*East Bay*	84
Mormon Temple	*East Bay*	86
Oakland Museum of California	*East Bay*	88
Marin Museum of the American Indian	*Marin*	90
Crocker Art Museum	*Sacramento*	92
Towe Ford Museum	*Sacramento*	94

TOWNS TO EXPLORE   97

Half Moon Bay	*Peninsula*	98
Gilroy & Environs	*Monterey Area*	100
Monterey	*Monterey Area*	102
Benicia	*East Bay*	104
Sonoma Plaza	*Sonoma*	106
San Anselmo	*Marin*	108
Sausalito	*Marin*	110
Mendocino	*North Coast*	112
Locke	*Delta*	114
Old Sacramento	*Sacramento*	116
Truckee	*High Sierra*	118
Volcano	*Gold Country*	120

LITERARY LANDMARKS 123

Robinson Jeffers' Tor House	*Monterey Area*	124
Eugene O'Neill's Tao House	*East Bay*	126
Heinhold's Saloon	*East Bay*	128
John Muir Historic Site	*East Bay*	130
Jack London State Historic Park	*Sonoma*	132
Mark Twain in Gold Country	*Gold Country*	134

GARDENS 137

Japanese Tea House & The Conservatory	*San Francisco*	138
Hakone Gardens	*Peninsula*	140
Saso Herb Gardens	*Peninsula*	142
UC Berkeley Botanical Garden	*East Bay*	144
Luther Burbank & California Carnivores	*Sonoma*	146
Mendocino Botanical Gardens	*North Coast*	148

HISTORIC HAUNTS 151

Alcatraz	*San Francisco*	152
Mission San Francisco de Asis	*San Francisco*	154
Peralta Adobe & Fallon House	*Peninsula*	156
San Jose Historical Museum	*Peninsula*	158
Carmel Mission	*Monterey Area*	160
Wilder Ranch State Park	*Monterey Area*	162
Ardenwood Historic Farm	*East Bay*	164
Camron-Stanford House	*East Bay*	166
Shadelands Ranch	*East Bay*	168
Treasure Island	*East Bay*	170
Petaluma Adobe	*Sonoma*	172
China Camp State Park	*Marin*	174
Fort Ross State Historic Park	*North Coast*	176
Sutter's Fort	*Sacramento*	178
Columbia State Historic Park	*Gold Country*	180
Donner Memorial State Park	*High Sierra*	182
Pioneer Yosemite History Center	*High Sierra*	184

THE GREAT OUTDOORS   187

Marin Headlands	*Marin*	188
Muir Woods National Monument	*Marin*	190
Point Reyes National Seashore	*Marin*	192
Richardson Bay Audubon Center	*Marin*	194
Pinnacles		
National Monument	*Monterey Area*	196
Point Lobos State Reserve	*Monterey Area*	198
Mariposa Grove of Big Trees	*High Sierra*	200
Yosemite Camera Walk	*High Sierra*	202

A STATE FOR ALL SEASONS   205

Winter:
Gloria Ferrer Champagne Caves	*Sonoma*	206
Whale Watching	*Marin & North Coast*	208

Spring
Strybing Arboretum	*San Francisco*	210
East Bay Parks	*East Bay*	212

Summer:
Bocce, Baseball		
& Birdwatching	*East Bay*	214
Delta Drive	*Delta*	216

Fall:
Monarch Butterflies	*Monterey Area*	218
Salmon Run, Taylor Creek	*High Sierra*	220

WHERE IT'S AT   223
Maps and Cross-Reference by Geographical Region

FOR YOUR INFORMATION   250
Resources for Lodging, Dining and Regional Information

INDEX   255

ORDER FORM   261

ABOUT THE AUTHOR   262

Welcome

The first edition of this book began with a discovery. In reviewing the hundreds of travel stories I've published on northern California, I discovered that the majority of them—many of my favorites—are surprisingly affordable. More than half are free!

The second edition is inspired by people like you. The enthusiastic response we received from readers of our sold-out first edition prompted this updated version. We are delighted that this guide sparks the spirit of exploration and helps people enjoy our backyard treasures.

San Francisco and Beyond is more than a region. It is a bounty of fun activities, fascinating histories, intriguing cultures and unparalleled natural beauty. Best of all, these precious gems can fit anyone's budget.

More than a quick listing, here are the in-depth stories behind these top-notch sites. *San Francisco & Beyond: 101 Affordable Excursions* is a storybook, keepsake and where-to guide all rolled into one. It will entertain you and inspire you to explore facets of California you may never have known existed.

These excursions are organized by "get out and see it" topics, followed by a geographical cross-reference section for easy planning.

You'll go "Behind the Scenes" at a glassblower's studio, an ice cream factory and one of the world's largest orchid growers.

"Kids of All Ages" will climb aboard antique railroads, defy gravity and design a bike on computer.

You will explore cultural enclaves, "Historic Haunts," hidden gardens, authors' homes and much more.

Make a day of it. Many of these excursions take less than two hours. With the spotting maps in the "Where It's At" cross-reference section, you can plan to visit more than one site in an area, perhaps bring a picnic lunch along.

If you want to spend even more time in a certain area, the "For Your Information" chapter lists unbeatable sources for information on activities, restaurants, inns and hotels—all free for the asking.

The trend is clear. More of us are enjoying shorter, activity-filled trips. If you have a free day or weekend, this guide is your key to spur-of-the-moment excursions that are fun, intriguing, exciting, enlightening and, best of all, surprisingly affordable!

☜ *Levi Strauss Factory*

It carries America's oldest apparel trademark. It was declared an essential commodity by the U.S. government during World War II. It's been enshrined in the Smithsonian. It's been worn by toddlers, teenagers and presidents. Today, it's sold in more than 60 countries.

It is none other than Levi's denim jean. You can learn the history of this American fashion icon and see how they are stitched together in San Francisco at the oldest functioning Levi's factory in the world..

The man behind these world-renowned pants is German-born Levi Strauss. In 1853, his brother-in-law, sensing opportunity in San Francisco during the booming gold rush years, convinced Strauss to join him here and expand the family's dry goods business.

Like any good salesman, Strauss soon discovered that what his clients, the miners, really wanted were heavy, sturdy pants that wouldn't wear out in the diggings. "Cotton duck" canvas was swiftly transformed to what Strauss called "waist-high overalls." He never liked the term "jeans," a word derived from the cotton trousers worn by sailors from Genoa, Italy.

The miners loved them, but, as legend has it, they complained that the weight of gold nuggets ripped their pockets. Nevada tailor Jacob Davis hit upon the solution. He began applying metal rivets to stress points—at pocket corners and the bottom of the button fly—but he didn't have the finances to pay for filing the patent. He became partners with Strauss, his fabric-supplier, and the rest is history.

If you're wondering where the name "501" for today's original shrink-to-fit, button-fly Levi's came from, it was the initial catalog number in the 1890s. Over the last century, the Levi's 501 design has become an American classic.

The factory tour begins with a ten-minute retrospective of Levi's commercials from the late 1960s to early 1980s to give you a taste of the Levi's mystique. Not just a durable working pant, Levi's came to represent the ideals of the rugged west and the uniform of the counterculture.

A small museum contains historic photos, a copy of Strauss' patent, a pair of brown duck pants from the turn of the century, original 501 jeans from the 1930s and other styles of Levi's clothing through the years.

Upstairs, you can peek into the styling department where designs for next season are created. This room is devoted to the Dockers line.

You also look in on Levi's laboratories. One is devoted to product evaluation. You may see an employee tugging and inspecting new materials to see if their quality matches Levi's needs. The second research laboratory, with its bottles of colored liquids, is where innovative treatments are concocted, such as the trendy stonewashed jeans.

Downstairs, you can walk past rows of workers piecing blue jeans together. Some sew just the pockets, others press open seams or punch in rivets, still others inspect the finished pants. By the time you finish your tour of Levi Strauss, you'll have a new appreciation for your old blue jeans.

Reserve as early as possible for the tour. Groups book ahead and individual spots often sell out in advance. Some overseas visitors reserve months in advance just to be sure they can get on the tour during their visit to San Francisco. Allow about 1 1/2 hours for the tour.

Levi Strauss Factory Tour
250 Valencia at 14th St., San Francisco
415/565-9159
Tours Wed. 10:30 & 1
Free

👁 *Walking Tours of San Francisco*

Did you know that San Francisco's financial section is built on hundreds of sunken ships abandoned by gold-seekers? That Robert Louis Stevenson wrote a goodly part of *Treasure Island* and *Kidnapped* in Portsmouth Square? That Mark Twain met the original Tom Sawyer where the Transamerica pyramid now stands?

You may learn these fun facts about San Francisco and much more on the free Friends of the Library City Guides walking tours. This is certainly one of the city's best bargains, led by enthusiastic guides who know and love San Francisco as well as anyone. More than a dozen different tours are offered, including City Hall, Haight/Ashbury, Pacific Heights Mansions and Historic Market Street. Each tour is unique.

The financial section isn't exactly on the top of the typical tourist's list, but the Gold Rush City walk sheds new light on the fascinating history of the area. The group meets in front of the Transamerica pyramid on the corner of Montgomery and Clay, an appropriate location to begin a talk about how San Francisco burst into a major metropolis.

In 1848, Montgomery Street was the shoreline of a sleepy mission town called Yerba Buena. Clay Street was a pier, when suddenly—Gold! The discovery in the Sierra sparked a rush like none ever seen. By 1850, California's population exploded from 10,000 to more than 100,000 men and several hundred women.

Sailing ships deluged the harbor, but captains and crews deserted them to head for the golden mountain. Some masts were torn down and used as tent poles. Other ships became laundries, hotels and brothels. Eventually, the remains of about 400 ships were scuttled and used as landfill, along with garbage and sand, for the growing city.

A rooming house once stood on the Transamerica pyramid site. Some of the renowned guests include writers Mark Twain, Robert Louis Stevenson and Bret Harte. Twain met a fireman in the public baths downstairs whose name he took a fancy to—Tom Sawyer.

A walk across the street reveals often-overlooked plaques celebrating the Pony Express. During the Express' short heyday, riders carried the mail as far west as Sacramento, where it was ferried by ship to Clay Street pier.

Robert Louis Stevenson enjoyed spending time in nearby Portsmouth Square, now the heart of Chinatown. From a bench here, he could look out and see the many sailing ship masts that inspired *Treasure Island* and *Kidnapped*. Today, a monument commemorates the site.

The group heads north on Montgomery to see some of the finest examples of San Francisco's earliest streets. Two brick buildings constructed during the gold rush were some of the few that survived the 1906 quake, but had to be abandoned after the 1989 quake.

Gold Street is one of the few remaining narrow, originally waterfront alleys. It's connected to Jackson Street by short Balance Street, whose name is from the ship, Balance, upon which it was built.

Gold Rush City is just one of more than a dozen different tours offered year-round. Some meet on weekdays. Most are scheduled on weekends. For a schedule of tours, send a self-addressed, stamped envelope to the address below or call to hear a recording of upcoming tours. Expect to spend about 1 1/2 hours for each walk.

City Guides, Friends of the Library
Main Library, Civic Center, San Francisco 94102
415/557-4266
Generally, tours scheduled Tu.-Th. Noon;
Sat. & Sun. at various times
Free

👁 *Acres of Orchids*

From happy, golden "dancing dolls" to bridal white "snowdrift," orchids are the largest and arguably the most beautiful flowering group in the plant kingdom.

About 30,000 species and more than 1,000,000 hybrids of orchids flourish in every country in the world except the polar regions. Thousands of new varieties have been created at Rod McLellan's Acres of Orchids in South San Francisco, the world's foremost orchid hybridizer.

Neophyte gardeners and orchid aficionados alike shouldn't miss the Acres of Orchids tours held at 10:30 and 1:30 daily. You can see how these intricate flowers are cultivated, enjoy the colorful variety of blooms in their stunningly beautiful visitor center and purchase a favorite for your home with complete instructions on care and feeding.

Plan to spend about an hour for this look into the horticulture of orchids and the history of the McLellan family in California's floral industry.

The family business began back in 1859 when Rod McLellan's grandfather, David, came west with his new bride to explore the gold country. They soon discovered that panning for gold wasn't the road to riches. Instead, they started growing vegetables and sold them to prospectors.

The love of growing was passed through the generations. David's son, Edgar, delved particularly into flowers. He realized the enormous potential in the San Francisco area's fine growing climate and the high demand for flowers back East. The McLellan family was instrumental in developing the state's air freight industry and new packaging methods in the shipment of perishable products.

One popular item was the gardenia corsage, which was invented here. On the tour, you can watch workers carefully assemble and package these delicate, sweet-smelling corsages for shipment around the country.

Greenhouses cover a good part of McLellan's 35 acres of land in South San Francisco, the base of operations which also handles products from a 112-acre Watsonville farm.

Although they grow gardenias, eucalyptus and a variety of cut flowers, they are best known for their orchids, thanks to the third generation of McLellans, Rod, known as "the orchid grower's orchid grower."

The tour winds through the maze of greenhouses where orchids are hybridized, cultivated and repotted. One greenhouse is "the nursery in the nursery."

The plants begin with a fine, powdery substance, the tiniest seed in the world. The seeds are placed in a jar with a gel-like mixture of water, sugar and agar, which is powdered seaweed.

Acres of Orchids also uses a cloning process to reproduce orchids, but either way, the cultivator must be meticulous and patient. In a sterile lab, specialists in white coats use a tweezers to thin tiny leaves half the size of your baby fingernail from one jar to another. It takes four to seven years before the plant is mature enough to bloom.

Allow time to browse in McLellan's visitor center. Its conservatory setting perfectly displays an enticing selection of floral-inspired gifts and orchids. Although 80% of their plants are sold wholesale, you can buy one for your home here or through their mail-order catalog. Contrary to popular belief, orchids are not difficult to grow, according to McLellan's experts. The confusion stems from the wide variety of orchids. Knowledgeable sales associates recommend the best plants for your climate and lifestyle.

Acres of Orchids
1450 El Camino Real, South San Francisco
Open daily 9-6; tours daily 10:30 and 1:30
415/737-2452
Free

👁 *Sunset Magazine*

Did you ever wonder why the recipes in *Sunset Magazine* taste so good? This behind-the-scenes tour of the magazine's offices reveals the answer. You're invited to look in on their busy kitchen, where every recipe is tested and retested three or more times before finding its way onto the pages of *Sunset*.

The tour begins in the main office building, which feels more like a home than corporate headquarters. If not for the reception desk in the lobby, you'd think you were entering a tastefully decorated living room, complete with 16th-century antiques.

Picture windows frame Sunset's famous gardens. Comfortable sofas invite you to relax and browse over *Sunset* books and magazines. They are displayed proudly but unobtrusively on the bookshelves and coffee tables.

Finely woven Native American rugs warm the desert tile floor. Western paintings, including the 1884 "Among the Giant Redwoods" and 1881 "Grisly Giant" by renowned landscape artist Thomas Hill, often are displayed. Sunset embraces its motto as "the magazine of western living."

Sunset first appeared in May 1898 as a publication of the Southern Pacific Railroad, who designed it to entice settlers to the west. Its name is derived from the Sunset Limited, the train that ran from New Orleans to Los Angeles. Its first front cover, displayed as a poster near the lobby, shows one of today's most recognized west coast landmarks, a view of the Golden Gate—but without the bridge.

In 1928, it was bought by the Lane family and became a regional magazine emphasizing gardening, cooking, home improvement and travel. *Sunset*

Magazine now boasts more than one million subscribers and produces how-to and travel books, instructional videotapes and language workbooks. Although Sunset was bought by Time Warner, its goals, editorial direction and working ambiance remain the same.

On the tour, you can pick up hints on how to display colorful, healthy plants throughout the year on your patio. Containers brimming with bright blossoms are interspersed throughout Sunset's secluded courtyards.

Inside, the spicy aroma of western cooking entices the tour group to the test kitchen. Visitors can peer through the glass wall as Sunset's five food editors test their own recipes and recipes sent in by readers.

What happens to all that delicious food? On one counter, plates of prepared recipes are laid out for the lucky employees at Sunset. If the counter displays a green flag, it means their tastebuds are in for a treat. If the flag is red, it means that the dish must be saved for photography or another special purpose.

Sunset is famous for its gardening advice, and you can learn first-hand tips as the gardener leads you through the beautifully landscaped grounds.

The gardens form a semi-circle around Sunset's perfectly trimmed, 18-hole putting green lawn. The plantings are a mini-version of the west coast from Canada to Mexico, moving from the north coast rhododendrons at one end, through the forests of Monterey to the cactus garden representing Mexico.

It's the perfect inspiration to cultivate Sunset's gardening tips into your own landscape. For even more inspiration, peek into the gift shop, with its selection of garden supplies, cooking gifts and, of course, all the *Sunset* books.

Sunset Magazine Tour
Corner of Willow and Middlefield Rds.,
Menlo Park
415/324-5479
Mon.-Fri. 10:30 & 2:30
Free

👁 *Long Marine Laboratory*

How do marine mammals think? What do they eat? How is their physiology affected by diving into the ocean depths? Just how deep can a dolphin or sea lion dive? Students at the UC Santa Cruz Long Marine Laboratory are researching the answers to these types of questions. You're invited to share in this intimate learning experience.

Long Marine Lab is located just beyond Natural Bridges State Park, along the coast north of Santa Cruz. You have to drive off the beaten path past fields of Brussels sprouts to get here, but you'll be rewarded with a compact aquarium, small museum and friendly docents to show you the sequestered tanks of sea lions.

One impressive exhibit is Long's 85-foot blue whale skeleton, one of only two blue whale skeletons in California. The docent will tell you that the blue whale is the largest animal that ever lived— larger even than a Brontosaurus. This whale washed ashore at nearby Pescadero. The immense skeleton is displayed in the courtyard, dwarfing the lab's small work trailers that encircle it.

Inside the museum is a piece of baleen, the fibrous material through which whales eat. The largest animal eats some of the world's smallest creatures—krill—thousands of pounds of them each day. A collection of scrimshaw recalls the era when these extraordinary animals were extensively hunted.

The museum is squeezed into a trailer, but it holds several intriguing pieces. The sea otter skeleton reveals a bone structure similar to dogs and cats, especially the legs. The otter is one of the only sea animals that depends solely on its fur for warmth. Other sea creatures have blubber to keep warm. The otter was hunted almost to extinction for its dense coat, with some 600,000 hairs per square inch of fur.

Long's cozy aquarium focuses on life in nearby waters. Tanks are filled with rose-colored anemones, a slithering eel and camouflaged fish. Kids plunge their hands into the cool water of the touch tank to feel its seastars and anemones and see them close-up.

If you're lucky enough to be visiting on a day when it's allowed, a docent will escort you to the marine mammal research area. You may see a California sea lion, harbor seal or bottle-nose dolphin. Students conduct hands-on research here to investigate such areas as cognitive thinking, diving physiology and eating habits.

The students' first goal, no matter what the animal, is to teach them to become used to humans so they can be hand-inspected periodically for illness. Once comfortable, the animals here seem to truly enjoy the company of the students who clean the pools or conduct studies.

This is a working laboratory, and you may not get to see all the animals close-up if a training experiment is in progress, but a path up the hill above affords an overview of all the lab activities and a unique peek at our friends from the sea.

Long Marine Laboratory
End of Delaware Ave. (along the coast)
Santa Cruz
408/459-4308
Tues.-Sun. 1-4
Free

☞ *Dreyer's Grand Ice Cream Factory*

How many licks does it take to polish off your average ice cream cone? Dreyer's official answer is 50, but I think we all should chip in and devote more tastefully conducted research to this savory question.

A great place to start is at the Dreyer's Grand Ice Cream Factory, where you're invited to watch this luscious dessert being made. Best of all, by the end of the tour, you'll graduate to official "ice cream taster for the day." Your first duty—to taste a generous sampling of two favorite flavors.

California produces the most ice cream in the United States, a good chunk of it right here in the East Bay. Dreyer's Grand Ice Cream Factory creates some 65,000 gallons of their frozen specialty every 24 hours.

It all began in 1928 with confectioner Joseph Edy and ice cream maker William Dreyer, who is credited with inventing Rocky Road, Toasted Almond and Peppermint ice creams. Over the decades, some 300 unique flavors have been introduced commercially. About 100 different flavors are distributed each year.

The "Grand" refers to their original store on Oakland's Grand Avenue. Now, the company retains the name as a reminder of their commitment to quality. Just how committed are they? The tastebuds of their discriminating "Official Taster," who has the final say in quality, are insured for a cool $1 million.

As you can see, becoming an "ice cream taster for the day" should not be taken lightly. Your tour begins in the brightly decorated ice cream parlor tasting room. A video fills you in on the company history, then walks you through the production process, showing close-ups of the machines.

Once you've donned your official taster cap, you head up the Marble Fudge stairs to Rocky Road

Lane. Windows overlook the grand production floor below, with its shiny silos, computerized measuring machines, flavor vats and freezers. The distinctive Dreyer cartons glide along conveyer belts, are filled, capped and shrink wrapped.

When is the best time to eat ice cream? You'll find out when the guide takes you downstairs and passes around a just-filled carton. It is in this "soft-serve" stage that you can immediately distinguish flavors. This is the "ATT" test for Appearance, creamy and smooth Texture and, of course, Taste. We tested "Strawberry Cheesecake Chunk." Need I say more?

Once filled, the cartons move into the hardening room, where they stay at minus 40°F for about six hours. The next stop for the ice cream, and those on the tour, is the minus 20°F Cold Box warehouse. You can take a quick, frosty walk into the Cold Box, which can hold more than 1,000,000 gallons of ice cream.

The best part of the tour is dessert. Back in the tasting room, you can choose two of about a dozen flavors. You may get Chocolate Chip Cookie Dough, a comparatively new flavor that's risen to #2 in popularity after Vanilla. Chocolate lovers are sure to be satisfied with their choice. And the diet-conscious can indulge in the frozen yogurt, no sugar added or lactose-reduced flavors. Congratulations. You are now an official ice cream taster for the day.

Call as soon in advance as possible to reserve this tour, especially if you're bringing a group. Individuals can sometimes hook up with groups on shorter notice. Children younger than first grade are not permitted on the tour.

Dreyer's Grand Ice Cream Factory
1250 Whipple Road, Union City 94587
One mile east of Hwy. 880, Whipple Rd. exit
510-471-6622
Tours Mon.-Fri. 9:15, 11:15 and 2, by appt. only
Tours confirmed two months in advance
$2 per person

👁 *Glass Blowers of Benicia*

The Pope and Robin Williams may not see eye-to-eye on much, but they do share one thing in common. Both have used the stylish art glass of Yuba Arts, three small, unassuming studios located in the outskirts of Benicia, about an hour's drive east of San Francisco. Nourot Glass created 2,000 communion bowls for the 1987 Papal Mass in San Francisco. Williams imbibes from Smyers' distinctive glassware.

Smyers was the first studio to move to Benicia more than twenty years ago. Now, two more studios, Zellique and Nourot, share this off-the-beaten-path location.

During the week, you can visit these three studios, known collectively as Yuba Arts, and watch the artists blow molten glass into enviable masterpieces. Usually, at least one glassblower is at work on any given weekday from about 10 A.M. to 4 P.M. In their showroom, you can purchase finished pieces and one-of-a-kind creations. Seconds sell for near wholesale prices.

Although they share the love of glass, blowing technique and a common location, each studio has a unique style, distinctive in look and sensation.

Nourot encompasses the talents of three artists, Michael Nourot, Ann Corcoran and David Lindsay. Michael Nourot studied at the respected Venini Factory in Italy. He incorporates traditional Italian glass blowing techniques into his contemporary designs. Nourot creations are exhibited in galleries across the United States, in Europe and Japan.

This studio creates perfume bottles and vases in deep jewel tones of cobalt blue, emerald green and ruby red. When First Lady Hillary Rodham Clinton traveled overseas, she brought a small collection of Nourot's perfume bottles to present as gifts that showcased some of the best of American artistry.

Next door to Nourot is Smyers Glass. Smyers' distinctive glassware has been featured in *Bon Appetit, Gourmet, Architectural Digest* and *Metropolitan Home*. Bette Midler, Tina Turner and Richard Dreyfuss are a few of the celebrities who entertain guests with Smyers pitchers and stemware. Their Morocco line of glassware features 24-karat gold accents. Like all Yuba Arts glass, each piece is individually handblown.

Zellique Art Glass is the creation of Joseph Morel, who opened his studio in Benicia in 1980. He has spent more than twenty years perfecting his craft, but still strives to give people "a moment out of the ordinary."

His "Seascape" paperweights, perfume bottles and vases seem almost alive in capturing the gracefulness of the underwater world. The Cupriz Collection incorporates stunning but soothing colors with elegant shapes. Zellique glass is sold in many galleries, gift shops and fine art museums as well as upscale department stores like Nordstroms. Prince Andrew and the Queen of Holland are some of the luminaries who have received Morel's art as gifts.

After you visit the studios, stop by the showroom to see the exquisite finished products. Some pieces are seconds. They sell for as little as a third of retail. They aren't defective, but have some cosmetic fault, such as a small bubble in the glass. Some may be slightly larger or smaller than standard. You also can find perfectly made prototypes, one-of-a-kind experiments that aren't sold to retailers. It's an excellent place to find a unique gift or begin your collection of art glass.

Yuba Arts Glass Studios
East end of H St., near 6th St., Benicia
Nourot 707/745-1463
Smyers 707/745-2614
Zellique 707/745-5710
Glass Blowing Mon.-Fri. 10-4
Showroom open Mon.-Sat. 10-4, Sun. Noon-5
Free

☜ *Takara Sake USA*

Takara Sake may be the most unusual "winery" in California. First, it's in Berkeley, far from the vineyards of wine country. That's because sake is made from rice, not grapes. Unlike grape wine, sake is traditionally served warm, although trendsetters now enjoy it at room temperature or chilled. And sake should be drunk right away rather than aged— the fresher, the better.

You can learn more about this popular Japanese drink and try a free taste of the pungent, potent potable at Takara Sake USA. The tasting room is a threshold to old Japan, with low-slung wooden benches, an oriental-motif mural on the rich wooden walls and immense screened lanterns hanging from the ceiling.

Before stepping up to the tasting bar with its five types of sake and three different plum wines, ask to see the short slide show. It gives you a behind the scenes peek into how tradition and technology combine to create today's sake.

The Japanese first enjoyed sake about 2,000 years ago. In the beginning, it was reserved for only the most holy of religious events. The "Toji," or sake master, was considered an artist whose skills were revered. Over the centuries, it has become a standard in Japanese celebrations. Today, sake is the second-most consumed alcoholic beverage in Japan, after beer.

Sake is made with the simplest of ingredients: rice and water. Brown rice from the Sacramento Valley is milled and finely polished, then soaked and steamed. A culture, or "moyashi," is added to create a "rice koji," which converts the rice starch to sugar. More cooked rice, a special yeast and water is added and the mixture ferments at 59°F for 20 days.

After fermentation, solids are removed, leaving behind the raw sake. The sake is then pasteurized and aged in stainless steel tanks for five to six months.

The final step blends batches of sake to perfect the flavor and body. Where most vintners use descriptions like mellow, fruity or full-bodied, sake balances five unique characteristics: sweetness, sourness, bitterness, astringency and pungency.

Sho Chiku Bai is their most popular brand. At the tasting bar, it's served warm, just a touch above body temperature. The silky Ginjo Sake, made from a highly polished rice, is the connoisseur's choice. It has a longer, colder fermentation and is more aromatic than other sakes.

Most unusual is the Nigori Sake, which is unfiltered and appears thick and milky. They also offer a dry sake and draft-style Nama Sake.

The Takara Mirin is a cooking sake, used in marinades, glazes and teriyaki sauce. Plum wines are much sweeter, appropriate as a dessert wine.

You can buy reasonably priced bottles and gift sets here. Bottles sell from $5 to $9 and gift sets, with a bottle, china serving pitcher and four cups, sell for $12.

To taste your Sho Chiku Bai in the Japanese tradition, drink it warm. Pour the sake into the china pitcher, or "tokkuri," and place it in a pan of boiling water. Remove pan from heat and let the sake warm for about 5 minutes. Then pour the warmed sake in the small cup, or "sakazuki," and enjoy.

Takara Sake USA Inc.
708 Addison St. at University Ave.
just off Highway 80, Berkeley
510/540-8250
Tasting daily Noon-6
Free

☜ *California Cooperative Creamery*

Do you know someone crazy about cows? Then you'll find that perfect gift at The Creamery Store in Petaluma. Herded into one compact boutique are more than 600 items inspired by the distinctive black and white markings of California's dairy cows, from coffee cups to soap dispensers, cocktail napkins to gift wrap.

The gift shop is a spin-off from one of the area's leading businesses—the California Cooperative Creamery. The cooperative's dairies produce more than one million gallons of milk every day. On the creamery's behind-the-scenes tour, you can see how that milk is made into our state's favorite cheeses.

A 15-minute video illustrates the cooperative's history and the massive inner workings of the creamery. It all began in 1913 with 33 Sonoma and Marin County dairies. Their 1,900 cows yielded about 6,650 gallons of milk each day, which was brought to the fledgling cooperative in horse-drawn wagons. Most of the milk was churned into butter for the San Francisco market.

Today, you'll see immense, two-tank stainless steel trucks bringing the milk from the dairies to the creamery. At last count, their 540-plus dairies milked more than 125,000 cows twice a day, yielding more than a million gallons. The guide will lead you back into the working creamery. You can watch through a window as ultra-modern machinery transforms 5,000 gallons of milk at a time into one batch of your favorite Monterey Jack or Cheddar.

Everything is shiny stainless steel, from the heating tanks to the mixing tables. After the milk is heat pasteurized, a secret starter culture is added. Only the creamery's master cheesemakers know its precise ingredients. The milk is then heated in large tanks until, at a certain temperature, it becomes curds and whey.

Most of the whey, which is liquid protein, is sent back to the dairies to feed the cows. The curds, more the consistency of scrambled eggs, are pumped onto long, 5,000-gallon mixing tables where the remaining whey is drained off. Pailfuls of salt and hot peppers, for hot pepper jack, are added by hand.

The cheese is then vacuumed off the table and sent into 23-foot-high chutes where it is fashioned into huge blocks. These blocks are sold wholesale or cut and packaged into the familiar random-size portions we buy in our local supermarket. All together, the process from milk to a block of cheese takes about six hours.

Back at the gift shop, you can taste free samples of the freshly made cheese, buy your favorite brands to enjoy at home and order gift boxes to be sent to those on your gift list along with, perhaps, a 12-ounce, chocolate fudge cow pie.

California Cooperative Creamery
711 Western Avenue, Petaluma
707/778-1234
Store open Mon.-Fri. 9-5; Sat. 10-5
Tours Mon.-Sat. 11-3, starting every hour
Large groups should book ahead
Free

Extra Tip...Did you know that cheddar cheese, like fine wine, is aged? Cheddars are aged in large refrigerated warehouses kept between 35° to 40°F. Mild cheddar is aged about 30 days, Medium three to six months. Sharp is aged six to nine months and Extra Sharp for more than one year. Monterey Jack, on the other hand, usually is best eaten within 120 days. Generally, Monterey Jack gets bitter with age. Cheddar gets better. But your palate is your best guide.

👁 *Anheuser Busch Beer Brewery*

When you tour this massive plant in Fairfield, you'll know why Budweiser is the "King of Beers." This is the largest brewery in the world. You're invited to walk above, around and through the fermenting and bottling buildings. At the beginning of the tour, you can taste free samples of Anheuser Busch's diverse line of beers, with sodas for the kids. And the gift shop has a wide selection of logo key chains, steins, cooler paks and more.

This brewery produces about 4 million barrels of beer every year. Their three bottle lines and two can lines fill about 7,000,000 bottles or cans every twenty-four hours, the equivalent of more than one million six-packs of beer. The brewery is abuzz with activity and whirring machinery 24 hours a day, seven days a week, 365 days a year.

The company has come a long way since Eberhard Anheuser acquired a small, debt-ridden brewery in St. Louis, Missouri. His son-in-law, Adolphus Busch, turned it into an industry giant.

Busch introduced Budweiser in 1876 as a new brand created with traditional, time-consuming methods and the finest barley malt, hops and rice. Following that success, he added the Michelob brand in 1896 as "a draught beer for the connoisseurs."

The famous Budweiser Clydesdales first pulled the bright red and green beer wagon in April, 1933 to mark the end of Prohibition. The Clydesdales traveled from the St. Louis brewery to New York's Empire State Building and on to the White House to deliver one of the first post-Prohibition cases of Budweiser. You won't see the Clydesdales at this brewery. Although frequently seen in parades and at fairs, they're kept in other parts of the country.

Today, Budweiser is the largest selling beer in the world, the guide will tell you. A video illustrates the 13-step process involved in creating this King of

Beers, from grinding the barley malt and rice to beechwood aging to cold filtering.

The beechwood aging takes place in immense, stainless steel aging tanks stacked three levels high. Just how much beer is in one of these tanks? If you were to drink one case of beer every day for 60 years, you'd just about finish it. A strong odor welcomes you as soon as you step into the aging room. It smells, well, like a brewery.

Before filling the tanks, a worker walks through placing a layer of beechwood chips, which come exclusively from Tennessee, and yeast on the bottom. The beer is added and allowed to age in the tank for 23 to 27 days, depending on the brand. Then it is filtered twice and sent on to bottling.

Most of the process you'll see on the tour is bottle filling and the packaging of beer. Machinery takes up almost all of this cavernous room. Armies of bottles are mechanically removed from boxes and clink and teeter along conveyor belts.

Huge, rapidly spinning silver domes fill the bottles. They are crowned with the metal caps, then march along a conveyor belt to the pasteurizer. Here, they are heated gradually to 120-140° for 45 minutes. Next, they continue to labeling and packaging.

The tour also includes close-ups of the can and keg lines, even the machine that makes case boxes out of flat, printed pieces of cardboard.

Wear comfortable, closed-toe, closed-heel shoes and bring a sweater for the cool aging room. Also, the machinery is LOUD. And children under 5 are not allowed on the tour. But don't worry if you're the designated driver. Anheuser Busch also makes a non-alcoholic beer you can taste.

Anheuser Busch Brewery Tour
3101 Busch Drive, Fairfield
Chadbourne Rd. exit off I-80, right to Busch Dr.
707/429-7595
Tours Tu.-Sat. 9-4; Shop open Tu.-Sat. 8-5
Free

👁 *Jelly Belly Factory*

This is the sweetest deal anywhere. The fascinating tour of the Jelly Belly factory alone is worth the trip. But you also get free samples at various stops on the tour. You receive a free souvenir bag of jelly bellies. And you can buy goodies to bring home from the gift shop, including "belly flops," odd-shaped but just as delicious Jelly Bellies sold at about two-thirds less than retail price.

Jelly Belly's new "Candyland Tour" takes you along an elevated walkway with a fantastic view of the factory below. Children of any age are invited to journey down Candy Corn Alley, Blueberry Boulevard and Dutch Mint Drive. Windows are at kid-height so they can see without stretching. Handicapped-accessible tours also are available.

Jelly Bellies are not an ordinary jelly bean. Standard beans only have flavoring in the shell. Jelly Bellies are flavored in the center and in the shell. The secret to their intense, true-to-life taste is the use of all-natural flavors whenever possible. Fruit purees are used in Raspberry, Blueberry and Peach, real peanut butter in Peanut Butter and jalapeno peppers in Jalapeno Jelly Belly beans.

Jelly Belly beans come in 40 gourmet flavors, including Chocolate Fudge, Mai Tai and Toasted Marshmallow. The most popular include Very Cherry, Green Apple, Coconut and Cinnamon.

The Herman Goelitz company, who makes the Jelly Belly, even created a new flavor for their most famous fan, former president Ronald Reagan— Blueberry, in honor of the red, white and blue. Their business boomed during the Reagan years, when a jar of Jelly Bellies was de rigueur in the White House. This is one highlight of the company's long history.

The Goelitz family first began making candy commercially in 1868. Their most popular product was candy corn, now a Halloween standard. Today, the fifth generation of Goelitz's runs the company.

Jelly Bellies, introduced in 1976, are one of their most successful confections. Today, this factory can create more than one million beans per hour and about 100,000 pounds a day at full capacity.

Before the tour begins, watch the 8-minute video. It's a fun introduction to what you'll see and learn from your guide. Once in Candyland, sweet aromas welcome you as you walk by the kitchen and peer over the production floor. The first stop is the moulding process, where candies are shaped in trays, 1,260 beans at a time. The guide hands out samples of this first stage of Jelly Belly, the center with a light sugar coating.

As you walk along, you'll be able to see, and taste, the entire production process of the jelly belly, as well as watch some of their other confections being produced. You'll see brightly hued taffies cooling on the table below you. You'll marvel at the stacks and stacks of jelly belly trays that attest to the 40,000,000 beans they can produce each day. You'll smell chocolate as you pass the area where the chocolate-covered nuts and confections are created. You'll watch as stainless steel barrels spin thousands of Jelly Bellies while the colorful, flavored coating is sprayed on. You'll see packaging machines funnel the brightly colored beans into various packets, sampler bags and gift boxes.

After the tour, indulge in the jelly bellies, packages and gourmet confections in the irresistible candy shop. But remember, although it takes up to ten days to create a Jelly Belly, if you buy a bag, it won't take that long to finish it!

Herman Goelitz Candy Company, Inc.
2400 North Watney Way,
in Solano Business Park, Fairfield
Chadbourne Rd. exit off I-80;
left on Courage Dr.; left on North Watney
707/428-2838
Tours Mon.-Fri. 9-2, no reservations needed
Gift Shop open Mon.-Fri. 9-5; Sat. 10-4
Free

👁 *Hershey's Chocolate Factory*

How many times have you been heading to Yosemite, drive by the Hershey Visitor Center in unassuming Oakdale and say, "next time we should stop and take a tour?" Next time—stop!

This is more than a convenient place to break the drive from the Bay Area to the mountains. It is one of the best factory tours anywhere. And, in their tantalizing shop, you can load up on "high energy" chocolate bars for all those outdoor activities ahead.

Tours begin at the Visitor Center Gift Shop. You may have to wait a few minutes, but you can watch the chocolate-making video or browse among hundreds of chocolate bars and novelty gifts.

A shuttle van transports you the short distance to Hershey's immense plant. Hundreds of thousands of pounds of chocolate are moulded into chips, kisses, Reese's cups and candy bars here every day.

This is the legacy of Milton Hershey, the company's founder and a name now synonymous with chocolate. By all accounts, Milton didn't show much promise as a young man. He tried and failed at many ventures in such far-flung places as Denver, New York, Chicago and New Orleans. When he returned to his native Pennsylvania in 1886 at the age of twenty-nine, he was virtually penniless.

Hershey's luck changed when family and friends helped him develop a "melt in your mouth" caramel made with milk. By 1894, he was living the sweet life as one of his city's most substantial citizens.

Hershey tasted his first chocolate at age 36 at the World's Fair Colombian Exposition in Chicago. One bite convinced him that this is where his fortune lay. He immediately bought the German chocolate-making machinery at the Exposition and was soon producing 114 varieties of fancy candies.

Today, you'll see Hershey's popular chocolates being produced by the thousands at this plant. The luscious aroma of chocolate greets you at the door. Inside awaits a multitude of magical, moving machinery that would make Willie Wonka proud.

One of the first things you'll see is row upon row of chocolate chips gliding along a conveyer belt. You watch through windows as chips are formed and sent into the cooling tunnel. Each pound you buy in the store has about 1,000 chips, so you can imagine how many are needed for all those cookies and ice creams.

One immense room encompasses an army of huge "conche" machines. Each contains up to 10,000 pounds of smooth, liquid chocolate. Large granite rollers push chocolate back and forth. The friction of this movement generates heat up to 200°F.

You'll walk along a conveyer belt moving cans or bottles of Hershey's Syrup at lightning speed as they are filled, sealed, boxed and lifted up elevators.

A mezzanine offers an overview of many of the production lines. You'll see hundreds of Reese's cups being packaged in the bright orange wrapping and dropped down to workers who neatly box them. Another, futuristic computerized production line can create some 1,500 Reese's cups every minute.

Moulded chocolate bars exit their cooling tunnels and ride down elevator systems, are dropped onto belts and wrapped.

As you head back downstairs, you watch as some 4,000 pounds of chocolate kisses come out of their cooling tunnel every hour, are quality checked and wrapped in their distinctive foil. First introduced in 1907, Hershey produces about 9,000,000 kisses each day in this plant.

If all this whets your appetite, you're in for a sweet treat back at the Visitor Center. You can trade in your tour pass for a free chocolate bar. Enjoy!

Hershey's Chocolate USA, Western Plant
120 South Sierra Ave., Oakdale
209/848-8126 (recording)
Tours Mon.-Fri. 8:30-3
Visitor Center open Mon.-Fri. 8:30-5
Free

Notes

For Kids
of All Ages

Academy of Sciences

The California Academy of Sciences in Golden Gate Park is rated one of the top five natural history museums in the country. You can travel to outer space via the Earth and Space Hall and to the ocean depths through the Steinhart Aquarium. You can even travel back in time through their award-winning exhibit on evolution, then marvel at the diversity of life on Earth today through their natural history dioramas.

An eerie blue aura sets the tone for the Earth and Space Hall. Overhead, our solar system's planets spin as they orbit the sun. Below, a Foucault Pendulum appears to rotate as it swings methodically back and forth. In fact, the pendulum moves along a straight line while the Earth rotates beneath it.

One hands-on exhibit guarantees instant weight loss just by finding out your weight on other planets. Simply step on the scale and push the button. On the moon you'll slim down to low double digits, but on Jupiter you'll be more than twice your weight on Earth. Climb the stairs to the shake table of the Safe Quake exhibit to experience two major earthquakes. Scenes from the disaster movie, "Earthquake," flash on the screen as the floor jolts beneath you.

A walk through the Steinhart Aquarium is the next best thing to SCUBA diving. Dolphins somersault and nod playfully at the children who peer into the tank. Smaller tanks contain everything from the Four-eyed Fish, that can see simultaneously above and below the water as it skims the surface, to the Blind Cave Tetra that has no eyes at all.

The crown jewel of the Aquarium is the 100,000-gallon Fish Roundabout. This circular tank swirls around you as you climb the spiral ramp. Sharks, rays and massive deep ocean fish cruise by inches from where you stand.

To see how this diversity of life evolved, don't miss "Life Through Time." It was named the finest exhibit on evolution in the world by the National Science Foundation. A fossil wall, stretching from floor to ceiling, is the threshold to this voyage back in time. Layers of sediment are dotted with fossils, from the stromatolites of 900 million years ago to a 208-million-year-old theropod dinosaur.

What do a horse and a rhinoceros have in common? Learn about evolutionary ancestors on the CD-ROM, interactive computer screens. This state-of-the-art system uses color photos, quizzes and "Life Map" graphs to make learning fun.

As you walk through the millenniums, exhibits show how the first marine vertebrates evolved, why gills became lungs and fins became limbs. Displays include living examples of these evolutionary stages including a lungfish and the amphibious Chinese giant salamander.

A replica of 300-million-year-old forest is inhabited with 8-foot-long millipedes and immense scorpions and dragonflies. The dinosaur age is illustrated with bones, fossil casts and holograms. Weird creatures populate the first stages of the age of mammals.

To find out more about today's mammals, visit the Academy's Wild California room, with its life-like dioramas. Fish swim in the Farallon Islands rookery scene. A fiberglass depiction of "beach wrack" shows a 50-times life-size view of a piece of seaweed cast upon the beach at high tide, where a rove beetle becomes a three-foot monster, offering a new perspective on something most of us overlook. It's just the beginning of what the Academy of Sciences, and the world around us, have to offer.

Academy of Sciences
Golden Gate Park, San Francisco
415/750-7145 (recording)
Open daily 10-5, until 7 P.M. July 4-Labor Day
$7 Adults; $4 seniors and ages 12-17;
$1.50 ages 6-11
Free first Wed. of each month

Cable Car Barn Museum

A trip to San Francisco wouldn't be complete without clinging onto a cable car as it clangs up the steep city streets. But how does it work? And what is that man doing with the huge set of pliers in the middle of the car?

Both kids and adults will have fun learning the answers at the Cable Car Barn Museum at the corner of Mason and Washington streets. Just ask the conductor to call out the stop.

This circa-1907 brick building holds the brawny heart of the world's first mechanized mass transit system, and the last surviving system of its type—the beloved cable car. It's our nation's only moving National Historic Landmark.

As you enter the Museum, head downstairs to the underground viewing room to see the cable enter the powerhouse from beneath the street. Then, follow the constant, vibrating hum upstairs to the balcony overlooking its source. Below, you will see a massive machine. Eight wheels, each 14 feet in diameter, guide and pull the cables for the entire system at a constant 9 1/2 miles per hour.

The cable cars, themselves, have no locomotion. They are pulled by the cables that run beneath the streets of San Francisco. That man on the cable car operating what looked like a huge set of pliers was actually gripping onto the cable to propel the car and letting go of the cable to stop the car. The gripman's job is best demonstrated in the color graphics of the 16-minute video shown continually at the Museum.

It all began in the 1870s with tenacious inventor Andrew S. Hallidie, whose company manufactured wire ropes for the cable railway systems he invented to transport ore in mines.

After witnessing a runaway wagon drag a team of four unfortunate horses down one of the city's steep hills, Hallidie hit upon a new use for his wire rope.

His cable railway system could pull ore up the steep mining grades. Why couldn't an enlarged version transport people over the hills of San Francisco? But like Noah's ark or Tucker's automobile, Hallidie's vision ran into a wall of skeptics who dubbed it "Hallidie's Folly."

Undaunted, Hallidie persuaded a few friends to invest in his dream, threw in all the money he had and sold stock to finance a working model of a cable car.

The official first passenger run of the cable car took place on August 2, 1873. Designed to hold 12 passengers on the grip car and 14 on the coach, 90 glory-seekers squeezed onto the car, starting the tradition of hanging on to the poles. The cable pulled the loaded car successfully up the steep grade. The era of the cable car was launched.

By the late 1800s, San Francisco boasted about 500 cable cars on seven cable car lines requiring 103 miles of track and plenty of Hallidie's wire rope. Cities as far flung as New York, Denver, London and Sydney adopted Hallidie's invention.

At the museum, you can see the first cable car ever built, the same one Andrew Hallidie jockeyed down Clay Street in 1873. The collection of antique cable cars and models illustrates design changes through the years. The cable car you rode on today is the same car our city's forefathers rode at the turn of the century.

After visiting the Museum, take a quick peek into the Cable Car Barn, about 25 feet up Washington Street. It garages the more than 40 cable cars in San Francisco's fleet.

The Cable Car Barn Museum is on both the Powell-Hyde and the Powell-Mason lines. Allow about 1/2 hour for your visit. Cable cars operate from 7:00 A.M. to 12:45 A.M. Rides cost $2 adults (for 2 hours); $1 children 5-17; $.15 for seniors over 65. All-day ride passes cost $6. Tickets can be purchased from the machines at the terminus of each line.

Cable Car Barn Museum
1201 Mason Street, San Francisco
415/474-1887
Open daily 10-5 Nov.-March; 10-6 April-Oct.
Free

Hyde Street Pier

What's the most intriguing site at the San Francisco waterfront? A) Ghiradelli Square B) Pier 39 C) The Cannery D) Hyde Street Pier.

The answer is Hyde Street Pier, a time capsule waiting to be discovered by anyone who veers off the well-traveled tourist beat. Located across the street from the Cannery, thousands of people walk by its unassuming entrance everyday. They don't know what they're missing.

A small fleet of historic ships is berthed here, from the massive, three-masted 1886 Balclutha to the 1890 paddle-wheel ferry Eureka. You're welcome aboard to explore the ships, from the pilot house to the elegant captain's quarters to the cool, dark hold.

Each ship is restored to reflect its heyday. Once aboard the ferry Eureka, you are easily transported to the 1930s when this side-wheeler plied the waters of the Bay. At the time, it was the world's largest passenger ferry, carrying as many as 2,300 people and 120 autos at a time.

Vintage automobiles rest on the wooden planks of the ferry's platform, as though their drivers will return at any moment. Among others, there is a bright red 1937 Diamond T pickup, a blue 1924 Express Wagon, a 1933 Packard sedan, a 1931 Model A Ford U.S. mail truck, even a horse-powered wooden wagon marked "D. Ghiradelli Co. Chocolate•Cocoa•Mustard" and stocked with milk cans.

Through doorways and windows, you can see the ferry's four-story steam engine and its barnacle-encrusted paddlewheels. Upstairs, you can roam through the rows of passenger seats and peer over a counter at the vintage goodies they used to sell during the Bay crossings.

Across the pier, the three-masted 1895 C.A. Thayer sailed as a lumber cargo ship from the Pacific northwest to California, then, from 1925, as an Alaskan cod fisherman in the Bering Sea. The ship is one of two surviving schooners from a fleet of 900 that once transported lumber to California's rapidly growing cities. Its final trip in 1950 was the last commercial voyage by a west coast sailing vessel.

The 256-foot-long, three-masted Balclutha is an iron and steel sailing ship built in 1886 in Glasgow, Scotland. It sailed around the treacherous Cape Horn seventeen times bringing coal from England and returning with grain. From 1903 to 1930, it made yearly voyages between San Francisco and Alaska to bring salmon south and men and supplies for the canneries north. In the hold, crates of fish are stacked from floor to ceiling.

A museum is in midships, with such artifacts as a helmet-diver's outfit, a collection of anchors and a world map showing the Balclutha's travels to exotic ports like Rangoon, Calcutta and Sydney.

One display describes the unfurling of the top-most sail. This duty usually was handed to a young sailor, who had to climb 130 feet up the mast while the ship pitched and yawed. "Keep your eye on your job," older sailors advised, "and don't look down."

Find out more about the sea at the pier's Maritime Store. It offers one of the west coast's best selections of books, prints, postcards and more on maritime subjects. You can take a bit of the salt air home with you in one of their audiotapes with music of the sea.

Historic Ships
Hyde Street Pier, San Francisco
415/556-3002
Open daily 10-6 April-Sept.; 9:30-5 Oct.-March
$3 Adults; $1 ages 12-17; all others free

Extra Tip... Another fascinating ocean vessel is docked nearby at Pier 45 near Fisherman's Wharf. This is the USS Pampanito, a World War II balao class submarine. You can tour its cramped living quarters and view its arsenal of ten torpedo tubes and a 5-inch deck gun. An audio tour describing the submarine and its history is included in the price of admission. Tel. 415/929-0202. (Open daily 9-6; $4 Adults; $2 Seniors and ages 12-17; $1 ages 6-12)

Musée Mécanique & Cliff House

If you want the Nintendo generation to see what mechanical games were like when their grandparents and great grandparents were kids, take them to the Musée Mécanique. This compact fun house is jam-packed with what is probably the largest private collection of coin-operated antique amusements in the world.

All of these 160 or so machines are museum-quality, but instead of ensconcing them behind glass walls, the Musée Mécanique has a hands-on approach. You put coins in the machines to make figures move, find out your fortune or play an early version of pinball, just as your ancestors did more than half a century ago.

Edward Zelinsky and his son, Daniel, are the enthusiastic rescuers and restorers of these mechanical marvels. Some of the games and musical instruments are from Playland-at-the-Beach, which was located nearby. Others came from Europe. The Zelinsky's are constantly adding to the collection.

One of the oldest amusements is the mutoscope from the turn of the century. This was the precursor to motion pictures. Pictures are printed on cards. When the cards are rapidly flipped, the pictures appear to be in motion.

Two of the most intricate and fun machines are the Mechanical Carnival and Mechanical Farm. Other devices predict your fortune, measure your sexual prowess or play a tune with piano, snare drums, flutes or xylophones.

Two unusual miniature working models, dating to 1930s and 1940s England, will seize your attention. One recreates an execution by guillotine, the other a bizarre opium den.

Most of the machines leap into motion at the drop of a quarter, but some cost as little as one cent, bringing back the days of the penny arcade. Old-timers will be glad to see six-foot-tall, red-headed "Laughing Sal," who chortled her way through three decades at Playland-at-the-Beach.

The museum is located downstairs from San Francisco's Cliff House, which is a prime tourist spot in its own right. Today, hundreds of people stop for the majestic scenery and to explore the ruins of the Victorian-era Sutro baths.

This area perched above the rugged Pacific coastline has been attracting visitors for more than 130 years. Where automobiles now vie for parking spaces, carriages once lined up to enjoy the scenery. A character named Captain Foster ran a restaurant here and was well-known for his hospitality and fine food.

Cliff House's popularity weathered financial ebbs and tides in the 1870s. When on the decline in 1883, Adolph Sutro, a Nevada silver king, bought the property. He was determined to make it a top landmark again for the benefit of San Francisco. A journey to the "Cliff" became de rigueur for the Victorian elite.

One of Sutro's most magnificent improvements was the grand, glass-enclosed bathing houses. Swimmers delighted in six sea water and fresh water pools, heated to varying degrees. Bleachers provided seating for thousands of onlookers. Art galleries exercised and cleansed the mind as well.

But the financial tide turned again. The Sutro Baths began losing money and finally closed. A fire burned the abandoned structure in 1966. Today, the ruins below Cliff House are silent reminders of the thousands who once frolicked there.

Musée Mécanique
1090 Point Lobos Ave. (Cliff House)
San Francisco
415/386-1170
Open daily 11-7 weekdays;
10-8 weekends and holidays
Free; Bring change for the machines

🚂 *Barbie Doll Hall of Fame*

She was an astronaut long before women dreamed it possible. She rides horses, hosts barbecues, drives a sports car, acts on the stage and screen, boasts more shoes than Imelda Marcos and never in her 35 years has grown out of her stunning, cutting edge wardrobe. She is every American's dream girl—Barbie.

At the Barbie Hall of Fame Doll Studio in Palo Alto, you can do more than relive girlhood memories of dressing Barbie in frilly evening gowns and mod bathing suits. Adults discover how the fleeting fads of fashion reflect the current culture. Children marvel at the largest collection of Barbie dolls and accessories in the world.

Owner and operator Evelyn Burkhalter has amassed more than 16,000 items of Barbie memorabilia, "just about everything they've made," she said. She began collecting Barbies in the early 1970s. By 1984, she was able to open her Barbie museum in honor of the doll's 25th anniversary. By 1986, the size of the exhibition doubled. She continues to collect every new Barbie item she can find, which is no easy task. Mattel Toys, Inc. releases at least 50 different Barbies every year.

Display cases are brimming with Barbies dressed in everything from nun's habits to mini-skirts. A short tour around this compact museum will take you from the conservative 1950s to the gold-sequined '90s. There are Ken dolls, diminutive, wide-eyed dolls made for the Japanese market, and white, black, Hispanic, Asian and Native American Barbies. Some commemorate historic events, such as the Friendship Barbie released when the Berlin Wall came down.

Barbie's curvaceous figure first appeared in American toy stores in 1959. Only 1/2 million dolls and 1 million costumes were made. All the original dolls' faces were hand-painted by three artists. They lasted just two months on the market before they were sold out.

Before long, one of Barbie's most popular outfits was the "Suburban Shopper," a starched cotton jumper, wide-brimmed hat, straw tote overflowing with fresh fruits and Barbie's first telephone. In the early 1960s, the Friday Nite Date called for a corduroy jumper with a patchwork scene of a birdhouse in a tree and flowers.

In the late 1960s, Barbie went mod, with a new hairstyle and psychedelic clothes, like the 1969 "Flower Wower" mini-dress in a colorful, giant flower print.

In the 1980s, "they even came out with a Yuppie Barbie," said Burkhalter. Barbie's 1986 Day to Night outfit looked like a business suit by day, but at night the jacket comes off to reveal a shiny dancing dress.

Gift sets also show the history of our culture, ranging from backyard barbecue scenes to a workout gym. Special fashions reflect actual uniforms of the day. Through the years, Barbie has been a flight attendant on a number of airlines. Today, she is the pilot.

Burkhalter has greeted people from around the world to her Barbie Hall of Fame Doll Studio. Her museum has been featured on television and in magazines in Japan, Italy, Amsterdam, France, Sweden and Russia, proof that Barbie, the "All-American Girl," is truly a world celebrity.

Barbie Hall of Fame Doll Studio
433 Waverly St., Palo Alto
415/326-5841
Tu.-Fri. 1:30-4:30; Sat. 10-Noon & 1:30-4:30
$2 Adults; $1 Children under 12

Tech Museum of Innovation

You can command a robot arm to spell your name in building blocks. Take an air shower and step into the simulated "clean room," where silicon chips are produced. Design a bike on a computer, then use a computerized marketing program to calculate how many to stock. These are just some of the fun learning exhibits in this innovative museum. It's crammed with activity and the weird noises of working machines.

Your first encounter is one of the third kind. A huge model of the Hubble Telescope explains exactly what went wrong. An interactive video screen allows you to direct a flight across the surface of Mars, dipping into valleys and coursing over hills.

Mars may seem far away, but just How Big is Our Universe? A display explains that if our solar system were the size of a postage stamp, then our Milky Way galaxy would be the size of California and the universe would be the size of our solar system.

Back on earth, see how silicon is transformed to mechanical intelligence. You'll have to take an air shower. It's like walking through an airport security metal detector with puffs of air blowing at you from all sides. This is to expel any dust particles. Chips the size of your fingernail may have one million transistors and even one microscopic particle can ruin the chip.

Just took a shower this morning, you say? Step into the phone-booth-sized particle detector and a meter will reveal how many particles your body is emitting. Scratch your head or jump up and down and watch the meter soar.

A six-foot long, enlarged model of a chip shows how it works. Type in your birthdate and it will calculate the day of the week as you follow the steps on the computer screen. The process is slowed to 87 seconds. Normally, it would take 0.012 seconds.

Robotic arms can be a boon to the handicapped. One on display is programmed to be voice-activated and can answer the phone, get a drink, place food in the microwave and feed a quadriplegic.

An intriguing look into genetic research reveals how these microscopic particles make us who we are. Deformities in genes may be responsible for mental retardation, cataracts and other health problems.

One of the most popular exhibits, especially with high school students, is the bike factory. A three-dimensional imaging system allows you to choose a frame, wheel-type, handlebars and color, then print out your creation to take home with you. You also can sit on a life-size, high-speed, pedal-powered vehicle. The 1986 "Gold Rush," ridden by Fast Freddy Markham, went over 65 mph for 660 feet.

One exhibit is a provoking collection of industry "artifacts." In 1971, the Victor, a bulky calculator larger than a typewriter, was considered top of the line. It could add, subtract, multiply, divide and remember and sold for $1,995. By 1972, a pocket-size calculator with many more functions sold for $395. Today, a solar-powered, credit-card-size calculator sells for $7.

At the Materials Bar, a volunteer shows you how disposable diapers and bulletproof vests are made. You can access CD-ROMs and on-line services in the Info Lounge. You can even enjoy an Astronaut ice cream or a low-tech sandwich at the Cafe or take a piece of fun science home with you from the Gift Store.

The Tech Museum of Innovation
145 West San Carlos, San Jose
(across from Convention Center)
408/279-7150 (recording)
Tues.-Sun. 10-5
$6 Adults; $4 Seniors and ages 6-18
Discounted rate for groups of 12 or more

Mystery Spot

Calling all skeptics! Can a golf ball roll uphill? Does a person shrink when nearing the center of the Mystery Spot? Is it all an optical illusion?

Even its name is hokey, but the Mystery Spot is not only fun but intriguing enough to attract the attention of scientists from NASA and Stanford. It is listed in Ripley's Believe It of Not and was photographed for LIFE Magazine. The day I entered the Mystery Spot, visitors from Japan and Hungary as well as the States were thoroughly enjoying this quirky phenomenon.

Deep in the forested hills above Santa Cruz, the Mystery Spot is a 150-foot circle in which gravity seems to be defied. Trees, people and buildings all lean towards the southwest, as though some force was trying to push them downhill. Why?

The scientists have come with their instruments for 50 years, but not one has a definitive answer. Some believed that "The Force" was actually carbon dioxide escaping from a fissure, which would explain why many visitors feel dizzy or seasick.

The most popular explanation is that a very dense meteor crashed here many centuries ago and now lays underground emitting the force that refracts gravity.

It all started when the land was bought for a summer home site. The surveyors' compasses went wild and the workers felt dizzy and top-heavy. Eventually the owner gave up trying to build his home here and opened this strange place to the public.

The enthusiastic guide begins your tour at the outer limits of the Mystery Spot. Two cement blocks are placed about three feet apart. One person stands on the first block, another on the second. When they exchange places, one person shrinks while the other grows taller. Why? One of the cement blocks is inside the Mystery Spot.

A steep climb up a slippery hill—wear non-slip shoes—brings you closer to the center of the Mystery Spot. A ramshackle wooden cabin here is slanted so severely that, if not for the trees holding it up, it would tumble down the hill. The guide leans a board across the windowsill and places a golf ball on it, but instead of rolling down the board, it rolls up it.

An optical illusion you say? The house is crooked so the board looks like it's slanting up when it's really slanting down? The guide pulls out his level. Sure enough, the ball is rolling uphill, or "the force" is pushing it uphill. The guide invites you to try it out with your own level. Unfortunately, I had left mine at home.

Inside the cabin, the guide offers more demonstrations of the mysterious force. Hanging from a handle in the ceiling of the doorway, he looks like someone is pulling his legs to the side. You can try it, too, to see if you look like someone is pulling your leg. A weight hanging from the ceiling in the next room appears heavier when pushed away from the force and lighter when pushed towards the force.

On either side of the cabin are more spots for shrinking and growing as people exchange places. Maybe it's an excess of carbon dioxide, but even skeptics have trouble explaining this one and I can't deny that this really works. Either the guides are very good magicians or there is indeed an unexplainable force inside the Mystery Spot. In any case, this is a fun, unique attraction, "believe it or not."

The Mystery Spot
1953 Branciforte Dr., 4 miles north of Santa Cruz
Exit Ocean St. from Rte. 17 in Santa Cruz;
Left on Water St.; first left on Market;
Follow Market 3 mi. until it becomes Branciforte
408/423-8897
Open daily 9:30-5
$3 Adults; $1.50 ages 5-11

Lawrence Hall of Science

Have you ever wondered how supermarket scanners work? How primitive Polynesians could navigate across vast stretches of ocean? Or how you can detect the scent of fresh-baked cookies?

With a fun, hands-on approach, the Lawrence Hall of Science shows how science affects everyday lives, even before the word "science" was invented. You can sail an ancient Polynesian craft by computer, create your own laser show, walk inside a huge, electrified model of the human brain and much more. Younger children will delight in some of the displays and games. Most exhibits are geared to complicated processes that will fascinate the serious student and intrigued adult.

This modern, low-slung building sits on a lofty perch high above the UC Berkeley campus. The view alone is worth the curvy drive up the hill. On a clear day, you can see San Francisco, parts of Marin and almost the entire East Bay.

Take time to enjoy the view. The kids will have a blast climbing on the plaza's colorful, 60-foot-long, scientifically accurate model of a DNA helix— the structure that makes each one of us unique.

The Lawrence Hall presents science on a human level. In The Wayfinding Art, models of Polynesian sailing ships illustrate the simplicity in design—a platform stretched between two hollow pontoons.

How do we know where these people sailed? The study of linguistics and archeology determines the common roots of the residents of many south Pacific lands. Press a button to hear how similar the word "fish" or "eye" is in Tagalog and other languages. "Canoe Do It?" challenges you to sail to an island via computer. You're given a limited number of days and provided with daily reports on wind and weather changes.

Another room is devoted to the laser. A cut-away of a supermarket scanner reveals how lasers are used in this fast, new method of totaling the cost of your groceries and keeping inventory at the same time. The laser "reads" the UPC code, that square of black and white vertical lines on the carton, that carries all this information.

Lasers also create holograms, three-dimensional images that defy their flat frames. As you walk by one hologram, a hand stretches out to grab you then waves as you cross by. The most confounding hologram is a pair of binoculars protruding from the wall. Lean forward and peer into the nebulous eyepieces to see a binoculars' magnified point of view of a snake and parrot on the branches beyond.

The key to learning these fun aspects of science is centered in your brain, the subject of another fascinating exhibit. A video shows a woman dissecting a human brain, explaining how certain sections of this mass of tissue help you smell, see, hear and learn.

Inside an immense model of the brain, an interactive computer shows how the simple actions of Little Red Riding Hood employ parts of the brain. When she smells cookies baking, a light flashes on the section of the brain model that controls smell.

On weekends and weekday holidays, seek out the Discovery Labs, where you can stand your hair on end with static electricity, compare your heartbeat with a rabbit's and experiment with pendulums and motors.

The Planetarium offers shows on the constellations. On Saturday nights, you can see the stars and planets first-hand when amateur astronomers meet on the museum's plaza, weather permitting.

Lawrence Hall of Science
Centennial Dr., UC Berkeley
510/642-5132 (recording)
Open daily 10-5
$6 Adults; $4 ages 7-18, Seniors and Students;
$2 ages 3-6

Lindsay Museum

Miracles occur daily at the Lindsay Museum in Walnut Creek. Here you may see a bobcat, who would have died in the wild, play hunting games in the sun-splashed exercise room. You can see a young boy, at first terrified of snakes, reach out to pet one. You may be closer than you've ever been to a bald eagle.

These are some of the more than 7,000 injured, mistreated or abandoned native wild animals that are brought to the Lindsay Museum each year. Whether it's a deer hit by a car, a raptor that struck electrical wires or a nestling that fell from its nest, the ultimate goal is to heal the animal, then return it to the wild.

The 150 native wild animals that reside permanently at the Lindsay were saved but would not survive if returned to their natural habitat. Some are irreparably injured. Others have been "imprinted," which occurs at an early age when the animal bonds to a person, rather than its own kind.

Today they greet 100,000 visitors each year and are vital to the Lindsay's goal to teach people to live responsibly and in harmony with nature.

The Lindsay is a natural history museum for all ages, where adults are just as intrigued and can learn just as much as children.

Interpretive guides bring snakes, owls and other animals out of their glass-enclosed homes to give visitors an "up close and personal" approach. You may learn how a tarantula mates or sheds its exoskeleton or discover that snakes are smooth, not slimy, and they smell with their tongues.

Some animals, like the bobcat, are strictly for viewing. The animals' care, comfort and safety is #1 at the Lindsay, before any educational programs or display plans. They are loved, but they're treated like wild animals.

The Lindsay's permanent residents include an opossum, a raven, a red fox, squirrels, a black-tailed hare, a raccoon, a painted turtle, a kestrel and more. About 75 animals are on display on any given day. Others are on routine "rest and recreation" vacations on a ranch in Martinez or other volunteers' homes.

Displays explain the dangers that local wildlife confronts, from garden pesticides to over-development. Aquariums, a 35-foot-tall replica of Mount Diablo's Balancing Rock, complete with mountain lion and deer, and "please touch" drawers filled with fossils, minerals and more all teach us to take a closer look at our partnership with nature.

Local children can check out "Natural History to Go" specimens, such as a mounted tree frog. Members of the Pet Library have access to 80 domestic rabbits, hamsters, guinea pigs and rats. They can take these animals home for a week of intimate learning, if they follow instructions and pass a written test on the animal's care.

The Lindsay Museum's phone consultation service receives about 20,000 calls each year. They advise people who have found injured opossums or baby birds dropped from the nest. Sometimes, the animal needs to be brought immediately to Lindsay's hospital. Often the caller should leave the animal alone and observe it. For example, fledglings, baby birds that have developed feathers, need several days on the ground before they learn to fly.

The "Especially for Children" discovery room, designed to look like your own back yard, invites you to find snakes in the woodpile, raccoons under the deck, fawns under the tree and other examples of wildlife in an urban setting. It reminds us all that you don't need to travel far to share in nature's small miracles.

Lindsay Museum
1931 First Ave. (in Larkey Park), Walnut Creek
510/935-1978
Wed.-Sun. 1-5 Sept.-May;
Wed.-Sun. 11-5 June-Aug.
$3 Adults; $2 ages 3-17

Tilden Regional Park

Tilden is perfect for families with small children, romantic couples, hardy hikers, nature lovers—anybody who enjoys a day outdoors. This regional park boasts an 18-hole golf course, Little Farm complete with goats, a pig and other animals, a swimming beach, old-fashioned carousel, scenic picnic grounds, botanic garden, miniature steam train and miles of nature and wilderness trails.

Tilden covers 2,078 acres, so you may have to drive to different activities. You can start at the south end of the park and take a ride on the miniature steam train. It delights kids of all ages as it chugs through the trees. (Open Sat., Sun. & holidays 11-6 year-round; Mon.-Fri. 12-5 during Oakland schools' spring and summer vacations, weather permitting. $1.50/ride, $6/5 rides, tel. 510/548-6100.)

You can follow South Park Drive through Tilden past a series of picnic grounds to the Botanic Garden. It was founded in 1940, making it almost as old as Tilden, itself. This garden is devoted to the collection, growing, display and preservation of California's native plants.

Gardeners have squeezed 160,000 square miles of California into this 10-acre botanic monument. Paths meander through a surprising diversity of shapes, textures and colors in the plant kingdom.

Regional plant communities include Shasta-Cascade, Channel Islands, Pacific Rain Forest, Coastal Dunes and many more. Every month offers something special, whether it be March's California poppies, August's evening-primroses or the first manzanita blooms in mid-December. (Open daily 8:30-5 except Christmas; tel. 510/841-8732; Free)

On a hot day, enjoy a dip in cool Lake Anza. There are picnic grounds nearby and a small sandy beach for laying in the sun. Lifeguards are on duty from 11 A.M. to 6 P.M. (Open daily May-Oct.;

Swim fee $2 Adults; $1 ages 1-15, 62 and over and disabled persons; under 1 free; tel. 510/848-3385)

Don't miss the old-fashioned merry-go-round near the end of Lake Anza Road. This treasure was built in 1911 and is one of the few existing "menagerie-type" Herschell-Spillman carousels. It once delighted visitors to San Bernadino Ocean Beach. For $1, you can ride on a fantastical tiger, ostrich, giraffe, lion, a traditional horse, a rocking carriage and many more unique creatures and seats. Afterwards, you can indulge at the espresso bar, soda fountain and delicatessen or browse through the gift shop's collection of old-fashioned toys.

The vintage pipe organ plays gay tunes as the carousel twirls around. In front, a carved wooden band leader keeps time by waving her baton. Take a peek in back to see the percussion system at work. Mechanisms cause sticks to hit drums to the beat.

Another favorite with kids is the Little Farm, with all the sights, sounds and smells of the country. It even has a kid-size red barn and wind mill. Cows, sheep, pygmy goats, a pig and more domestic animals welcome visitors to their farm. Ducks have found a home in the pond nearby.

You can bring lettuce and celery to feed the cows, pigs and other animals, but please don't give them fruit, crackers and bread products and don't pick plants here—some may be poisonous.

In the Environmental Education Center next door, walk through the Wildcat Creek watershed in miniature, learning about the area's flora, fauna and human history along the way. (Open Tues.-Sun. 10-5) Naturalist programs are offered on weekends.

This is all part of the 740-acre nature study area, which also encompasses several short (1/2-mile to mile-long) trails ranging from gentle to steep. You're sure to find a walk that's just what you are looking for to get back to nature.

Tilden Regional Park
Berkeley Hills
(follow signs from Grizzly Peak Blvd.)
510/525-2233
Free

Snoopy & Skating

Who is one of the most recognizable Americans in the world today? That ace pilot, bird-loving beagle, Snoopy! He was on the cover of LIFE, went to the moon with Apollo 10 and shook hands with Prince Charles. Every day, more than 100 million people around the world enjoy Snoopy's antics in over 2,000 newspapers translated into 26 languages.

You'd think a beagle of such bearing would be created in New York, Paris or Milan, but he's drawn right here in Santa Rosa by one of the town's most famous residents, Charles Schulz.

Schulz, the creator of Snoopy, Charlie Brown and the rest of the Peanuts gang, has provided the public with a slice of Peanuts paradise in his hometown.

You can relive the history of Peanuts through the awards, original drawings and memorabilia in Snoopy's Gallery. You can buy a Peanuts toy in the gift shop, which features the largest collection of Snoopy merchandise in the world. And you can enjoy Schulz' second love, ice skating, in the rink next door.

Since he was a small child growing up in Minneapolis, Schulz knew that only one career was right for him—that of a cartoonist. He was inspired by his father, who made sure they bought all four Sunday papers published in the area so they could read the comics. Schulz realized his dream when he sold his first Peanuts comic strip to United Feature Syndicate on October 2, 1950.

The original drawing for this first strip, hanging in the gallery, reveals that the initial Peanuts gang was much more simply drawn. The characters have full, round faces and Charlie Brown's jersey has no trademark zig-zag stripe. Through the progression of original drawings, you can see how the kids developed.

Other memorabilia includes a model of Apollo 10, in which Snoopy and Charlie Brown went to the moon as mascots in 1969. Color animation cels, layers of plastic sheets with a series of drawings, show how Peanuts television specials are made. A note from Ronald Reagan contains his sketch of a cowboy. Its postscript reads, "As you can see, I'm no threat to you in your chosen work."

Downstairs, Peanuts and Snoopy toys span every marketing idea imaginable. Neckties, alarm clocks, magnets, fire engines, embroidery kits, plush toys, t-shirts, mugs, rubber stamps and many more items feature the familiar Peanuts figures.

Next door, Schulz' Redwood Ice Arena looks like a colorful Swiss Chalet. Like the Peanuts gang, Schulz created this rink to provide hours of fun, old-fashioned entertainment for the whole family. It's a good idea to call ahead to confirm the rink's public hours, especially in December when it hosts a show of world-class skating stars. If the kids have more energy than Mom and Dad on the ice, a coffee shop offers a place to relax looking out on the skaters.

Snoopy Gallery and Gift Shop
1667 West Steele Lane, Santa Rosa
707/546-3385
Open daily 10-6
Free

Redwood Empire Ice Arena
next door to Snoopy Gallery
Winter Hours (Sept.-April):
Mon. 12:30-2 & 8:30-10:30 (Adults only);
Tu. & Th. 4-5:30 & 7:30-9; Wed. 12:30-2;
Fri. 4-5:30 & 8-10:30;
Sat. 12:30-2:30, 3-5 & 8-10:30;
Sun. 12:30-2:30 & 3-5;
Also open Mon.-Fri. 2:30-5 in summer.
Call ahead. Rink may close for special events.
707/546-7147
$5.50 Adults; $4.50 ages 11 and under
Includes Skate Rental

🚂 California State Railroad Museum

This is one of the largest and finest railroad museums in the world.

In 100,000 square feet of exhibit space, you explore above, on board and below 21 beautifully restored locomotives and cars. The collection includes Central Pacific's first locomotive, Lucius Beebe's luxurious private railcar, a post office car where you can try sorting mail, a huge, 1,051,200-pound steam engine and the St. Hyacinthe sleeping car that recreates high-speed night travel through deceivingly realistic special effects.

On weekends, you can experience the sights, sounds and smells of railroad travel first hand during their excursion train's 45-minute ride along the Sacramento River. Its Locomotive #4466 is the oldest coal-burning steam locomotive in regular service west of the Mississippi.

The California State Railroad Museum is located where railroading in the west all began—in Old Sacramento. With the financing of the Big Four, the labor of 10,000 Chinese, the determination of Manifest Destiny and the inspiration of a nation, California was linked to the rest of the country via the transcontinental railroad on May 10, 1869.

The first room in the museum is dedicated to this astonishing accomplishment. The shiny black, gray and brass 1862 "Gov. Stanford," Central Pacific Locomotive No. 1, appears to chug through a snowy Sierra scene. Chinamen lift barrels of blasting powder up perilously steep cliffs. A whistle blows in the background, heralding a new era in transportation and history.

The main exhibit hall showcases most of the restored locomotives, some more works of art than machine. Late 1800s passenger cars are equally elaborate. Peek into Nevada Central Railway's "Silver State" to see ornately painted details, upholstered seats, wooden louvered shutters and a wood stove. Even Virginia and Truckee's 1873 freight locomotive, "Empire," boasts brass trim, bright red wheels and gold-emblazoned lettering.

The giant of all steam locomotives is Southern Pacific's No. 4294. Towering three times taller than the average person, this 1944 million-pound, 6,000 horsepower Goliath is the sole survivor of these unique cab-forward engines.

Step aboard Canadian National Railways' "St. Hyacinthe" Pullman to relive train travel of the 1930s. The gentle rocking of the car, crossing lights flashing by the window and sounds of the rails and whistles all add to the illusion. Berths are lowered from the ceiling, hand towels wait by the stainless steel sinks in the washroom and thick, burgundy curtains are pulled closed for privacy.

Lucius Beebe's railcar, "The Gold Coast," marked the epitome in private rail travel. In 1948, this bon vivant hired a Hollywood decorator to refurbish an 1890s business car. With opulent furnishings, chandeliers, a fireplace and fine china, Beebe brought back rail travel in a grand manner.

You can try sorting mail on the Great Northern Railway Post Office Car. It operated as a complete U.S. Post Office on wheels between Chicago and Tacoma, Washington. Armed clerks sorted letters while the train sped as fast as 80 mph. An ingenious arm swings out to catch sacks full of mail hanging on poles by the side of the track.

In addition to this exceptional collection, films, artifacts, souvenirs, informative displays, hands-on quizzes and enthusiastic docents all add to this unique monument to the railroad and its place in American history.

California State Railroad Museum
2nd and I Sts., Old Sacramento
916/448-4466 (recording)
Open daily 10-5
$5 Adults; $2 ages 6-12; under 5 free
Includes same-day admission to
the Central Pacific Railroad Depot (see p. 116)
Train fare: $4 Adults; $2 ages 6-12; under 5 free

Travis Air Force Museum

If man were meant to fly, he'd have wings like these. More than 20 aircraft of every size, shape and design are on exhibit in front of the Travis Air Force Museum. There's a Globemaster II C-124 large enough to carry a tank, a double-rotor rescue helicopter, a huge B-52D bomber and a sleek Phantom II jet.

Inside the museum, you'll find more airplanes, from the Gonzales Aeroplane No. 1, dating to 1910, to World War II-era trainers. There's even a collection of NASA spacecraft models. You can climb into one capsule and flip toggle switches to feel what it was like to be one of our first astronauts.

This surprising collection is located on Travis Air Force Base in Fairfield. As you tour the historic planes, you often see and hear their modern-day counterparts taking off and landing on a nearby strip.

One of the museums' newest additions is a Russian-made Iraqi anti-aircraft gun captured after a major tank battle at Kuwait City International airport. Many more of the exhibits are from World War II and the 1950s and 1960s.

The collection includes a series of bomb casings, including the stubby, 10-foot, 8-inch long "Fat Man" casing for the atomic bomb dropped on Nagasaki on August 9, 1945.

One intriguing artifact is the cockpit of a Waco CG-4 Assault Glider. With canvas stretched over steel, these lightweight gliders were towed by C-47 aircraft to a target area. Once there, they could land silently in an open field. The gliders could carry 15 troops or eight troops and one jeep and 90% made only one assault landing.

The Gonzales Aeroplane No. 1, used in San Francisco in 1910-1912, looks like something the Wright Brothers flew. It is little more than a seat and 35 horsepower engine attached to a 36-foot wingspan and a tail, totaling 28 feet long. Designed primarily as a trainer, the plane boasted a top speed of 30 mph and a range of 10 miles.

Compare this to the impenetrable-looking B-52D, one of the huge aircraft parked outside the museum. B-52s, used extensively in the late 1960s and early 1970s, have a wingspan of 185 feet, more than five times wider than the Gonzales. They reach speeds up to 638 mph and weigh more than 220 tons.

Another giant is the Globemaster II C-124, the first of which flew in 1949. This aircraft is almost five stories tall and could transport tanks, bulldozers and trucks or carry 200 soldiers in its double-decker cabin. A door in its nose lowers for easy loading and there's an elevator under its aft fuselage.

One of the most contemporary aircraft on display is the McDonnell Douglas F-4C Phantom II. It entered into service in 1961 as a fleet defense interceptor for the U.S. Navy. This jet could reach 1,400 mph and boasted a range of 1,750 miles. When used by the Air Force in Southeast Asia, it could carry twice the bomb load of the World War II-era B-17.

This is just the beginning of what the Travis Air Museum has to offer. You also can see aircraft under restoration, engines, a collection of pilots' helmets through the years or watch movies that show many of these planes in action.

Travis Air Force Museum
Travis Air Force Base, Fairfield
707/424-5605
Mon.-Fri. 9-4; Sat. 9-5; Sun. Noon-5
Closed on federal holidays
Free

Western Railway Museum

Clang, clang, clang goes the trolley—straight into nostalgia and fun at the Western Railway Museum. It's like playing with your old train set, but this is life-sized.

People line up at the depot. The trolley pulls away with a clickety-clack and a gleeful ring. It rumbles past an immense locomotive and freight cars stretching into the prairie, then circles back to the stop at the railroad barn with its impressive collection of antique and unusual engines and coaches.

The museum isn't exactly on the beaten path, but it's worth the drive along Highway 12 past rolling hills and sheep herds. When you arrive, you'll find several enthusiastic volunteers, complete in conductor uniforms. They are part of the 1,000-member, non-profit Bay Area Electric Railroad Association who share their love of railroads through this museum.

Begin your tour with a ride on one of the antique electric railway cars, such as the car that originally ran across the San Francisco Bay Bridge. These cars have been completely restored, some to the tune of 10,000 or more volunteer man-hours. Inside you'll find polished wood paneling and vintage advertisements. You can watch and ask questions as the conductor works the crank and bell.

The trolley rumbles past a yard piled with rusted railroad parts, but "whatever you do, don't call that junk," our conductor, Al Lingo, explained. "That's gold." The association avidly collects old railroad cars and parts that have been left to rot in yards and fields.

In the carbarn, you can see how these "junked" cars can come back to life. Some have pictures that show their original state. Of the thirty cars in the barn, several have been restored. Others may never be revived.

Children especially enjoy climbing onto and through the cars. You can even ring the bell on some, if you do it gently. Old-timers will recognize the design of several of the cars that used to be part of the Bay Area's Key System. The System, which included some of the cars here, dates back to the turn of the century, and encompassed San Francisco ferry boats that connected with East Bay electric trains and streetcars.

An unusual specimen is the Blackpool Corporation Transit or Boat Car. This open-air, boat-shaped car was built in England in 1934 for use in Blackpool, a seaside resort. Tourists enjoyed this unique form of transportation along the coast, complete with slatted wooden seats to accommodate wet bathing suits.

Another passenger car had traveled more than 1.2 million miles on the streets of Melbourne, Australia before coming to San Francisco for the 1983 Historic Trolley Festival. A Koala painted on the side of the car invites people to "Hop Aboard, Mate."

A favorite with the kids is the classic caboose, this one from the Great Northern Railroad. Built about 1899, cabooses originally were used as quarters for the train crews. A person riding in the cupola could watch the freight cars for mechanical problems. Today, the crew rides in the diesel locomotive and cabooses are no longer needed.

If the Railway Museum has sparked your enthusiasm for the rails, stop by their bookstore with its extensive collection of railroad publications or picnic at their landscaped grounds by the trolley tracks.

The Western Railway Museum
Highway 12
(a little more than 12 miles from I-80)
Solano County
707/374-2978
Sat. & Sun. 11-5
$5 Adults; $2 ages 4-12

Mercer Caverns

More than a century ago, the curious and daring descended into these hidden caverns. They discovered a fantasy land of graceful rock spires, gaping maws and crystalline jewels. Today, you still do.

Electric lights have replaced candles and you climb on stairs rather than ropes, but Mercer Caverns are timeless in their inspiration. Delicate tubes called "soda straws," sheer, flowing "angel wings," jewel-like "iron flowers" and eerie stalagmites and stalactites decorate this series of underground galleries. Adults will appreciate their beauty. Kids will thrill at the adventure of it all and have fun pointing out shapes in the rocks.

Ever since Walter Mercer discovered the caves in 1885, people have been paying to see them. Mercer stumbled onto the find while prospecting for quartz. Tired and thirsty after a long day, he noticed some bay bushes and thought he might find water there. Instead of water, he noticed a slight breeze blowing through a hand-sized hole.

Before long, Mercer hacked away an opening big enough to crawl through. Armed only with a candle, he lowered himself into the dark void. When he reached the bottom, he felt something odd beneath him—a human skeleton. Fearing that these poor souls were men like him who had been trapped in a cave-in, he quickly scrambled out.

The first cavern you enter on your tour is the same one that Mercer first discovered. This "Gothic Chamber" stretches 234 feet long and 60 feet wide. The bones, that of four adults, a child and an infant, turned out to be those of local Yokuts Indians, who frequently buried their dead by throwing them into caves. The skeletons were 1,500 to 2,000 years old. They're now in the Smithsonian.

These "water solution hole caves" began forming nearly 3 million years ago. Underground creeks ate away at the stone, creating subterranean caverns.

Over the centuries, slow-moving water, first from the creek and later from raindrops seeping through the surface, blended with limestone and formed the intricate shapes that fascinate today's visitors.

Mercer named many of the shapes. Although some stretch the imagination and your sense of humor, these historic monikers still stick today, including the Cave Twins, the Chinese Meat Market, with its sausages and vegetables, an upside-down Rapunsel and the Beehive.

Along with the majestic stalagmites and stalactites, many rock formations are gracefully beautiful. The translucent calcite Angel Wings look like silk ruffling in a soft breeze. They are 9 1/2 feet long and 3 1/2 feet high but only millimeters thick.

The most stunning rock formations are Mercer's famous aragonite flos ferri, a very rare mineral that is found in its greatest abundance on the North American continent at Mercer Caverns. Mercer won the Grand Prize Award for this "Flower Garden" in the 1900 Paris World's Fair. The room seems to glow with the sparkle of these crystals, like stepping inside a diamond in the rough.

During your hour-long tour, you'll explore ten rooms, see an abundance of stunning formations, experience a brief time in total darkness and climb down 208 steps and back up 232 steps. When you return to the surface, you'll arise with a new appreciation of the unseen earth beneath your feet.

Mercer Caverns
1665 Sheep Ranch Rd.
One mile north of Murphy's,
follow signs from downtown
209/728-2101
Open Weekends and school holidays 11-4 Oct.-May
Open daily 9-5 Memorial Day-Sept.
$5 Adults; $2.50 ages 5-11

Notes

We Got Culture

Asian Art Museum

The largest museum outside Asia devoted to Asian art is right here in San Francisco. The Asian Art Museum in Golden Gate Park has an estimated 12,000 works spanning more than 6,000 years. The works are intriguing, from bronze vessels dating to 13th century BC to Liao Dynasty death regalia to the world's oldest dated Buddha known to exist.

Even if you're a not a Buddhist, several works are supplemented with fascinating histories that will enlighten you. Whether it is pieces currently on display from the permanent collection or one of the museum's splendid temporary exhibits, you're sure to come home with a better understanding of the extraordinary Asian cultures.

Downstairs, this museum's collection of bronzes showcases vessels that are masterpieces in the media. Crafted long before many western civilizations were born, they display an unsurpassed artistry and skill. One favorite piece is the bronze Rhinoceros wine vessel from 2000 BC.

The pottery collection contains beautiful works in shimmering turquoise, green and deep red, crafted in the late 1600s and early 1700s. The display explains how these rich colors all result from a copper glaze. Different hues are dependent on the kiln temperature at which the pottery is fired. The glaze requires an intense 1200° F to produce the crimson red.

One unusual piece is the death regalia from the Liao Dynasty, dating to 937 to 1125 AD, which "evokes the Liao version of eternity, where the quality and details of life were believed to be preserved forever," according to the display.

Metal wire is formed into a net-like suit to wrap the body of a wealthy man. The highest ranks were wrapped in gold or silver, the lower ones in bronze. Fragments of silk show that the body was first wrapped in silk before being enclosed in the metal suit. A rare jade death mask, which was placed over the face of the deceased, hangs on the wall nearby.

Be sure to explore the special exhibition galleries, which feature excellent temporary displays of Asian art themes.

Upstairs, thoughtfully organized galleries travel through Southeast Asia, Persia, ancient India, Tibet and Japan . Almost all the works are inspired by religion. Many are Buddhas or Bodhisattvas, those who have renounced the rewards of enlightenment to remain on Earth and help mankind.

On Sunday afternoons, storytellers breathe new life into the sculptures of the Indian galleries. They share the tales of gods and goddesses and relate the ancient myths and legends of characters like Ganesha, the elephant-headed boy.

In the Tibet room, one unusual collection features 18th-century human bone implements, such as thigh-bone trumpets and skull bowls. To the Buddhist, the display explains, human bones are reminders that life is brief and death inevitable. Tibetans saw the skull as a "natural container" unshaped by human hands. It represents the fundamental goodness that is the natural condition of the mind.

Artworks from Japan are refined, elegant and graceful. A large, mid-19th-century kago, used to carry a person, is black and red lacquer with gold highlights. Painted screens show the beauty in simplicity, a concept that prevails in many of the works exhibited in this exceptional museum.

Asian Art Museum
Golden Gate Park, San Francisco
415/668-8921
Wed. 10-8:45; Thurs.-Sun. 10-5
$5 Adults; $3 Seniors 65 and over;
$2 ages 12-17; under 12 free
Includes same-day admission to de Young
$1 suggested donation first Sat. 10-Noon
and first Wed. of each month.

☼ Chinese Historical Society

Did the Chinese land in America before Columbus? The Spanish recorded a Chinese presence in California as early as the 1630s. After the gold rush, the Chinese made up 90% of the Central Pacific's workforce during the construction of the transcontinental railroad. In 1882, 75% of California's agricultural workers were Chinese.

You can learn this and more about the Chinese role in California's history at the Chinese Historical Society in San Francisco. Don't be put off by its unassuming entrance and off-the-beaten-path location. Despite its humble size, the museum offers a horizon-expanding view of the Chinese experience through displays, historical photographs and such artifacts as a life-size fishing boat, a century-old altar and a traditional braid of hair, called a queue.

Displays look into the good and bad sides of Chinese history. A long opium pipe is symbolic of the many troubles that nation suffered because of this drug. Widespread addiction led to the First Opium War, ending in defeat to England and a century of foreign domination.

Gold! It lured white settlers from across the country and thousands of Chinese from across the Pacific. In 1850, only 450 Chinese lived in San Francisco. Two years later, the number exploded to 20,000. After 1852, an average of 10,000 Chinese immigrated every year.

Most came from Canton, the only open port in China. Because of the country's closed door policy, the rest of China didn't know about the gold rush, or couldn't get out if they did.

Those that did come held on to their heritage, culture and language. The queue, a long braid of hair, was worn by men as a symbol of their allegiance to the Manchu Emperor of China. After a revolution in 1911, some cut their queues. Another display shows the tools and plants used by a traditional herb shop for medicinal uses.

The most colorful artifact is the immense dragon head. Made in Canton, it was shipped here in 1915 for use in parades and was one of the first dragon heads to be equipped with electric lights. The century-old, deep red altar was carved by Chinese laborers for their temple in Napa.

Through hard work, the Chinese were able to create new and successful industries only to be forced out by discriminatory practices and laws. One such industry was shrimp farming, as represented by the massive, wooden winnowing machine.

Some Chinese brought the skills they learned in America back home with them. Displays tell the stories of people like Chin Gee Hee, who worked on the railroad here. He returned to his home town in 1905 to build a railroad for his countrymen. It served the community until 1938, when locals were forced to destroy it so the Japanese couldn't exploit it for their war effort.

From the museum, it's a short walk to the heart of Chinatown. Portsmouth Square, now landlocked by the financial district, was once the harbor where Chinese first landed in San Francisco during the gold rush. Today, groups of Chinese men cluster around boisterous games of tiles and cards.

On the busy streets of this community, you'll find colorful vegetable stands filled with such unusual produce as lotus root or mile-long beans. In a tea shop, try a cup of ginseng tea, believed to have many health benefits. Shops are brimming with fun, inexpensive Chinese imports and reasonably priced gifts, embroidered linens and silk clothing. To top it off, sample the exotic foods of the orient for a true taste of San Francisco's Chinese heritage.

Chinese Historical Society
650 Commercial St., near Kearny, San Francisco
415/391-1188
Tu.-Sat. Noon-4
Free, contributions appreciated

Coit Tower

Coit Tower was never intended to resemble a firehose nozzle, but there is no better way to describe this cylindrical, fluted tower that tops Telegraph Hill. There is, however, much more to this structure than its art deco shape and panoramic view from the top.

Lining both sides of Coit Tower's circular lobby are provocative murals that immortalize one of our nation's most difficult eras. It was the 1930s, a time of harsh, industrial working conditions for those who had jobs and little hope for those who didn't. The murals portray the working class, from the factories to farms.

The murals were painted about sixty years ago. A massive and meticulous restoration process has pumped new life into the artworks' vibrant colors. For $1, the Coit Tower brochure describes each of the murals and the history of the tower. Although its map is a bit confusing, the text offers a deeper appreciation for the murals' message. To learn even more about the artworks, join a mural tour.

Coit Tower was originally built as a monument to Lillie Hitchcock Coit, one of San Francisco's most colorful women. In the late 1800s, Lillie often dressed as a man to gamble in North Beach saloons. She smoked cigars and publicly ice-skated in shortened skirts.

Lillie was best known for her passion for firefighting. In 1863, Knickerbocker Hose Company #5 declared Lillie their mascot and she rarely missed a blaze. Coit Tower is a result of her $125,000 bequest to San Francisco.

The murals were commissioned by the U.S. Government as a Public Works of Art Project, but they later regretted it. The social criticism prevalent in these artworks caused a controversy that delayed the opening of the tower from May until October 1934.

Although 25 artists worked on the murals, they are surprisingly homogeneous in style and theme. These actually are frescoes. They are the result of a time-consuming, tricky process in which dry pigments are applied with a wet brush to fresh plaster.

The social realists combined scenes of everyday life with sobering touches of unadorned reality. The colors are bold, the portraits stark, the expressions somber. Each tells a story of the working class.

One depicts the stages of a newspaper, from reporters gathering news, to typesetters, to the newsboy selling the finished product on the street. Another shows a crowd of stone-faced unemployed men. One holds a paper announcing a Mayday labor protest.

In a city street scene, people walk apathetically by a major accident on the street, implying citizen's lack of concern for each other during these tough times.

The most cheerful mural presents a panoramic view of California agriculture. Here, at least, the workers are outdoors, collecting bright cut flowers and laying apricots out to dry. Other murals are not entirely humorless. In the mural depicting Banking and Law, take a close look at some of the titles. One reads the *Laws of Fresco Painting*.

An old-fashioned elevator and a narrow spiral staircase takes you up to the very tip of 180-foot Coit Tower. Here you can enjoy a panoramic view of San Francisco. Far below, you'll see the 12-foot bronze statue of Christopher Columbus gazing over the waters of the Bay.

Coit Tower
Telegraph Hill, San Francisco
415/362-0808
Open daily 10-6
Free to see murals
Elevator: $3 Adults; $2 Seniors 64 and over;
$1 ages 6-12; under 6 free
Mural Tour: Tues. & Th. 10:15; $5 ages 18-64;
$3 Seniors and Children

de Young Museum

The de Young is more than a fine art museum. It is a walk through our nation's history and culture. From the austere 17th-century "Mason Children" to 20th-century realist William Glackens' rambunctious working class picnic scene, the collection illustrates our heritage in a new light—through art.

The best way to see the de Young is to join a free guided tour. Several are offered each day, focusing on different aspects of the museum. The enthusiastic, informative docents tell the story behind the artwork and point out details usually overlooked. Each tour is unique.

The de Young's masterworks include portraits by Copley, Sargent, Whistler and Mary Cassatt. There are landscapes by Bierstadt and Frederic Church. Trompe l'oeil paintings include William Harnett's "After the Hunt" and Alexander Pope's "The Trumpeter Swan." You'll see sculptures by Frederic Remington and William Story, silver by Paul Revere, furniture by Stickley and much more. Some of these may be covered on your guided tour. Allow time afterwards to see those you missed.

The galleries are arranged chronologically. Some are illuminated with the glowing natural light of wall-to-wall skylights.

The 1670 "Mason Children" is one of the few paintings created in the burgeoning colonies. The clothes are simple, but a touch of wealth is shown in the boy's gloves and silver-handled cane. The girl holds a gaudy red necklace, thought to ward off witches. The Salem witch trials took place just 20 years later. This painting was passed down for three centuries through descendants of the girl in the painting.

Nearby is a portrait by John Singleton Copley, considered the first accomplished painter born in

America. This 1770s painting of a New England gentleman and his son exhibits more graceful, life-like figures than his 17th-century predecessor. The shoulders of the man's colonial vestments reveal traces of white powder from his powdered wig, that era's fashion statement. The wigs were valued so highly that thieves snatched them off heads of gentlemen on the street.

In the mid-19th century, landscapes came in vogue, to show God's works, not man's. One gallery wall is devoted to Albert Bierstadt. With the westward expansion, people back east were intrigued with scenes from the new frontier. Works here include the 1871-'72 view of Donner Lake, commissioned to show the building of the transcontinental railroad.

The 1895 bronze sculpture "The Bronco Buster" by Frederic Remington shows another side of the west. Both man and horse reveal their fight and fury.

By the early 20th century, artists expanded beyond portraits and landscapes to the heart of their subject. Georgia O'Keefe's 1925 "Petunias" shows the supple, sensuous beauty in a simple flower.

From the Puritans to the free spirits, a tour of American art in the de Young is sure to give you a new understanding of our culture.

The de Young Museum
Golden Gate Park, San Francisco
415/863-3330
Wed. 10-8:45; Thurs.-Sun. 10-5
$5 Adults; $3 Seniors 65 and over;
$2 ages 12-17; under 12 free
Includes same-day admission to Asian Art Museum
Free first Sat. morning and first Wed. of each month

☼ *Fort Mason*
Ethnic Museums

What happens when a military base becomes defunct? A small miracle in the case of Fort Mason in San Francisco. Ex-military buildings have been transformed into offices for such cultural organizations as Make-A-Circus, Friends of the River and the National Poetry Association. Best of all, several rooms are now ethnic and folk museums.

Within short walking distance are the San Francisco Craft and Folk Art Museum, the African American Historical & Cultural Society, the Museo ItaloAmericano and the Mexican Museum.

These museums are small but sharply focused. They primarily feature changing exhibits. Call ahead to find out about the current exhibit and to make sure the museum will be open on the day you visit. They sometimes close when setting up a new exhibit.

Each museum also has a gift shop with unique items from their cultural groups, from carved wooden African animals to bright Mexican pottery. You can see just one museum or all of them in an afternoon, then indulge in a goodie from the Tassajara Bakery or Greens vegetarian restaurant.

The San Francisco Craft & Folk Art Museum is devoted to contemporary craft, American folk art and traditional ethnic art. Some exhibits here have traveled as far as New York, Chicago and Washington, DC. You might see a display of hand-painted third world billboards or finely crafted handmade porcelains.

The African American Historical & Cultural Society lends unique insight into the traditions, heritage and diversity of Africans and African Americans. Special exhibits focus on everything from contemporary art to West African textiles.

The Museo ItaloAmericano showcases contemporary works by Italian artists while the

Mexican Museum features changing exhibits by Mexican craftspeople.

There is always something interesting happening at Fort Mason. During any given month, events may range from a Bay Area Tarot Symposium, to Story-telling, to an International Beer Festival. Lectures range from Metaphysics to Music Publishing. You may be able to hear a poetry reading or enjoy a one-woman play or watch a Flamenco dance.

To get the most out of the amazing diversity offered by this cultural collective, pick up the free, monthly Fort Mason Center schedule of events while you're visiting. Or you can get one free sample copy in advance by calling the Fort Mason Center office.

Fort Mason Center
entrance at Buchanan St. & Marina Blvd.
415/979-3010 (24 hr. recording-info & events)
415/441-5706 (for Calendar of Events sample copy)
Free
SF Craft & Folk Art Museum
Bldg. A, Fort Mason, San Francisco
415/775-0990
Tu.-Sun. 11-5; Sat. 10-5
$1 Adults; $.50 Seniors over 62 and ages 13-17
Free on Sat. 10-Noon
African American Historical Society
Bldg. C, Fort Mason, San Francisco
415/441-0640
Wed.-Sun. 12-5
$2 Adults
Museo ItaloAmericano
Bldg. C, Fort Mason, San Francisco
415/673-2200
Wed.-Sun. 12-5
$2 Adults; $1 Seniors and Students
Mexican Museum
Bldg. D, Fort Mason, San Francisco
415/441-0404
Wed.-Sun. 12-5; first Wed. of each month 12-8
$3 Adults; $2 Seniors and Students
Free first Wed. of each month

Haas-Lilienthal House

A new popularity in Victoriana has brought about magnificent restorations of San Francisco's Victorian houses. Many are elegant bed and breakfast inns, others elaborate private residences. But the Haas-Lilienthal House is a home where you feel more like an old friend than a tourist.

Generations of the same family have lived in this grand Victorian since it was built in 1886 until it was donated to the Foundation for San Francisco's Architectural Heritage in 1972.

Almost all of the family's furnishings are still here, reflecting the home's Victorian origins as well as the changes that the family had introduced over the years. Family members still return to the home for a celebration every Christmas.

The house was built originally for William Haas, a Bavarian native who sought his fortune in the gold mines, but found it in the wholesale grocery business in San Francisco. He married Bertha Greenebaum in 1880 and built this home six years later.

The other half of the house's name comes from their daughter, Alice, and her husband, Samuel Lilienthal. The happy couple was wed in the formal parlor of this home in 1909. After Alice passed on, her heirs donated the house in its remarkably unchanged condition.

From the outside, the Haas-Lilienthal House looks fit for a queen, but this was actually an upper middle class home. In 1886, the family invested $18,500 for the house and $13,000 for the land. At the time, several grand Victorians graced the neighborhood, most of which have fallen beneath the developer's hammer.

This is a fine example of transitional architecture. The dining room's rectangular bay windows are

Stick Eastlake style, popular in the late 1880s. The front parlor's faceted bay window is Italianate. The gables, varied shingles and graceful round tower reflect the Queen Anne style, in vogue in the 1890s.

As you walk through the front door, the house immediately emits a lived-in rather than staid museum feel. The foyer and main hallway are dark by today's standards. Deep green wallcovering is patterned to simulate grained leather highlighted with gold embossing. An intricately detailed grandfather clock comes from the family's native Bavaria.

As in many Victorian homes, the hallway leads from the front to the back of the house, opening on one side to a formal parlor, center parlor and dining room with 13-foot-high ceilings. Oriental vases decorate the parlor's mantel. Goods from China took a mere six weeks to arrive compared with months for decorative ware from the east coast or Europe.

The dining table could seat 22 people. The hutch's glass-enclosed cabinets still showcase the family's gold-laced stemware. A 1927 stove and oven is in the kitchen, along with an original marble-topped table where the cook could roll out strudel.

A later influence also is found upstairs in the bedroom that Bertha converted to her sitting room. Alice and Samuel's bedroom still has the furniture they received as a wedding gift. It's a twin bed set, but the pattern shows that the beds were meant to be placed together.

In the children's room is a charming white bassinet which is still used by the family when a baby is born. Other delightful furnishings include child-size, fully upholstered Stick Eastlake chairs.

As in other rooms in the house, you almost expect a family member to come in at any moment and offer you a cup of tea.

Haas-Lilienthal House
2007 Franklin St. (at Washington), San Francisco
415/441-3004
Tours Wed. Noon-4 (last tour at 3:15);
Sun. 11-5 (last tour at 4:15)
$5 Adults; $3 Seniors over 65 and Children under 12

North Beach

Caffe Roma, Biordi Art, Stella Pastry, Bocce Cafe, Fior d'Italia. The names of North Beach bring back the old country, a slice of Italy right in the hub of San Francisco. And if the names don't transport you to Europe, the sights, sounds, delicious tastes and scents will.

Washington Square is the soul of North Beach and the best place to begin a walk around our city's "Little Italy." Now landlocked, the name "North Beach" dates to the 1850s when a finger of the Bay extended here. If you come early in the morning, you'll see dozens of Chinese men and women performing the slow stretches of T'ai Chi on the soft grasses of the Square. Once exclusively Italian, North Beach has become a cultural melting pot, with Chinese, Basque, Persian and even Afghani restaurants among the Italian cafes.

The Romanesque, cathedral-style Church of Saints Peter and Paul, completed in 1924, reigns over Washington Square. Its twin spires soar 191 feet high, flanking a 14-foot-wide rosette window and a large arched doorway. Inside, glowing white and intricately carved statues, domes and spires rise above the main altar of Carrara marble. Candles flicker in the shrines. Mosaics line the walls.

From the church, cross the square and walk up Columbus Avenue. Small Italian, family-owned shoe-shine shops, delis and cafes line the street.

Coffee lovers shouldn't miss the Caffe Roma Coffee Roasting Company at 526 Columbus. Dominating the shop is the immense, sparkling brass and burgundy machine that roasts beans fresh on the spot, creating that heavenly aroma. Enthusiastic owner Tony Azzollini studied with the roasting maestros in Italy and he's happy to show you how he creates his own perfect blend.

Indulge in a sweet cookie or cake at Stella Pastry at 446 Columbus. Look in their inviting display case to find Amaretti and Pignolati cookies, Napoleons, Sacripantina and Tirami Su cakes. At 412 Columbus, browse through Biordi Art Imports' collection of stunning Majolica pottery. These are classic, intricately hand-painted patterns, many from the town of Deruta, Italy's largest pottery center.

The North Beach Museum, on the mezzanine of the EurekaBank at 1435 Stockton, illustrates the far-reaching influence of the neighborhood's Italian and Chinese residents on the burgeoning city.

For more than 40 years, curator Alessandro Baccari has collected historical photographs, family heirlooms and vintage books to tell their story. You'll discover that the Bank of America began as the Bank of Italy. You'll realize that it's no coincidence Italian names reign over seafood restaurants on the wharf. You'll know why the Chinese choose Washington Square for T'ai Chi.

The first Italians immigrated here in the 1840s to a small village named Yerba Buena. But the discovery of gold in 1848 created an overnight boomtown and it was renamed San Francisco. By the 1880s, North Beach was predominantly Italian. Many worked as fishermen and produce farmers.

The museum's exhibits change periodically, but generally focus on the family life of North Beach. Among the heirlooms is a complete 1870s table setting with china, silverware, wineglasses and candlesticks. The richly embroidered priest's vestments were presented to Baccari's great, great uncle by the devoted parishioners of Saints Peter and Paul in 1917. Chinese residents have donated Chinese books used in San Francisco schools. Historical photographs set the scene.

Despite its compact size, the North Beach museum presents an intriguing, new perspective on the family life, history and cultural heritage of San Francisco's "Little Italy."

North Beach Museum
EurekaBank, 1435 Stockton St,. San Francisco
415/391-6210
Mon.-Th. 9-3:30; Fri. 9-4
Free

☼ Old Mint & Ansel Adams Center

In the quieter side of The City, south of Market Street, you can take in two of San Francisco's unique cultural collections. The Old Mint is a treasure house of California history and our nation's numismatics. The Ansel Adams Center, just two blocks away, focuses on the world's foremost and upcoming photographers.

The massive, Greek Revival building which houses the Old Mint opened in 1874 to accommodate the influx of gold from the Mother Lode and San Francisco's booming financial market.

With brick and stone walls, a granite floor and interior cast iron columns supporting a cast iron ceiling, the Mint was constructed to withstand earthquakes and fires. It proved its mettle in 1906, when it stood unscathed while the city collapsed and burned around it. Recently, when seismic experts decided it needed work to keep up with today's standards, local citizens rallied to keep it open until finances could be raised.

Everyday coins are no longer produced here, but you can still stamp out your own commemorative medal on the circa-1869, 160-ton press for $1. Commemorative medals, honoring presidents, historic anniversaries and statesmen, are big business with collectors. The Old Mint's gift shop offers a fine selection of them. These, along with proof sets of everyday coins, are produced in the new San Francisco Mint, located a short distance away.

Coins are miniature works of art when produced as proof sets. Each cent, nickel, dime and quarter is painstakingly created by hand. First, the dies, which stamp the picture onto the coin blank, are polished with several grades of diamond polish, then buffed.

Coin blanks are burnished with thousands of steel beads and cleaning chemicals before being sent to the press. The combination of custom-made dies and blanks results in gleaming, high-relief coins worth several times their face value.

Only one-quarter of the building is devoted to museum space, but there's plenty to see. One room recreates a Victorian bedchamber, another the Superintendent's Office with original furnishings from 1874. Memorabilia, including typewriters, Victrolas and quilts, are part of their collection.

A beautiful six-foot scale, with gold leaf highlights and ivory handles, stands in the hallway. Scales of this type still are used to weigh bags of coins in the new mint.

The Ansel Adams Center is a short walk away. It's run by the Friends of Photography, founded more than 25 years ago in Carmel and now one of the oldest photography organizations in the world. The museum encompasses several galleries, one devoted to Adams prints. Others showcase changing exhibits of major photographers and young, emerging artists.

Adams is best known for his black-and-white nature shots. The play of light and shadow in Yosemite was one of his favorite subjects. His images of Half Dome and Yosemite Valley are two of the most widely recognized photographs in the world. A staunch conservationist, Adams' photographs were not only works of art, but a call to preserve America's wilderness.

The Old Mint
Fifth and Mission, San Francisco
415/744-6830
Mon.-Fri. 10-4; Tours every hour on the half-hour
Free

Ansel Adams Center
250 Fourth St.
between Howard and Folsom, San Francisco
415/495-7000
Tues.-Sun. 11-5
$4 Adults; $3 Students with ID;
$2 Seniors 62 and over and ages 12-17

☼ *Rodin Sculpture Garden*

The second largest collection of Rodin sculptures in the world is not in the museum of a great metropolis. It belongs to Stanford University. The collection encompasses 125 of Rodin's masterpieces, though not all are on display all the time. Several, including "The Thinker," are found throughout the campus, but the best place to see the sculptor's work is in the Rodin Sculpture Garden next to the Stanford Museum.

The garden design is simple, an open, quiet setting for the 20 bronze sculptures exhibited here. The pieces have been placed to receive the maximum benefit from sunlight, which accentuates the figures' fluid lines and facial expressions.

Auguste Rodin (1840-1917) was a master sculptor from a small town outside Paris. He created his figures in clay, then crafted plaster molds for the bronze casting. The sculptures in this garden are authentic and original, but not unique. They are cast in molds that Rodin created.

Rodin wanted his sculptures to be distributed around the world. His will authorized the French government to cast with his molds after his death, but this has been strictly controlled with limited editions.

The most intricate work in this garden is The Gates of Hell. It is a provoking, nightmarish vision of Pandemonium. Two massive bronze doors are alive with anguished men and women struggling to escape the flames.

Many of the figures are not much larger than a human hand, yet each features a unique expression of anguish and fear as they plummet downward. Above the gates is a small-scale figure of The Thinker. On either side, life-size figures of Adam and Eve turn away from the searing heat of the flames.

Rodin worked on The Gates of Hell on and off for 20 years. Since the first bronze castings weren't made until the 1920s, he never saw the finished masterpiece cast in bronze.

There are only five castings of The Gates of Hell in the world today: in Paris, Philadelphia, Tokyo, Zurich and right here at Stanford. The Stanford piece took over four years to cast, from 1977 to 1981. It is the fifth and last cast made of The Gates of Hell, cast using the lost wax method.

While working on The Gates of Hell, Rodin enlarged some of the figures to exhibit as sculptures in their own right. These are found in the East Court of Stanford's Rodin sculpture garden. The South Court focuses on Rodin's monuments and tributes to artists.

The boundaries of the Terrace trace the foundations of the wings of the Stanford Museum lost in the 1906 earthquake. On the Western Terrace are the partial figures of Rodin's famous Burghers of Calais. Four more full-size figures from the Burghers stand in Stanford's quad, a short walk away.

Just beyond is Memorial Church, one of the most beautiful buildings on campus. This is the centerpiece of the Main Quadrangle, Stanford's first buildings. The front facade of the church frames a sparkling gold mural of "Christ welcoming the righteous into heaven." It is a striking contrast to Rodin's tormented Gates of Hell.

Rodin Sculpture Garden
Stanford University
415/723-3469
Garden open 24 hours daily
Tours offered Wed., Sat. & Sun. 2:00
Free

:☼: ***Rosicrucian Egyptian Museum***

The dim beam of the guide's flashlight leads the way through the dark and narrow hallways of the tomb to the room holding the sarcophagus. It flashes on colorful wall paintings depicting everyday life of the dead noble's estate. On the rock ceiling above the sarcophagus, an immense, gracefully serene image of a goddess has been painted to protect the deceased from grave robbers. It didn't work. A corner of the sarcophagus has been hacked out and valuables stolen.

This is one of the unusual highlights of the Rosicrucian Egyptian Museum in San Jose, which is devoted to artifacts of the ancient world. The tomb is a life-size composite replica of Egyptian rock tombs from 4,000 years in the past. The building of these grand structures sometimes began at the noble's birth. Wall paintings of bakers, fishermen and cattle being led to market bring back the times of the deceased. Some sketches have not been colored in yet. The noble died before the tomb could be completed.

Many more cedar sarcophagi and mummies are displayed in the museum's exhibit rooms. Although thousands of years old, they are still nearly perfectly preserved. On some mummies, like Usermontu, a priest buried in Thebes in 600 BC, you can still distinguish the man's facial characteristics and see his fingernails and toenails. Animals also were mummified, including a baboon, from about 525 BC and a gazelle, from 1400 BC. Three cat mummies represent hundreds found. Cats were sacred to Bast, one of the more popular goddesses.

Writing, in the form of hieroglyphics, is one of the most important legacies of the ancient world. A replica of the Rosetta Stone is on display. The original was found in 1799 near the Nile. Since it was written in both Egyptian hieroglyphics and Greek, it was key to understanding Egyptian history and culture.

Scribes were considered some of society's most important members. Their work is exhibited on the dozens of clay tablets, some no bigger than your palm, that fill the museum's display cases. Many of these are religious writings, invoices, receipts and medical texts from 2800 to 200 BC.

Babylonian businessmen dictated messages which a scribe engraved onto a wet clay tablet. After authenticating the written message with the businessman's stamp, the tablet was dusted with a fine powder, then sealed in a clay "envelope." It was addressed by the scribe and baked to harden. A Pony Express-style system delivered the package to its recipient who cracked open the envelope to retrieve the message.

Ancient musical instruments reveal another lifestyle of the ancients. Ivory castanets in the shape of two hands date to 1400 BC. A bronze sistrum, shaken like a noisemaker, was used in temples for the adoration of Isis and became the symbol for cosmic motion. Present-day priests still believe the rattling sound drives away evil spirits.

For an extra fee, you can cruise the "Celestial Nile" in their planetarium and discover astronomy's influence on ancient Egypt.

Plan to spend some time exploring the park surrounding the museum as well. Its Egyptian-style buildings, verdant lawns, obelisk and statuary make a peaceful sanctuary to ponder the ancient world.

The Rosicrucian Egyptian Museum
At Rosicrucian Park,
Corner of Park and Naglee Avenues, San Jose
408/947-3636
Daily 9-5
$6 Adults; $4 Seniors 65 and over
& Students with ID; $3.50 ages 7-15

☀ *Behring Auto & UC Berkeley*
Museums at Blackhawk

Before the assembly line robot came the artist. This simple fact inspired real estate magnate Ken Behring to create a collection of classic cars which is one of the finest of its kind in the world.

These are the crown jewels of their era—the customized Packards, Cadillacs and one-of-a-kind sports cars. Like jewels, they are displayed in a magnificent setting—the opulent Behring Auto Museum in Blackhawk Plaza.

A gilded gate and low rising stairs past fountains and waterfalls lead to the museum's faceted smoked glass facade. Inside, two showrooms house more than 100 automotive masterpieces. Subdued lighting and classical music set the tone. Spotlights highlight the ruby, sapphire, silver and gold colors of the cars.

The collection, valued at millions of dollars, includes some of the rarest cars on Earth. Signs point out unique design details, outline outstanding engine performance or relate fascinating historical facts. Some cars belonged to Hollywood celebrities. Others were custom-made for royalty. Cars on display change periodically, but here are a few that you might see when you visit.

The first floor gallery is arranged chronologically, a walk through automotive history. It begins with an 1897 three-wheel Leon Bollee Voiturette. The 1901 Oldsmobile curved dash runabout was one of America's first production cars. With seven horsepower, it chugged along at 20 mph.

One area is devoted to race cars, like the 1912 Stutz Bearcat Series A. Another focuses on 1950s "Dream Cars," each one handcrafted for Chrysler by the Italian Ghia company.

One-of-a-kind cars include the 1941 Lincoln Continental by industrial designer Raymond Loewy, one of only two ever built. Loewy is known for designing the Shell Oil logo, Frigidaire appliances and Studebakers. Video displays tell the story of nine famous automobile designers, including Frank Hershey, who introduced the fins of the '50s.

The third floor showcases unique automobiles with fascinating histories. The most extravagant car is the 1926 Daimler Salon Cabriolet, custom built for the Maharajah of Rewa's tiger hunts. Its silver body has horns in the form of snakes rising over the front wheels and a hood ornament resembling a Grecian bust. They just don't make them like that anymore.

The UC Berkeley Museum, next door, focuses on nature's marvels, rather than man's. One popular exhibit showcases fossils uncovered just up the road. Nine million years ago, you might have encountered a Mastodon, camel, turtle or hyena-like dog while visiting here. The full reconstruction of the "Blackhawk Mastodon" makes it easier to imagine.

You'll also see California's official state fossil— a saber-toothed cat skeleton from the La Brea tar pits. A cast of Lucy and the "first family's" footprints illustrate what our own ancient ancestors looked like. Children enjoy searching through sand to uncover ancient shark's teeth, which they can take home.

In the multi-cultural displays, you may see life-size Papua New Guinea tribal figures, an Eskimo canoe or an Egyptian mummy case. Special exhibits range from a one-woman contemporary art show to hands-on, interactive science exhibits.

Behring Auto Museum
UC Berkeley Museum of Art, Science and Culture
Camino Tassajara and Blackhawk Rd., Blackhawk
Exit I-680 in Danville at Sycamore Valley Rd.
Head east 4 1/2 miles. Museum on left.
510/736-2277 (recording)
Open Tu.-Sun. 10-5; Wed. until 9 PM
$7 Adults; $4 Seniors (65 and over) and ages 6-17,
$4 for all ages on Wed. after 5 PM

☼ *Judah L. Magnes Museum*

Housed in a 1908 mansion on one of Berkeley's prettiest streets, the Magnes is the third largest Jewish museum in the United States. Its permanent collection encompasses 10,000 objects. Its Judaica Library contains 10,000 volumes. Its Western Jewish History Center includes 20,000 items.

The museum's "Holiday Room" is an intriguing place to start discovering the basics of Chanukah and other Jewish celebrations.

Illustrating a calendar year of Jewish holidays, the exhibits contain objects found in Jewish homes as well as synagogues. Jewish ceremonies are very home-oriented.

In the Sabbath display case are Kiddush goblets, Challah knives for cutting braided egg bread and intricate silver spice boxes. The Kiddush is the blessing said over the wine. Another blessing is said while cutting with the Challah knife.

The spice box contains cinnamon, cloves or nutmeg, so the sweetness of the Sabbath can linger throughout the week. The spice boxes displayed here are intricately crafted silver, mostly from 19th-century Russia and Germany. One resembles a castle's turret with waving flags.

Sabbath objects like these are used today in many Jewish homes. An interesting assortment of spice boxes is available at the museum's gift shop.

The Chanukah exhibit illustrates the extraordinary diversity of Chanukah lamps. Some are the familiar Menorah-style, a candelabra with eight curved arms. Many show the influence of different cultures on the religion. A 14th-century Chanukah lamp from Spain has a cut-out rose window above a colonnade of Moorish arches. One from 19th-century Iran is a flat brass sheet that looks like a pavilion with two small side towers.

Chanukah is a historic holiday, not actually mentioned in the Torah, that celebrates a resistance movement at the end of Alexander's empire, about 165 BC. When Jewish freedom fighters recaptured and rededicated their synagogue, the perpetual light had enough oil to burn only one more day. The light is never supposed to burn out, but it would take eight days to create more lamp oil. Miraculously, the perpetual light continued to burn for those eight days.

This event is just one of the cycles when Jews were persecuted then rose again. The museum's "Room of Remembrance" illustrates other eras of anti-Semitism. Most prominent are objects from Nazi Germany. One case displays a burnt Torah scroll from Kristalnacht. The Torah scroll, containing the Holy Word, is the Jew's most sacred object, to be treated with the utmost reverence. Another display shows a defiled segment of Torah scroll used as a canvas for an oil painting.

One of the Magnes' missions is to preserve Jewish artifacts; many were lost during times of anti-Semitism. In the upstairs hall is a large stained glass window representing the 12 tribes of Israel, probably from a synagogue. Someone found it in an antique store. The Torah and Synagogue Room contains artifacts spanning five centuries and objects from around the world.

In addition to the permanent collection, the museum's temporary exhibits celebrate works by contemporary Jewish artists, art with Jewish themes and Jewish lifestyles in other cultures.

After touring the museum, you can relax in the picnic area, surrounded by roses and palms in a garden designed by John McLaren, the landscape architect for Golden Gate Park.

Judah L. Magnes Museum
2911 Russell St., between Pine & Claremont,
Berkeley
510/549-6950
Sun. - Th. 10-4; Tours offered Sun. & Wed.
Free, $3 Donation suggested

☼ *Mormon Temple*

You can see it from the freeway, a glowing white monument high in the Oakland hills. Ships and planes use it as a landmark. Visitors from around the world are attracted to it like a beacon.

Next time you have an hour to spare, satisfy your curiosity and drive up to the Oakland Temple of the Church of Jesus Christ of Latter-day Saints. Members of the Mormon Church will be on hand to show you around this inspiring setting and explain the basics of their religious beliefs.

The gleaming white granite Temple follows an Oriental motif, with five pinnacle spires reaching heavenward. A long walkway lined with colorful flowers, tumbling waterfalls and splashing fountains draws the eye to this most sacred of the Mormons' meeting places. Beyond is a cloud-high view of Oakland, the Bay and the San Francisco skyline on the horizon. The sweet scent of flowers and piped-in music of the Mormon Tabernacle Choir enhance the site's peaceful aura.

You begin your tour at the Visitor Center, where you can pick up brochures on the Church's history and choose from a list of 20 to 30-minute films to watch. Rather than preaching, the films focus on common sense questions, such as the purpose of life, and illustrate them with everyday, feel-good people and stories. As the tour guide will tell you, they're not trying to convince you but simply want to share what they've found.

The architecturally unique Temple is the beacon that draws people from the freeway, but don't expect to see its interior. Because it is sacred, only Church members in good standing are allowed to enter. Even then members only use the Temple for four highly sacred purposes: marriage, certain baptisms, a "sealing" ceremony to unite families and certain promises with God.

Regular Sunday meetings are held in the Inter-Stake Center, the long building next to the Temple, which is open to the public. This Center encompasses 170 rooms, with two gymnasiums, three chapels, two kitchens and a 2,000-seat auditorium and its well-used genealogical library.

In the chapels, Sunday sacrament meetings are conducted in many languages, including Tongan, Samoan, Vietnamese, Cambodian, Laotian, Chinese, Spanish and English. The auditorium's highlight is the immense organ with more than 4,500 pipes.

Have you ever wondered where your ancestors were during the Renaissance? The popular Family History Center, a genealogical library located in the Visitor Center, is a branch of the world-renowned Salt Lake City library . About 80% of its users are non-Mormons researching family trees. Volunteers and a short film will show you how to get started.

Even the non-religious find it's well worth the trip to the Oakland Temple to see the architecture, to study in the Family History Center and to learn more about the Mormon religion.

While you're in the area, visit Joaquin Miller Park, a short drive east of the Temple off Joaquin Miller Road. Miller was an Indian fighter, pony express rider, judge, gold prospector and writer, but he is best known for his trees. He and his friends planted 75,000 of them—Monterey pines, cypress, and, reportedly, California's first eucalyptus.

Today, you can hike in this 500-acre forest park and visit the stone monuments that Miller erected to those he most admired, such as poets Robert and Elizabeth Browning and Moses. Bring a picnic to enjoy at the shaded sites overlooking panoramic views of San Francisco.

Oakland Temple of the Church
of Jesus Christ of Latter-day Saints
4770 Lincoln Ave. at Highway 13, Oakland
510/531-1475
Guided tours daily 9-9
Family History Center: Tues.-Th. 9:30-9:30;
Fri. 9:30-5; Sat. Noon-5
Free

☼ *Oakland Museum*

What do the barn owl, Mickey Mouse and artist Thomas Hill have in common? They are all part of the unique heritage of the great state of California.

The Oakland Museum is a whirlwind tour of California's environment, history and art. This is one of the best organized museums anywhere. The first floor is devoted to California's natural history, cutting a swath of the state from seashore to mountaintop. The second floor encapsulates human history, from Native Americans to Hollywood. The third showcases California art through the decades, from 19th-century landscapes to modernism.

Begin on the first floor with the dizzying film, "Fast Flight." In five minutes, you rocket from the pounding surf, over the coastal mountains, across the central valley, up the crest of the Sierra and down to the deserts.

Now you can take a leisurely walk across California from west to east. Each mini-environment, from seashore to Sierra, captures life-like scenes of animal, plant and insect life to illustrate the interactions of nature.

The diorama of the mountain lion resting by its recently killed deer demonstrates the food chain. Energy from the sun is used by the green plants, which are eaten by the deer, which is eaten by the lion, then returned to the earth as waste.

Other exhibits include a redwood grove alive with bird songs, a weasel attacking a porcupine and a bear eating berries. There is one live display, a squeamish termite farm. Another is proof that "some living things survive mainly by irritating other livings things," that is, galls on trees.

The second floor's history collection boasts more than 6,000 examples of California memorabilia. Interactive touch screens introduce you to some of the stories behind our state's unique culture. You may hear a Native American basketmaker, a historian, even Alice Waters on California cuisine.

Along the three-dimensional time-line, you walk past Indian acorn granaries, ceremonial regalia and basketry to the Spanish missionary era's illuminated Bibles and embroidered garments to a carreta, or ox cart, built when California was Mexican.

The "Goldseekers and Adventurers" section showcases the original James J. Ott's Assayers Office from Nevada City, complete with counter, workshop, scales and log books. Playing cards, gold nuggets and much more is on display.

The crude lifestyle of the forty-niners contrasts sharply with the intricate, graceful Victorians. One fancy lady greets a dandy on his big-wheeled bicycle at her door, framed with delicate, etched glass.

As you walk through the 20th century, you realize that you, too, share a place in California's history. Peek into a 1940s kitchen, a 1960s patio barbecue with grilling steaks, a cheese tray, wines and peach pie, and a 1980s den with Scandinavian-style black leather furniture and Trivial Pursuit.

The 20th century is the most technically marvelous, and cluttered, of all, with customized motorcycles, surfboards, Apple computers, movie cameras and windmills. The hippies earned a display, with candles, psychedelic album covers and a guitar patterned with "Peace and Love." Even the Yuppies are represented by a woman's gray business suit, white blouse, red bowed scarf and a laminated I.D. card from Bechtel.

The third floor highlights California art and artists. The collection includes masterful landscapes of Yosemite by Thomas Hill. Early 20th-century work is characterized by the California Decorative Style, including a stunning, stained glass window. More recent works include flowing three-dimensional sculptures and the vibrant colors of contemporary artists.

Oakland Museum of California
1000 Oak St. (at 10th St.), Oakland
510/834-2413 (recording) or 510/238-3401
Wed.-Sat. 10-5; Sun. noon-7
Suggested Donation: $4 General; $2 Seniors over
62 and Students with I.D., under 7 free

☼ *Marin Museum of the American Indian*

The site is almost as old as history itself. Almost 1,000 years ago, Native Americans were born, lived and died on a patch of land we now call Novato, in Marin County. Little remains of their settlement, but archeological digs in the 1960s unearthed evidence of a thriving community here.

Today, the Marin Museum of the American Indian stands on the very site where the village existed in centuries past. Inside, you will find informative displays highlighted with such artifacts as obsidian arrowheads, shell beads, baskets and hunting and fishing tools. Surrounding the museum is a small park with a playground and compact garden of native American plants.

The best place to begin your tour of the museum is at the diorama. It depicts the Miwok village as it might have looked on this site, complete with thatch huts and earth shelters. One man paddles a canoe made of tule. Fish dry on a pole.

The earthen sweathouse, or lamma, was used for ceremonial purposes by men only. Before a hunt, the men gathered here to pray for good hunting. Sweating, followed by cleaning themselves, helped rid them of the human scent, essential to successfully stalking their prey.

A cross-section of earth shows how archeologists find layers of civilization in the depth of artifacts. In addition to carbon 14, which helps determine the age of a particular item, they can piece together history by the way an item is made. Shell beads, mortars and arrowheads become more refined over time.

About 400 AD, the bow and arrow replaced the spear as the primary hunting weapon. One case holds a sampling of obsidian arrowheads. This black volcanic glass was prized as it was durable and fractured easily to produce sharp edges.

The Indians lived in harmony with the land, taking only what they needed and using nearly everything they took. One display shows how a deer was used. They ate the meat and used the hide for clothing. Bones became scrapers, arrowhead-flakers and ornaments. Sinew was softened into cordage. The head and antlers could be used as a disguise for hunters. Even the hooves were hollowed into ceremonial rattles.

Fishing was another vital pursuit. One clever contraption was the long, cone-shaped fish trap, like the one displayed here. This was placed in the center of a dam, its narrow end pointing upstream. Fish swam in as they headed upstream to spawn, then could not turn around to escape.

Indians also made duck decoys out of tule, sometimes covering them with feathers. Dried mud balls, flattened on two sides so they could skip over the water, became projectiles and helped in capturing the ducks.

Clamshell discs were used as currency. One display illustrates how variations in style and the number of beads found at an archeological site indicate economic and social patterns. Glass beads, for example, came only after the Europeans.

This was the final era of the Miwok's traditional lifestyle. Disease and the encroachment of new settlements spelled disaster for the Indian. Today, their descendants still living in this area come to the museum to ensure that their heritage is preserved for all of us.

Marin Museum of the American Indian
2200 Novato Blvd., Miwok Park, Novato
San Marin/Atherton exit off 101 North, 3 mi. to Park
415/897-4064
Wed.-Fri. 10-3; Sat.-Sun. Noon-4
Free; Donations appreciated

Crocker Art Museum

The Crocker Art Museum is the oldest public art museum in the west. Housed in an Italianate Victorian mansion, the building, itself, is a masterpiece. Built in 1871 for Judge Edwin Crocker and his family, it served not only as their home, but also as an enviable entertainment center and art gallery. The mansion once boasted a bowling alley, skating rink, billiard room, elaborate ballroom and library.

While it was being built, the Crockers enjoyed a grand tour of Europe, collecting old masters to display in their new home. Many of the oils exhibited today are the works that the Crockers originally purchased. Crocker also acquired a worthy collection of paintings by the California artists of his time, including such greats as Thomas Hill, William Keith and Charles Christian Nahl.

No expense was spared in decorating the floors, walls and ceiling during the Victorians' elaborate heyday. Every detail has been restored to reflect its original appearance. You walk through immense carved wooden doors to an entryway with an ornate but tasteful tile floor and intricately painted ceiling. Curved staircases rise up either side to the European and California galleries.

In the European Gallery, you'll find the rich colors and dramatic figures of 16th-century Flemish works and 17th-century Dutch and Italian paintings. Many depict Biblical or mythical scenes.

This Gallery also exhibits highlights of the Crockers' collection of 150 contemporary German paintings acquired during their European travels in the early 1870s. These now comprise one of the largest collections of German popular art in the U.S. Many are scenes of the everyday life of the common man and are enhanced by excellent signs describing the paintings.

One of the grandest works in the Early California Hall is Thomas Hill's "Great Canyons of the Sierra—Yosemite," painted in 1871. It measures 6 by 10 feet. Light appears to glow on the cliffs, with a waterfall feathering into the valley and Half Dome looming in the background. Another landscape by William Keith shows what Mt. Tamalpais looked like in 1871.

On the first level, the Crockers' magnificent ballroom nearly overwhelms the artworks displayed. It features parquet floors, rich wood wainscoting and an intricately painted ceiling. Stand beneath the second chandelier and look up. You will see a patch of the original design exposed to show how closely the restoration matches.

A period room recreates the Crocker family parlor from 1870 through 1885. Furnishings include a rococo mirrored etagere with shelves for displaying yet more porcelain artworks. This room saw the wedding of Katie Crocker in February of 1874 and her funeral in October of that year.

You'll also find contemporary works at the Crocker and fine special exhibits at any time of year. Just six blocks from the heart of Old Sacramento, the Crocker is a don't miss for anyone touring the area.

Crocker Art Museum
3rd and O Sts., Sacramento
916/264-5423
Wed.-Sun. 10-5, Th. 10-9
$4.50 Adults; $2 ages 7-17

Towe Ford Museum

The "World's Most Complete Antique Ford Museum" isn't in Michigan. It's right here in Sacramento. More than 180 automobiles, from a 1903 Model A to a sporty 'sixties Mustang, fill this cavernous garage.

The cars are arranged chronologically. Walking through the museum is like walking through 20th-century American history and rediscovering the automobile's distinctive role in that history.

Period music from the various decades plays in the background. Displays list world events of selected production years to bring back the times of the cars' original owners. A few artifacts, such as vintage clothing and advertisements, personalize the machines. You can even climb inside and sit behind the steering wheel of a Model T.

From 1912 until 1924, Henry Ford was responsible for manufacturing half of all motorcars in use in the United States. It began in 1896 in his Detroit workshop. Ford pieced together bicycle chains, wheels and other parts to a buggy frame and attached a gasoline-powered engine. The first Model A, displayed in the museum, isn't much more than a modified horse carriage with brass headlights and a wood steering wheel.

You can see how the automobile evolved as you walk past the early cars. Almost every year and model produced by Ford in its first 50 years is on display. By the time the Model T was introduced, Ford was unable to manufacture enough cars to meet demand, despite his pioneering mass production methods that turned out 15 million Model Ts from 1908 to 1927.

Individuals customized Fords to their personal needs, as in the 1929 Model A mail truck and 1930 red Model AA dump truck. One rare adaptation is the 1931 Model A produce truck used in Hawaii to ship fruit around the island. The chassis, frame and engine were shipped to Hawaii, where a custom truck body was added. Only 25 of these were made. This is the only surviving "Banana Wagon."

One scene is straight out of *Grapes of Wrath*. A 1917 Model T truck is loaded with such depression-era goods as a disassembled windmill and prized mirror. A simple camp, with a coffeepot over a campfire, stools and a wash basin, is set up in front—a typical scene along Route 66 as families headed to California.

Another scene embodies the World War II era. Period music, newspaper headlines proclaiming the Pearl Harbor bombing and a collection of gas ration coupons form the backdrop for a 1943 Ford jeep with Army markings. The jeep is the "grandfather" of today's 4-wheel drive vehicles.

Roomy sedans from the 1950s are parked as though they're at a drive-in movie, with speakers attached to their windows. An enviable 1957 Skyliner convertible features a retractable hardtop that folded back into the car's trunk.

A 1964 1/2 Mustang and sleek 1955 Thunderbird are the stars of the southern California beach scene, complete with hamburger stand and surf shop.

Specialized non-Ford automobiles round out the collection, including Governor Jerry Brown's 1974 gas-guzzling blue Plymouth and a 1976 Cadillac armored limousine. Once used by the secret service, the door is open to reveal the nearly 2-inch thick window. Even though it weighed five tons, the limousine could top 80 mph on four flat tires.

Towe Ford Museum
2200 Front St.,
about one mile south of Old Town, Sacramento
916/442-6802
Open daily 10-6
$5 Adults; $4.50 Seniors;
$2.50 High School; $1 Grade School;
under 5 free

Notes

Towns
to
Explore

.- --*Half Moon Bay*

"You're only 25 miles south of San Francisco, but you're a world away," a Half Moon Bay resident sighed. This quiet coastal village is brimming with old-fashioned charm. You can browse through the fun shops of the quaint downtown, peek into a garden, picnic on the beach or visit a winery.

Half Moon Bay was founded in the 1860s by Portuguese and Italian farmers and fishermen. Today, fishing and agriculture remain two of the area's main industries. The foggy, coastal climate is ideal for growing Brussels sprouts, artichokes, cut flowers and its most famous produce—pumpkins.

Each autumn, the hills turn orange with a plethora of pumpkins. It's hard to dispute the town's claim that it is the "Pumpkin Capital of the World." Begun in 1970, the annual Half Moon Bay Art & Pumpkin Festival, held the weekend after the Columbus Day observance, now draws about 300,000 people to this tiny town.

Another popular festival is Chamarita, usually held the seventh Sunday after Easter. Chamarita is a holiday of thanksgiving dating back to Queen Isabel of Portugal. It has been celebrated for over a century in Half Moon Bay. A Catholic Mass, parade, carnival and barbecue are part of the festivities.

The area's bounty of beautiful bouquet flowers also is celebrated. On the third Saturday of each month from May through September, local floriculture wholesalers set up colorful booths downtown to sell flowers and house plants.

At any time of year, you can see one of the town's prettiest little gardens at Le Bouquet. Look for the fanciful painted door on Mill Street a half-block west of Main Street. Inside this shop, you'll find wreaths decorated with dried flowers and, occasionally, seashells.

On Half Moon Bay's eclectic Main Street, an art gallery and an animal feed store may be next-door neighbors. The Tin Palace is a mini-mall of artsy boutiques. Sidewalk tables invite you to people-watch with a coffee and treat.

The smell of leather greets you at the Half Moon Bay Feed & Fuel Co. You'll find beautifully tooled saddles, garden seeds, birdfeeders. You may even see their resident rooster.

Cavanaugh Gallery specializes in handcrafted American furnishings and folk art, including rag rugs, tole-painted dressers, upholstered double rockers, whimsical cow planters and wood chairs custom-made by the Amish.

Coastside Books offers a beautiful selection of titles on art, photography, metaphysical subjects and more. Brightly colored children's clothes fill the racks of P. Cottontail.

Take a one-block detour down Miramontes Street to the Community United Methodist Church, built in 1872. Look closely and you'll notice an unusual theme in one of the stained glass windows—pumpkins.

For a touch of old-fashioned Half Moon Bay, drop by Cunha's Country Store. The shop's been open for 100 years and run by the same family for 65 years. Upstairs is a regular emporium of kitchen gadgets, mixing bowls, plaid shirts, bandannas, straw cowboy hats, jeans, fancy cowboy boots, muffin tins, placemats, wrapping paper and much more. Downstairs is a grocery where you can buy local produce and a sandwich for a picnic. Top it off with cookies from the HMB Bakery next door.

Before taking the short drive to the coast's sandy beaches, you may want to detour to Obester Winery, about 2 miles east of town on Highway 92. It's open daily for tasting and sales from 10 to 5 (tel. 415/726-9463).

Half Moon Bay
Chamber of Commerce
520 Kelly Ave.
Half Moon Bay 94019
415/726-5202 (recording) or 415/726-8380

Gilroy & Environs

Welcome to "the only town in America where you can marinate a steak by hanging it on the clothesline," according to humorist Will Rogers. Just roll down your car windows and you'll know when you've arrived at Gilroy, the self-proclaimed "Garlic Capital of the World."

This area grows and processes 90% of all the garlic consumed in the United States. Each year, the Gilroy Garlic Festival in late July draws about 140,000 people to this small town. They eat about 5,000 pounds of garlic, 20,000 garlic rolls and 15,500 pounds of garlic-laced pepper steak sandwiches. But there's more to Gilroy than garlic.

Take a quick tour of the town's historic district to see what Main Street, U.S.A. looked like in the 1920s. Monterey Street, between 4th and 6th Streets, is lined with the brick and concrete shops of a working man's downtown.

Head up 1st Street towards the Hecker Pass for one of the most interesting drives in the area. You can't miss the stunning, colorful flower fields and greenhouses of Goldsmith Seeds, the second largest flower seed producer in the world. You're welcome to walk among the rows of well-marked petunias, marigolds and other blooms growing out front.

Within a short distance, you can visit seven wineries, small, family-owned operations run by the same families for generations. The owner may be the one to pour your samples. Surprisingly, this is one of California's oldest wine grape growing regions. The Franciscan fathers first planted vineyards here in the mid-1770s.

After visiting Hecker Pass Winery, the last on this route, double back and take a left on Watsonville Road. You will pass three more wineries, including historic Kirigin vineyards, before circling back to Monterey Street.

Just outside of town (Leavesley Road exit off 101), the Pacific West Outlet Center and Outlets at Gilroy are a bargain-hunter's paradise of more than 100 factory direct discount stores. Liz Claiborne, Anne Klein and Guess are some of the brand-name outlets here.

Next, drive further south on 101 to San Juan Bautista. Its mission, founded in 1797, has been restored. It offers a cool retreat into history on a hot summer day. Once known as "the Mission of Music," one room contains an old bass, two violins and choir books. A tall music stand features a box from which white doves were released during mass on Pentecost. (Open daily 9:30-4:30, $1 donation suggested, tel. 408/623-4528)

The State Historic Park preserves the San Juan Bautista of the 1860s and '70s, encompassing four major buildings along with courtyards and gardens. The 1840 Castro House is traditional Spanish architecture, with red-tile roof and a shaded balcony running the length of the adobe structure. Inside, it's furnished in the style of the 1870s. Across the street, the Plaza Stable houses an extensive selection of restored horse-drawn vehicles, from a Parisian coach to a 12-barrel beer wagon. (Park open daily 10-4:30, $2 Adults, $1 ages 6-12, tel. 408/623-4881) Fun handcraft shops, boutiques and restaurants entice visitors to the town's small but diverse main street.

A bit further afield, but well worth the drive for outdoor enthusiasts, is Pinnacles National Monument. You can hike up, around, above and beneath the odd-shaped rock towers that gave the park its name. Tarantulas, wild pigs and neon-colored rock climbers are some of the strange creatures you might encounter here. For more on Pinnacles, see The Great Outdoors chapter.

Gilroy & Environs
Gilroy Visitor's Bureau
7780 Monterey St., Gilroy, CA 95020
408/842-6436

.. •• *Monterey*

Most people visiting Monterey head for the same attractions: Cannery Row, the Aquarium and Fisherman's Wharf. Next time, take a detour.

Follow the Path of History to discover a side of Monterey that many miss—the surprising story of California's first capital. Pick up a map at the Custom House or join one of the docent-led tours. The Path wends past one of the state's most extensive collections of adobe homes and one of California's first brick houses, first theaters, first glass windows and the building where the state's first Constitution was written.

The Custom House is across from Fisherman's Wharf. This is the oldest existing government building on the west coast. At one time, while under Mexican rule, Monterey was California's chief port of entry. Each ship that harbored here had to unload their cargo for inspection and taxation. Inside the Custom House, you will find a sampling of goods that 19th-century Californians coveted: china, wood saws and burlap sacks full of flour, rice and salt. Nearby, the Maritime Museum features more exhibits on the area's nautical heritage.

The Stars and Stripes were first raised in California on the Custom House flagpole. Monterey was named in 1602, founded in 1770 by Father Junipero Serra and was the Spanish capital of Alta California until the Mexicans revolted in 1822. Then Monterey was the Mexican capital until 1846, when Commodore John Drake Sloat landed here, raised the American flag and claimed California for the United States without firing a shot.

Follow the Path of History to Monterey's first brick house and its delightful courtyard garden. A Virginian bought this land for $29, kilned his own bricks and built this simple home in 1847. Next door is the Whaling Station, headquarters of the Old Monterey Whaling Company from 1855 to 1885. At the time, whale blubber was sliced off and made into oil on the Custom House beach.

On the next corner is Monterey's first theater, built in 1846 as a boarding house for sailors. By the late 1840s, people doled out $5 to enjoy the plays featuring an all-male cast. Today, you, too, can watch a 19th-century melodrama for less than $10. Performances are held weekends year-round.

Walk half a block to the Joseph Boston Store. In 1849, Boston opened this store to serve the growing number of settlers brought in by the gold rush. Today, it's like walking into the late 19th-century, thanks to the Monterey History and Art Association.

Shelves are stocked with goods from that era: ribbons, tea, Victorian lace bags, rock candy, homemade bird houses and more. Proceeds from sales go to the Association. It is said that the safe in the corner once held prospectors' gold dust, as Boston's was the only safe in the region at the time. This is how a general mercantile store became a "Casa del Oro," or "House of Gold."

Walk down busy Pacific Street, past a series of quiet, simple adobes, to Colton Hall. A museum on the second floor recreates the room where California's first Constitutional Congress convened. Here they drafted the state's first Constitution and penned it in English and Spanish. Today, their top hats, quill pens and scattered papers remain as if the delegates had just taken a break.

These are a few of the more than 30 historic buildings on Monterey's Path of History. Other highlights include the Old Monterey Jail, with bleak granite walls from which no prisoner ever escaped and the Larkin House, a fine example of Mexican era residential architecture.

Monterey's Path of History
Most buildings open daily 10-4.
Some open by guided tour only.
408/649-7118 (Monterey State Historic Park)
$2 Adults; $1.50 ages 12-17; $1 ages 6-12
for guided walking tour or each home tour.
Two-day pass for all buildings and guided walking
tour is $5 Adults; $3 ages 12-17; $2 ages 6-12

Benicia

Benicia was named for a beautiful, charming woman from a family steeped in history. Nearly 150 years later, you'll see that Benicia was aptly named. This state capital turned small town boasts several important historic sites, a number of handsomely renovated Victorians and a charming downtown with antique shops, cafes and boutiques.

Begin at the State Capitol building on the corner of 1st and G Streets. This imposing red brick structure fronted with two white, fluted columns was California's State Capitol for 13 months beginning in 1853. Since then it's been everything from a grammar school to the city jail.

Today, it's a State Historical Park. The Senate and Assembly rooms appear as if the early politicians are on a lunch break. Inkwells and candles wait on the desks, with spittoons on the floor nearby. Some men even left their top hats. (Open daily 10-5; $2 Adults, $1 ages 6-12, tel. 707/745-3385)

On weekend afternoons when volunteers are available, you can tour the Fischer-Hanlon House next door. This circa-1858 home captures life in early California. It is fully furnished, complete with potbellied stoves, a creamery and an old-fashioned water pump in the pantry. The Fischer-Hanlon home is one of several restored Victorians along G Street.

The Brewery, a dark, cool saloon on H Street just north of the Capitol, is an unlikely spot for a history lesson. But its interior walls are covered with murals illustrating Benicia's grandest moments throughout the years. Browsers are welcome.

The colorful courtyard garden of St. Paul's Episcopal Church is two blocks north, at First and J Streets. This graceful edifice with Gothic details and colonial-style steeple was built in 1856 by shipwrights from Benicia's Pacific Mail and Steamship Company. The church's ceiling, with exposed, arched ceiling beams, resembles an upside-down ship's hull. If you phone ahead, you can arrange a guided, historic tour of St. Paul's. (Open Mon.-Fri. 10-3, Sun. 8-Noon; donations accepted for church; $2 for guided tour; 707/745-0307).

Walk back down First Street towards the water. You may be enticed into the many antique shops and gift boutiques. Several cafes offer delicious, creative meals at reasonable prices. For something fancier, try the Union Hotel. This 1882 hotel is the oldest three-story structure in Benicia. Until 1952, its 20 rooms "came occupied," a subtle description for a bordello. Today it's revamped as a B&B inn.

The renovated Tannery building, now filled with restaurants and boutiques, is a remnant of Benicia's tanning industry. This was once the principal tanning center of the Pacific Coast.

At a nearby spot on the waterfront, a spark began a wildfire that engulfed the entire nation. In May 1848, Sutter's messenger had stunning news: Gold discovered in the Sierra foothills. Before long, the thriving town of Benicia plunged to 14 families as men rushed to the Mother Lode.

Many of the buildings where First Street tapers into the water were bordellos. The abandoned green building was Jurgensen's Saloon in 1892. Jack London was among the regulars when he lived in a nearby houseboat.

The yellow building is the old transcontinental railroad depot. At the end of the pier, ferries carried thousands of passengers, including Pony Express riders, across the straits to and from Martinez. Today, park benches invite visitors to relax in quiet solitude overlooking the tranquil waters.

Benicia Chamber of Commerce
601 1st St., Benicia 94510
800/559-7377 or 707/745-2120

Extra Tip... Another fun, historic site in Benicia is the Camel Barn Museum, on the other side of I-780 from downtown. Camels, imported as part of a government experiment in transporting military supplies, were auctioned off here in 1864. (2060 Camel Rd., 707/745-5435; Wed.-Sun. 1-4; $1 donation requested.)

⚫⚫ ⚫⚫ *Sonoma Plaza*

The toast of Sonoma wine country, this is one of the largest and prettiest plazas in California. You can spend an hour or an entire afternoon here, browsing in boutiques, exploring historic buildings or indulging in delicious homemade treats.

As you stroll around the plaza, take time to read the plaques which tell the history of the buildings. Many were built by the Vallejos in the 1830s and '40s when Sonoma was under Mexican rule.

Several businesses also boast long histories. A third-generation cheesemaker runs the Sonoma Cheese Factory. At the back of the store you can watch their specialty being created in 10,000-pound cheese vats. A slide show illustrates the history and process of cheesemaking.

The next corner is devoted entirely to history. The Sonoma State Historic Park encompasses this neighborhood of buildings, from the Servant's Quarters to the Mission. Venture into the barracks to discover the history of Sonoma. Exhibit rooms focus on the area's Indian, Mexican and American residents.

Seven flags have flown over the Sonoma region: Spain, England, Russia, Mexican Empire, Mexican Republic, Bear Flag Republic and the United States. While under Mexican rule, Americans could not own land nor hold office.

In 1846, 30 Americans, self-proclaimed "Bears," revolted. They rode into town, surrounded Vallejo's home and, without firing a shot, seized the general and the town. They raised a muslin flag with a bear emblem, a symbol that evolved into our state flag.

Built in 1823, the Mission San Francisco Solano de Sonoma is the northernmost and last of the California missions. It marks the end of 300 years of Spanish-Mexican settlement. Inside you will find up to 4-foot-thick adobe walls. In the chapel, the whitewashed walls are highlighted with borders of blue and gold designs. (Open daily 10-5, $2 Adults; $1 Children, tel. 707/938-1519)

The ancient-looking building across the street was once the Blue Wing Inn. Built about 1840, it boasts many renowned guests, including Ulysses S. Grant, Kit Carson and the bandit Murietta.

While walking up First Street, explore the vine-covered alleyways. Down El Paseo you'll discover the Vasquez House. Built in 1856, the home was once owned by General Hooker, from whence the slang term originated for the ladies that catered to his soldiers. Today, you'll enjoy the friendly conversation and low-priced goodies baked by the Sonoma League for Historic Preservation volunteers.

Follow your nose to the Sonoma French Bakery, famous for their award-winning sourdough. Their secret? "Some people credit it to climate, but I think it's experience," said Josephine Morenzoni. She had been at the bakery for nearly 3 decades.

If you don't have time to visit the area's wineries, stop by the Wine Exchange. They offer some 14 different wines for tasting every day, at about $1 per taste. Other stores around the plaza include thrift shops, a kitchen store and much more.

Sebastiani Winery, established in 1904, is just two blocks from the plaza, at 389 Fourth Street East. They offer free tours and tasting from 10-5 daily, as well as another fun gift shop.

Two other wineries are well worth the short drive from the plaza. Ravenswood, at 18701 Gehricke Road, offers free tasting from 10 to 4:30 daily and barbecue lunches for under $10 on summer weekends. Buena Vista has free tasting, an art gallery and gift shop with enviable picnic accessories. This winery is located at 18000 Old Winery Road and is open 10:30 to 4:30 daily.

The best way to plan your trip is to call or write the Sonoma Valley Visitors Bureau and ask for their Official Visitors Guide. They'll send it to you free, or you can buy it for $1.50 in their Sonoma office.

Sonoma Plaza
Sonoma Valley Visitors Bureau
453 First St. (on the Plaza), Sonoma, CA 95476
707/996-1090

.. •• *San Anselmo*

When people visit the north Bay, they usually flock to Sausalito, Tiburon or the coast. But antique hounds will uncover a small paradise in San Anselmo, just a few miles west of the San Rafael Bridge.

Even if you're only a casual browser when it comes to antiques, you'll still find a slice of quintessential Marin County here. San Anselmo is small town America with a touch of open-minded eccentricity under an aura of affluence.

Antique shoppers don't have to go far to search out that special knick knack, brooch or curio cabinet. More than 130 dealers are clustered within a 1/2-mile. Sir Francis Drake Boulevard and San Anselmo Avenue, which runs one block to the west, are lined with antique shops, gift boutiques and cafes. Two-hour free parking is plentiful in the public lots and along the street. If you're planning to stay longer, park on the streets a few blocks west of town. It's not a far walk.

Pick up the free brochure, "Northern California's Antiques Capital," available at most San Anselmo antique stores. It lists the town's dealers, describes the kinds of items they carry and shows their locations on a map. You can follow along as you stroll through town or head directly for the kind of specialty antique store that interests you.

You may want to start your tour in The Pavillion, the distinctive building at the north end of town. Opened in 1980, their collective houses items from more than 30 dealers.

Amateur antiquers appreciate The Pavillion's goal to label their goods with country of origin, date and, at times, the item's purpose. You'll find everything from cribs to crystal. For those who don't like bargaining, an accepted practice in many antique stores, The Pavillion has "fair and firm" prices.

Nearby is the Modern i, which specializes in 1950s furniture and accessories. Oveda Maurer Antiques, on Greenfield, offers 18th-century and early 19th-century American furniture and accessories including pewter, early lighting, glass and folk art.

As you head down Sir Francis Drake Boulevard, you'll pass a dozen or so antique stores. For English country furniture, especially pine, try the San Anselmo Country Store. The Legacy, a collective of about 35 dealers, is the place to go for nostalgia and collectibles. Across the street, on Tunstead Avenue, you'll find Radio Activity, specializing in restored '30s and '40s radios, along with Sanford's Antiques' arts and crafts era furniture.

Head one block west to San Anselmo Avenue, the heart of town. You'll find dealers in old jewelry, out of print books, even antique bridal gowns.

Before leaving town, take a short drive up to San Anselmo's humble beginnings, the San Francisco Theological Seminary. To get there from San Anselmo Avenue, take a right on Bolinas at the south end of town, then take another right onto Kensington and follow the signs to Montgomery Hall.

The first stone building you'll see is the 1897 Montgomery Chapel with its lovely stained glass windows. Wind your way up a forested knoll to two surprising castle-like structures perched on the top. These are Montgomery and Scott Halls, built in 1892. The Seminary was the first real industry in San Anselmo. The 1906 earthquake convinced some people to settle down around it.

The completion of the Golden Gate Bridge in 1937 caused another influx in the population. In 1974, having grown to almost 13,000 residents, San Anselmo officially became a town. Today, the Seminary is a reminder of San Anselmo's quiet past while the town bustles below.

San Anselmo
Chamber of Commerce
P.O. Box 2844, San Anselmo 94979
415/454-2510

•• •• *Sausalito*

Sausalito combines the ambiance of a Mediterranean marina with a touch of Cape Cod clapboard and a history that's pure Marin. Just north of the Golden Gate Bridge, the town is an instant getaway.

Most visitors to this sunny tourist Mecca spend their time on Bridgeway Boulevard. Here you'll find stores that offer everything from the wacky to the sublime, including designer toothbrushes, art deco sculpture, board games, resort-wear clothing, fine jewelry, handcrafts, t-shirts and souvenirs. Hawaiian ice cream, cookies and plenty of restaurants, many specializing in seafood, renew your energy.

When you've had enough shopping, explore Sausalito's quieter side. You can stroll along the shore or climb steep backstreets to visit pleasant parks, a poet's bench and a century-old church.

Sausalito has changed dramatically over the years, except for its knack for attracting those looking for the good life. In the late 1800s, the wealthy attempted to duplicate the life of the English country gentry in their Victorian mansions here.

In 1875, the railroad came to town, bringing transients and other unsavories along with it. Before long, the town boasted 25 gambling dens and bordellos, whose guests included the infamous Baby Face Nelson. During Prohibition, Sausalito bootleggers catered to San Francisco speakeasies.

In the 1950s and '60s, Sausalito was a magnet for artists seeking a bohemian lifestyle. The beat generation, flower power and funky houseboats were Sausalito trademarks.

Today, you can see remnants of all these phases of Sausalito's history. From Bridgeway, walk along the shore past restaurants cantilevered over the water. Horizons restaurant, built in 1898, was the first yacht club on the Pacific coast.

Bridgeway eventually ends at Valhalla, now The Chart House restaurant. It was opened in 1893 as a beer garden by a German native and used by bootleggers during Prohibition. Its best known owner was the colorful Sally Stanford, a former San Francisco madam and Sausalito mayor.

If you don't want to walk that far, look for the flower-bedecked Tiffany Park and climb the steep stairs to the back streets. At the top, turn right onto Tiffany. The Poet's Bench is at the next intersection. Carved into the stone bench is a poem about a castle of silence where "walls are draped with legends woven in threads of gold."

From here, follow Bulkley until you see the Alta Mira Hotel. Its sprawling patio topped with white, wrought iron furniture and light-colored umbrellas is especially popular with the Sunday brunch crowd. It is one of the two fancy hotels in Sausalito built in the late 1800s.

Across the street is the circa-1909 Presbyterian Church, with its cedar shingles and charming, uncluttered architecture. Follow the hill down from the church to the stairs leading back to Bridgeway. Below you is the colorful Vina Del Mar park with its fountain and elephant statues from the 1915 Panama-Pacific Exposition.

You'll come out by the 1885 Casa Madrona Hotel, which was a Beatnik beerhall-boarding house in the 1950s. Now it is a delightful bed and breakfast inn.

Next door is the Village Fair. Over the years, this was a Chinese gambling hall and opium den, then a distillery for bootleg whiskey, then an indoor golf course. Today it is an open air mall, complete with splashing waterfall. The Cafe Sausalito on the third floor offers indoor and outdoor seating with superb views of the bay, a restful spot to enjoy a sandwich and milk shake.

Sausalito Chamber of Commerce
333 Caledonia Street, Box 566
Sausalito, CA 94966
415/332-0505

Mendocino

You may get a sense of déjà vu in Mendocino, even if you've never been here before. The town is Hollywood's favorite setting for shows set in charming New England towns, including "Murder, She Wrote," "The Russians are Coming," "Same Time Next Year" and "Summer of '42."

We can thank Mendocino's first settlers for this slice of the east coast on the Pacific. They were loggers from New England, here to reap the bounty of the redwood forests. They built their down-east style Victorians along this rocky bluff abutting the ocean to reflect homes left behind on another shore.

Today, tourism, not timber, is Mendocino's mainstay. The entire town is a State Historic Preservation District. Almost all of the late 19th-century Victorian homes have been restored down to their fancy finials and fish-scale shingles. Many are unique bed and breakfast inns.

The ruggedly beautiful setting is a magnet for artists. The hub of the village boasts several galleries exhibiting their finely crafted exotic woods, watercolors depicting local scenery, contemporary jewelry and hand-thrown pottery.

To find the historical side of Mendocino, begin your tour at the Kelley House Museum. Housed in an 1861 Victorian, the museum's historical photographs, artifacts and period furniture illustrate Mendocino's beginnings.

The house was built by William Henry Kelley, one of Mendocino's first pioneers. The promise of gold first lured him to California in 1850, but he soon discovered the untapped riches in the north coast's forests.

In the parlor, an impressive collection of historical photographs brings back the Mendocino of the late 1800s. A scene from 1865 shows lumber being sent down apron chutes from the top of the cliff at the end of town to the cargo ship in the waters below. Another from 1890 shows a 16-bull team pulling logs through the forest.

Society ladies began their long journey to San Francisco's shops by being lowered to the ship from the top of the headlands on a crude chair, which resembled a ski lift without the safety bar.

The Victorian era was not without its amenities, however, even in Mendocino. In the Kelley House guest room is a black horsehair loveseat and desk chair. Upstairs, the bedroom is highlighted with intricate stenciling along the top of the wall. This stenciling was meticulously reproduced from remnants of the original.

On Main Street, the 1854 Ford House has a visitor center, with brochures on the area, and a museum for the Mendocino Headlands State Park. The most distinctive building in town is the Presbyterian Church with its white, New England-style steeple. Built in 1867-'68, it is one of the oldest Protestant churches in continuous use in California.

The small, bright red Kwan Ti Temple, on Albion between Kasten and Osborne, is the last remnant of the 200 Chinese who provided services for mill workers in the late 1800s.

Fans of "Murder, She Wrote" will recognize the Blair House, on the corner of Little Lake and Ford Streets. It served as the exterior of Angela Lansbury's home in the popular television show. Interior scenes are shot in a Hollywood studio. It was built in 1888 for Elisha W. Blair who, like many of his neighbors, worked for the lumber mill.

All of these historic buildings add to Mendocino's welcome-to-the-past mystique, but it may best be found in what is not seen: no traffic lights, no parking meters and no mailboxes in this town where everybody seems to know their neighbor. Be forewarned, however, that many of Mendocino's residents were city folks who planned to visit for a few days, then moved here.

Mendocino
Fort Bragg/Mendocino Coast Chamber of Commerce
332 N. Main, Fort Bragg, CA 95437
800/726-2780 or 707/961-6300

.● -● *Locke*

The wooden buildings are ancient and
weatherworn. Oriental characters are painted above
the doors. In the Dai Loy gambling house, tables
laid out with cards and dominos await the next
player. Shops sell silk robes, embroidered linens
and coolie hats.

No, this isn't a travelogue of exotic small town
China. This is Locke, right here on the Sacramento
River delta.

Locke is delta country's most unusual town. It
was founded in 1912, the only rural town in the
United States to be built entirely by Chinese. Today
it is a ghost town that hasn't quite given up the
ghost.   Small shops sell inexpensive Chinese
imports, antiques and giftware. There are two fine
art galleries and a unique historic museum. To top it
off, stop into Al's Place, a boisterous saloon and
restaurant, one of the friendliest places on the delta.

Begin your tour of Locke on the street below the
levee road. On the eastern corner of this tiny town is
a Chinese school. It is just one vestige of Locke's
oriental heritage.

Tin San Chan founded this town on land owned
by the three Locke brothers.   Shortly after, he
constructed its first building. The town boomed in
1915, when a fire destroyed nearby Walnut Grove
and the displaced Chinese families moved to Locke.
In addition to the school, Locke once boasted a
church, theater, two saloons, five grocery stores, six
restaurants and five hotels and rooming houses. The
riverboat and train made regular stops here.

Today, Locke's Main Street is a photographers'
paradise of weatherworn, western front buildings.
Some are so rickety that they're buckling to the side,
as if a good gust of wind will blow them over.

The most intriguing spot in town is the Dai Loy
Museum. This is, literally, a time capsule of a
gambling house that operated here from 1916 to the

early 1950s. When the gambling house closed down, they simply locked the doors, leaving it all behind. When the doors were opened years later, everything in the room was still intact.

Inside, gaming cards, dominos and dice games wait on the tables. Displays explain the rules of each unusual game. Fan-Tan was played with ordinary white buttons.

The gamblers were heavy smokers. Strips of sandpaper were attached to the edge of the tables for lighting matches. The tables' cross braces are well worn by the years of nervous feet.

This unusual collection includes the butterfly harp that originally was played here. Any patron who wanted to grace the gambling hall with music could borrow it.

The Lottery Room, its twirling wire basket full of ping pong balls marked with Chinese characters, is not too unlike today's lotteries. Another exhibit room illustrates the importance of the Chinese laborers who built the levees and islands of the delta. Artifacts also include China bowls, small medicine bottles and an English and Chinese newspaper from the late 1930s that had been used as padding beneath a table top.

Near the Dai Loy is the River Road Gallery, specializing in fine art paintings and pottery. Next door, Locke Ness is a small but fun antiques store.

Lotus Gifts specializes in toys and embroidered silk clothing. At Peony Imports, you can buy crocheted placemats, patchwork guest towels or a coolie hat for a few dollars, all made in China. Climb the alley's wooden steps up to the main levee road to Locke China Imports for the most varied selection of Chinese goods. And if visiting the laid-back delta country hasn't relieved all your stress, a Chinese Acupressure practice on Main Street offers a 15-minute treatment for $20.

Dai Loy Museum
Locke, Sacramento River Delta
Sat. & Sun. 11-5
Free, $1 donation requested
For Locke info, call Al's Place, 916/776-1800

.◦ •• *Old Sacramento*

Where else can you determine your weight in gold, communicate to a friend via telegraph and guess the functions of odd-shaped iron hardware tools? Nowhere but Old Sacramento. Within two blocks are five fun history museums that focus on the capital's formative years.

The Central Pacific Railroad Depot is a reconstruction of where you would have arrived back in 1876. The new transcontinental railroad shortened the cross-country transit time from at least 3 months by ship or wagon to a breakneck 2 weeks. The depot bustled with travelers, freight wagons and hawkers. Shipments arrived by boat from San Francisco and were loaded onto trains for destinations in and beyond the Sierra.

Today, the station is restored to its 1870s heyday. An audio wand brings back the sounds of the era. Voices of passengers, a baggage man and others tell lively stories you might have overheard then. Locomotives wait on the tracks in this cavernous, shed-like building as if frozen in time.

The Discovery Museum is across the street. It's housed in a reconstruction of the 1854 City Hall and Waterworks building which originally occupied this site. Inside, you're taken on a chronological tour of local history. You pass a replica of an Indian hut made of tule leaves and willow, a miner's shack, a Japanese internment cabin and more. The agricultural exhibit room includes a recreated 1928 kitchen set up for canning fruit. Above your head, cans tumble along the working prototype of the Blue Diamond almond canning line.

One highlight is the museum's $1 million collection of Mother Lode gold. Nearby, stand on the large scale and find your weight in gold both by 1849 standards, when it sold for $20 per troy ounce, and in 1987, when it sold for $450 per troy ounce. Then try your luck at panning. Gold pans, covered with clear plastic, contain dirt with just enough water for swirling. Follow the instructions and, before long, real gold specks appear through the black mud.

Next door is the often-overlooked Huntington & Hopkins Hardware Store. This is a time capsule of the late 1800s. You can guess the function of the odd-shaped tools of the era and purchase baskets, iron nails, wash basins and other items that the store's original customers bought.

The B.F. Hastings building at 2nd and J Streets held the offices of the Alta Telegraph Company in 1859. Today, artifacts in the museum include a working telegraph. Sit in one booth and communicate to a friend in the booth across the room. Posters in each booth display the Morse Code.

This building also was the terminus for the Pony Express and has housed the Wells Fargo bank since 1854. Among the collection of antique handwritten receipts and a scale for weighing gold is the new juxtaposed against the old—a computerized automatic teller machine.

Central Pacific Railroad Depot
Front & K Sts., tel. 916/445-4209
Open daily 10-5
$5 Adults; $2 ages 6-12; includes admission
to California State Railroad Museum.

Discovery Museum
101 I St., tel. 916/264-7057
Memorial Day weekend-Labor Day, Tu.-Sun. 10-5
Wed.-Sun. 10-5 rest of year
$3.50 Adults; $2 ages 6-17

Huntington & Hopkins Hardware Store
115 I St., tel. 916/445-4209
Tu.-Sun. 10-5
Free

B.F. Hastings Building and Wells Fargo
2nd and J Sts., tel. 916/445-4209
Tu.-Sun. 10-5
Free

Truckee

In the 1870s, it had the second largest Chinatown on the Pacific coast, a testament to the manpower behind the transcontinental railroad's route through the Sierra. Today the railroad still stops in Truckee and the town clings to its old west flair.

Truckee is a favorite stop for people zooming along Interstate 80 or heading down to Tahoe. Many pause to stretch their legs, grab a bite to eat or peek into the boutique windows. But Truckee is fast becoming a destination in its own right.

Truckee is a working man's town on the verge of gentrification. A freight train clatters along one side of the street. A boutique plays soft, contemporary music on the other. An upscale gallery spotlights the newest art trend next to a general store selling children's card games.

The best place to start your tour of Truckee is in the train station. Here you will find dozens of brochures and information sheets on the town and the surrounding area. You can pick up everything from the North Tahoe/Truckee tabloid with its discount coupons on nearby attractions and restaurants to a Truckee Activity Guide that outlines a walking tour. For even more local information, a Visitors Bureau is located on the western end of town near the outlet stores.

Truckee's history dates back to 1844 when a Paiute chief whose name sounded like "Tro-kay" became a favorite guide for westward pioneers. Before long, the river and nearby lake were called Truckee. The lake is now called Donner after the ill-fated pioneer family who was snowbound near here in the winter of 1846. Many starved. The survivors lived by resorting to cannibalism.

In 1863, the first log cabin was built in what is now the center of town. The building still remains, though at the turn of the century it was rolled on logs to its present site on Church Street.

Truckee boomed in 1868 with the building of the railroad. The Chinese worked on its construction but were ostracized and forced to move across the river in the early 1880s. Less than a decade later, the whites drove away all the Chinese. Just across the river from downtown is the last remnant of their population. The white building on South East River Street was built in 1878 as a Chinese herb shop.

The avenue behind Commercial Row, now called Jibboom Street, was once Truckee's red light district. Today you can see the jail that was used from 1875 to 1964. It's rumored that Baby Face Nelson once spent the night here.

Shoppers enjoy the variety along Truckee's Commercial Row. One of the best places to buy athletic clothes is the Sports Outlet on the western end of town. Skiers, cyclists, hikers and joggers will find good quality outfits at discount prices.

In the next building, you can watch as artists create bronze ships and delicate glass flowers. With a flaming torch, James Hacker welds and molds metals into a deer, a skier or a hawk. Frank Rossbach uses a torch to form glass into graceful, slender wine glasses, hummingbirds or calla lilies.

A delightful break from the upscale boutiques and galleries, the Truckee Variety Co. is a favorite hang-out for local kids. This is an old-fashioned five & dime, with counters full of novelty toys, jars brimming with candy and basics like plastic foam hair rollers and glue sticks.

Don't miss the Earthsongs cellar shop if you're a tea-lover. Shelves of jars feature more than 40 different teas, from Vanilla to Mad Hatter to Treasure Island Mint. More jars contain exotic spices.

The ArtTruckee gallery features first-class works from area artists, including limited edition prints of local scenery, so you can bring a piece of Truckee home with you.

Truckee-Donner Chamber of Commerce
and Visitors Bureau
12036 Donner Pass Rd., Box 2757
Truckee, CA 96160
800/548-8388 or 916/587-2757

Volcano

Located 12 curvy miles off State Route 49, the beaten path in these parts, this is the gold country town that tourism forgot. Pick-up trucks have replaced freight wagons and mountain bikes are more prevalent than horses, but not much else has changed in Volcano since the 49ers' boom fizzled out.

Today, it recaptures the quiet post-gold-rush era, with a few fun gift stores and a couple of small restaurants along a cobblestone walk. Benches invite you to set a spell and soak up history.

As early as 1848, veterans of the Mexican War discovered gold here. They named their settlement Soldier's Gulch, a more accurate name than the later Volcano, inspired by the mistaken idea that the town lay in a volcanic crater.

By 1856, Volcano erupted into a boomtown of some 6,000 people. The town had daily mail service and the first telegraph service in the county. Buildings sprang up: the Adams Express Building, Sieble's Brewery, the Jail, the I.O.O.F. and Masonic Hall and the Union Billiards, Saloon and Boarding House.

Surprisingly, secluded Volcano became rich in culture as well. California's first circulating library, the Miner's Library Association, was established here in 1854. The Volcano Thespian Society initiated the state's first little theater group. Volcano also boasted California's first literary and debating society, first private law school and first private observatory.

As late as 1862, an optimistic entrepreneur built a three-story hotel, the St. George, at one end of town. At the time it was one of the tallest and most elegant hotels in the Mother Lode. But by the mid-1860s, the rest of the gold played out. Although enterprising Chinese successfully gleaned what was left behind, most fortune-seekers rushed to more promising veins.

As the dust settled, vacant stone buildings became the only reminders of the once-thriving village. Volcano was tucked neatly under a bell jar, preserved in time and spirit for generations to come.

Today, the St. George Hotel is still the largest and, for Volcano, the most elegant building in town. It rents out rooms decorated much the way that hopeful prospectors would have seen them.

Along one side of Volcano's short stretch of Main Street, stone ruins form the backdrop for Volcano's outdoor theater and small park. On the other side, weather-worn stone buildings house the town's few businesses. The Country Store is the local gathering place. Its warped shelves are packed with cans of stew, hunting supplies and other goods that could have been stocked 100 years ago. In the back of the store, a skylight brightens a small lunch room with an old oven built into the stone wall. They serve some of the best burgers around, according to one local.

Down the cobblestone sidewalk, shaded by a slumping wood overhang, is the Jug and Rose Confectionery. Inside, you'll find an old-fashioned soda fountain and a small cafe.

The small shed next to the mineral shop houses one of the two landmarks that symbolize Volcano's community pride and quirky personality. "Old Abe," a bronze cannon, was acquired by the Volcano militia during the Civil War to protect their gold from Confederate sympathizers.

Across the street, you'll find the historical landmark sign for Volcano, originally placed four miles away. In 1934, a proposed dam would have flooded Volcano, but the plan was negated by geology and water rights. In 1980, the residents placed their own plaque here proclaiming that historic Volcano didn't drown, "not by a dam site!"

Volcano
Amador County Chamber of Commerce
125 Peek St., Jackson, CA 95642
800/649-4988 or 209/223-0350

Notes

Literary Landmarks

⬅ *Robinson Jeffers' Tor House*

Robinson Jeffers is considered by many Californians to be one of our state's greatest poets. But even if you aren't a Jeffers fan, you'll enjoy touring his Tor House in Carmel.

Jeffers' rustic home and stone Hawk Tower are an oasis of old Carmel, when the natural beauty of the Pacific's rugged coast attracted artists, poets and writers rather than expensive shopping malls and exclusive resorts.

Jeffers chose the site and began construction on the Tor House in 1918, naming it for the craggy knoll, or "tor," on which it stood. He wrote all his major works and most of his poetry here and eventually died in this humble home in 1962.

With the Pacific for a backdrop, distinctive and romantic Hawk Tower is a scene out of ancient Ireland. Jeffers built the tower by himself, learning the art of making "stone love stone" by apprenticing with the contractor building his house. Begun in 1920, the tower took four years to complete. It became a treasured retreat for his beloved wife, Una, and a magical playground for their twin sons.

The tower walls are six feet thick at its base, enclosing two small rooms. One has Jeffers' sturdy chair, constructed from the burnt timbers of the nearby Carmel Mission. A narrow, spiraling secret passage climbs up the tower to Una's room.

Despite the rough stone exterior, this room is cozy with warm wood paneling and gothic-arched windows. In one corner is Una's organ. Pictures of towers in Ireland echo Hawk Tower's theme.

An epigram carved in the wooden mantle of the fireplace reads, "they make their dreams for themselves," truly reflecting the Jeffers' lifestyle.

Jeffers incorporated artifacts from around the world in his building. The porthole on the right in the stairway is from Napoleon's ship. The red stone at the tower's top is from the Great Wall of China.

His Tor house also is reminiscent of old Europe. It is modeled after a Tudor barn in England. The simple home is furnished as when Jeffers lived here. The Steinway is the same piano Gershwin played when he visited.

Books, many poetry or Thomas Hardy, crowd the shelves. Records show Jeffers had read almost all of his 3,500 volumes.

Pictures and statues of unicorns are placed throughout the home. The immense, spear-like horn of a narwhale, the closest thing to a unicorn horn that Una could find, hangs in the dining hall. This medieval room is furnished with a rough wooden table and benches.

Highlighting the stone walls are more intriguing artifacts, small Mayan and Inca masks. At the very peak of the A-frame wall is a stone from the great pyramid at Giza.

Throughout the tour, Jeffers poetry is read. "The Bed by the Window," a 1932 poem, was written about the bed where Jeffers died in Tor House. The window in this bedroom is built low in the wall so one could lie on the bed and just turn his head to see the rocky shore of Jeffers' cherished Point Lobos.

Originally, a small, understated sign reading, "not at home," hung on Jeffers' door to steer away unwanted guests, but friends knew enough to ignore it. Now, through the Robinson Jeffers Tor House Foundation, you, too, are invited into the poet's private sanctuary and a unique look at old Carmel.

Robinson Jeffers' Tor House
26304 Ocean View Ave., Carmel
408/624-1813 or 408/624-1840 when home is open
Open by guided tour only; reservations advised.
Tours on the hour, Fri. & Sat. 10-3.
$5 Adults; $3.50 College students;
$1.50 High School students
No children under 12 admitted.
No photography except during annual Garden Party,
held the first Sunday in May

Eugene O'Neill's Tao House

The Chinese characters riveted to the black courtyard gate of Eugene O'Neill's Tao House proclaim it is the "House of the Righteous Way." Cradled in the rolling hills of Danville, the troubled playwright believed he had found his beloved final home and harbor here.

During the Tao House years, from 1937 to 1944, O'Neill penned such classics as *The Iceman Cometh, Hughie, Moon for the Misbegotten* and *A Long Day's Journey Into Night*. He was honored with four Pulitzer Prizes and is the only American playwright to be awarded the Nobel Prize for Literature.

Both Eugene and his wife, Carlotta, were attracted to the precepts of Taoism and carried them through the design of their home. The brick courtyard walk makes four turns before reaching the front door, since Taoists believe that evil spirits only travel in straight lines.

The original green-hued mirror and a series of masks in the entranceway are the first indication of the house's brooding, introverted atmosphere. Oriental "Fu" dogs, believed to protect against evil spirits, guard the staircase.

Like the Fu dogs, Carlotta was fiercely protective of O'Neill. She routinely held back visitors and correspondence from O'Neill if she deemed it would interfere with his writing.

An oriental rug and ceramic elephant match those in the period photograph of the living room, once filled with Oriental-style furniture from Gump's.

Oona, O'Neill's daughter from his second marriage, was one of the few visitors to stay in the guest room. O'Neill virtually disowned Oona over her marriage to Charlie Chaplin, a thrice-divorced man O'Neill's age, who was involved in a scandalous paternity suit. O'Neill's first-born son, Eugene Jr., committed suicide. His only other child, Shane, was a drug addict. Shane also killed himself, though long after his father's death.

O'Neill and Carlotta enjoyed some of their happiest times in Rosie's room. Rosie was O'Neill's favorite entertainment, a player piano from a bordello. Their Dalmatian, Blemie, as cherished and pampered as any child, slept here.

Today, an exact model of Rosie stands along one wall, the original blue phonograph cupboard along another. Photographs of O'Neill's father, mother and friends fill the room.

O'Neill's study hides in a secluded corner on the second floor. With wood paneling and beams, it resembles a ship's cabin. A collection of sailing ship models are prominently displayed.

O'Neill's original blue velvet chair sits at the desk. A blank pad of paper seems to be waiting for the playwright to return. Even a crumbled pack of Lucky Strikes, found by the Park Service in the recesses of the fireplace, evokes O'Neill's presence.

But even as O'Neill was creating his greatest works, a serious tremor rapidly diminished his physical ability to write. O'Neill's entire manuscript for *The Emperor Jones* is little over five pages of virtually unreadable handwriting.

O'Neill's failing health and the lack of household help and transportation during wartime forced them to sell their home. O'Neill once told Carlotta if he could not write, he would die. They knew they were facing more than the end of their time at Tao House. Before they left, they burned several of O'Neill's unfinished works in the fireplace. O'Neill died in a Boston hotel room nine years later.

Eugene O'Neill National Historic Site
Tours meet in downtown Danville
Park shuttles tours to Tao House
510/838-0249
Tours Wed.-Sun.; maximum 11 per tour
By advance reservation only
Free

Heinhold's First and Last Chance Saloon

Listen carefully at Heinhold's First and Last Chance Saloon on the Oakland waterfront. You may hear the kind of high seas tales that inspired Jack London's books. For more than a century, sailors have haunted Heinhold's. Today's Navy now sits on stools worn by yesterday's oyster pirates.

Even if you've never set foot on a ship, you'll enjoy this fun step into history. The first dizzying experience is the floor that slants downward, a balancing test even for those with sea legs. The slant was caused when the pilings beneath sank into the mud during the 1906 earthquake.

The trembler also stopped the clock in the saloon. Like the floor, the clock has never been fixed. It's now part of Heinhold's unique personality.

Once something finds its way into Heinhold's, it's there to stay. Every inch of wall, ceiling and rafter is covered with an eclectic array of mementos in this cozy museum-cum-bar.

Built in 1880 with the timbers of an old whaling ship, the funky cabin was first used as a bunkhouse for men working nearby oyster beds. It became Heinhold's Saloon in 1883.

Today, you can sit at the same rough, wooden tables where Jack London, President William Howard Taft and Robert Louis Stevenson have imbibed over the years. The dim lights above are the original gas fixtures, making Heinhold's the only commercial saloon in California that still uses them.

The stove is original and was Heinhold's only source of heat until 1989. Also squeezed into this tiny saloon are the original movie machine and the timeworn bar and rail.

One wall is dedicated to photographs of Jack London. As a young boy, London studied his school books on the docks until Heinhold invited him in out of the rain. London's favorite spot was the round corner table, as evidenced by the photo of him sitting there studying.

London met the salty characters who peopled his books right here in Heinhold's. Alexander McLean, known for his cruelty on his so-called "Hell Ship," became Wolf Larsen in The Sea Wolf. Heinhold and his saloon are mentioned 17 times in John Barleycorn and The Tales of the Fish Patrol.

Heinhold also loaned London the money to attend college and helped London in his deals for his three ships, the Razzle Dazzle, the Snark and the Roamer. All three deals were struck in this saloon.

Through the years, customers have added their own mementos to Heinhold's collection. Money from around the world is signed and tacked to the wall so that sailors leaving port will have payment for a drink on their return. The plaques dedicated to Heinhold's saloon are from five aircraft carriers.

Most pervasive are business cards tacked one on top of the other on every free speck of wall. Many are blackened with decades of smoke from the stove, lanterns, cigarettes and creosote in the old wood.

On a sunny afternoon or balmy evening, pull yourself away from Heinhold's for a stroll around the waterfront. Next to the saloon is the 1897 log cabin where London lived while prospecting the Klondike gold rush. It was authenticated and moved here piece by piece.

Nearby, Jack London Village is a two-level wooden pier area with a fun selection of specialty shops and restaurants. Many have a superb view of the water and marina with the San Francisco skyline on the horizon.

Heinhold's First and Last Chance Saloon
Jack London Square, Oakland waterfront
510/839-6761
Mon.-Th. Noon-midnight;
Fri. & Sat. Noon-1 A.M.; Sun. Noon-8 P.M.
Free

John Muir Historic Site

"I care to live only to entice people to look at nature's loveliness," John Muir wrote to a friend. You, too, can share in nature's loveliness when you visit Muir's house and the small but thriving parcel of his original fruit ranch in Martinez.

Muir's tireless writing from his "scribble den" in this stately Victorian popularized a radical concept—conservation—at a crucial time when land exploitation was quickly depleting vast areas of forest. Proving that the pen was mightier than the wood saw, his letters and subsequent meeting in Yosemite with Teddy Roosevelt convinced the President to establish 148 million acres of National Forest, 5 national Parks and 23 National Monuments during his term in office.

Muir co-founded and was first president of the Sierra Club and was key in establishing the National Park Service. We enjoy Yosemite, Sequoia, Mount Rainier, Arizona's Petrified Forest and Grand Canyon National Parks today thanks to Muir's turn-of-the-century battles.

Appropriately, Muir's property is now part of the National Park Service. The imposing gray Victorian, its entrance flanked by towering century-old palms, was built by Muir's father-in-law, John Strentzel, in 1882. Ironically, although Muir lived here the last 24 years of his life, it does not reflect the mountain man's simple tastes. It's built almost entirely of redwood, the tree Muir devoted his life to protecting.

The home has been lovingly restored to the time when Muir lived here. Restorers relied on the memories of people who visited with Muir as their guide. A custom-made black horsehair sofa once again adorns the west parlor. Even the floor is finished in a technique thought forgotten.

The 1906 earthquake gave Muir a chance to show his architectural style. After the chimney of the coal-burning marble fireplace in the east parlor was destroyed, he replaced it with an immense, brick, mission-style wood burner. Finally, Muir was able to enjoy a "real mountain campfire" in his home.

But Muir spent his most precious time in the dining room. He treasured the moments with his family and employed a clever strategy to ensure his two daughters came to dinner on time. He told a continuing story at each meal, leaving off at a cliffhanger. One of these stories eventually was published as *Stickeen*, the endearing tale of his heroic canine companion in Alaska.

The most important room in the house is Muir's study, which he called his "scribble den." Muir's research papers, articles, book manuscripts and letters lay strewn about the floor as though he were still in the midst of a fight for conservation.

Symbols of two of Muir's proudest triumphs are displayed next to the desk—the yellow hood of his honorary doctorate from Yale and a spear presented to him by native Alaskans for his courage in exploring the living glaciers. A bowl of dried bread balls, Muir's favorite snack, waits on the mantel.

Beyond the orchard is the 1849 Martinez Adobe, built by Don Vincente on what once was his 17,000-acre Mexican land grant. Muir's daughter, Wanda, called the adobe home during the last years of his life. Muir would visit daily to dine and play with his grandchildren.

Here you can picnic among the fruit trees and reflect on Muir's belief that "the clearest way into the universe is through a forest wilderness."

John Muir National Historic Site
Alhambra Ave., just off Rte. 4, Martinez
510/228-8860
Wed.-Sun. 10-4:30
$2 Adults 17 and older; Children Free

Jack London State Historic Park

Jack London was, and still is, one of the most popular authors in the world. To many, he epitomizes the robust, adventuresome, free-thinking American. Nowhere is his style more evident than at the 800-acre Jack London State Historic Park in Glen Ellen.

Here, you can see the haunting ruins of Wolf House, London's dream castle. Nearby, the stone House of Happy Walls serves as monument and museum to the author. It houses such eclectic memorabilia as dancing sticks from the Solomons, London's photographs of the Japanese-Russian War and the first of his 600 rejection letters.

The sprawling grounds also encompass London's recently restored cottage, where he lived and worked while Wolf House was being built, a horse barn, the remains of his pig palace and a delightful picnic area.

Begin your tour at the House of Happy Walls. London's wife, Charmian, began construction of this house three years after London's death as a memorial to her late husband. Charmian was the first curator, so everything is authentic. London's books, letters, a scale model of his ship, the Snark, exotic souvenirs and other displays tell the story of London's adventurous life.

London's study has been relocated here from their modest cottage, a short walk from the picnic area, where he wrote all his later works and, ultimately, died. The roll-top desk, with paper and ink at the ready, appears as though London had just left after completing his 1,000-word-a-day ritual.

Be sure to explore the upper floor of the House of Happy Walls. Here you'll find more exotic memorabilia from the Londons' travels and displays illustrating the important influences and events in London's life.

Follow the half-mile forested trail to Wolf House. Visitors are dwarfed by the ghostly castle walls and chimneys that compete with the redwoods for a piece of the sky.

London sunk the bulk of his earnings from writing into this immense castle. He harvested monolithic stones from the surrounding Valley of the Moon and fortified them with mighty redwood timber, sure that it would shelter generations of his heirs. Tragically, a fire of suspicious origin burned Wolf House to the ground days before London and Charmian were due to take residence in 1913.

Today, the timbers are long gone and weeds blossom in the hearths. But you can imagine London's dream castle by studying the floor plans displayed by the ruins. A two-story living room, a dining room that could seat 50 and numerous guest rooms reveal London's gregarious nature. Wolf House was to have a gun and trophy room, a sleeping tower, even a stag party room.

London also glowed over his "Pig Palace," located near the cottage. He designed the innovative piggery with the hope that it would revolutionize pig farming. Instead, his stock died of pneumonia, but the ruins of the piggery and nearby silo, one of the first and biggest concrete block silos in the state, stand as testimony to London's audacious spirit.

Jack London State Historic Park
2400 London Ranch Rd., Glen Ellen
707/938-5216
Park open daily 10-7 during daylight savings time;
daily 10-5, rest of year; museum open daily 10-5
Museum closed Jan. 1, Thanksgiving and Christmas
$5 per car; $4 if senior is in car

⬅ *Mark Twain in Gold Country*

The gold rush was one of the wildest times in the west and no one had more fun chronicling it than Mark Twain. His yen for travel and wry sense of humor were an open book for the tall tales of eccentric miners.

Angels Camp and Murphy's proved to be gold mines for the writer's pen. Both towns still retain the flavor of the old west. Today, you can visit the 1855 Angels Hotel, where the bartender first told Twain the story that brought the author, and the county, immortal fame. Twain called it "The Celebrated Jumping Frog of Calaveras County."

Samuel Clemens (Twain's real name) first came west in 1861. After trying his hand at mining, he became a reporter for the *Territorial Enterprise* in Virginia City, Nevada. Here, he chose his pen name, Mark Twain, after a common riverboat pilot's call in his native state of Missouri. In 1864, Twain came to Angels Camp, already a bustling gold rush town.

The area boomed early in the rush. By 1849, some 4,500 miners were prospecting here. Angel was the name of a merchant who grew wealthy by digging into the pockets of the miners, rather than digging for gold in the mines. Clothing and tools sold for astronomical prices.

Before long, the placer gold played out and the boom might have busted but for a man named Bennegar Rasberry. Rasberry was hunting when his ramrod got stuck in his gun. Since he couldn't knock it out, he pointed his gun towards the ground and shot it out. The ramrod pierced the ground and revealed the unmistakable shine of gold-bearing quartz. Within three days, Rasberry mined $10,000 worth.

Rasberry's story is just one of the legendary tales to come out of Angel's Camp. While sitting in the Angels Hotel, a two-story brick building with iron shutters on Main Street on the south end of town, Twain was told the story that he'd later pen as the "Celebrated Jumping Frog."

It seems that a compulsive better, Jim Smiley, caught a frog. He "cal'klated to edercate him" and "learn that frog to jump." A stranger came to town and challenged Smiley to a jumping contest between his animal and an ordinary, "unedercated" frog. The stranger then deviously poured a load of quailshot down the throat of Smiley's frog. Sure enough, the frog couldn't budge and Smiley lost his bet.

When printed back east, this simple story propelled Angels Camp and Mark Twain to fame. Today, you'll see an "official" frog statue at the south end of the historic section of town and another frog statue at the north end of town and frogs painted on the sidewalks in between. In the shops, you'll find frog pins, patches, t-shirts, caps and stickers. Since 1928, Angels Camp has held an annual jumping frog contest the third weekend in May.

A quick detour off Highway 4 east of State Route 49 leads to Murphy's, one of gold country's best preserved relics. Twain stayed at Murphy's Hotel, once considered one of the finest hotels on the Mother Lode. Today, you can still visit Murphy's hotel or stroll along Main Street, which appears to have stood still in time, and imagine it as Twain saw it. While others around him mined for gold, Twain found his fortune in stories of the Mother Lode.

Calaveras County Visitor Center
1211 S. Main St., P.O. Box 637
Angels Camp, CA 95222
209/736-0049 or 800/225-3764
Free

Notes

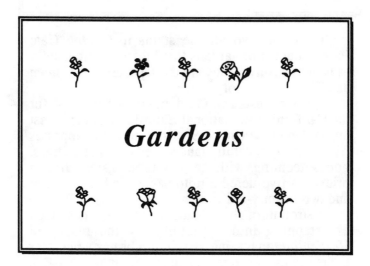

Gardens

❦ *Japanese Tea Garden & The Conservatory*

There are two unique stems in Golden Gate Park's bouquet of gardens that blossom with history as well as beauty. They are the Japanese Tea Garden and The Conservatory.

The Japanese Tea Garden, created in 1894 for the California International Exposition, is the oldest tea garden in the United States. It now encompasses five acres of gracefully landscaped ornamental trees, ponds teeming with carp, temple gates, arched bridges, a five-tiered Shinto pagoda, a bonsai forest and two-century-old Buddha.

A stroll through the gardens was aptly described as "stepping into a picture" by the respected *Horticulture* magazine. Each turn brings you closer to the beauty of nature and your place in it.

Japanese maples, Oriental magnolias, camellias, azaleas, dwarf cypresses, cedars and pines blend in perfect harmony. Although this is one of the most popular spots in Golden Gate Park, a sense of solitude and tranquillity pervades.

Amidst this oasis of serenity, the open air Tea House serves tea and cookies. Now a standard in any oriental restaurant, fortune cookies were invented here by the garden's creator, Makoto Hagiwara, in 1914 to amuse his guests.

The Conservatory is one of Golden Gate Park's crown jewels. This graceful crystal palace is the park's oldest structure and is the oldest growing house in California. It is listed on the National Register of Historic Sites.

The Conservatory's more than 20,000 panes of glass were shipped around Cape Horn to San Francisco in the early 1870s at the behest of millionaire James Lick. But Lick died shortly after and the crates remained unopened on his estate in San Jose.

Public-minded citizens made the Conservatory a reality for all to enjoy. The greenhouse was purchased in 1877 and erected in the park. Tragically, their efforts were dashed by a fire in 1883 which destroyed the dome. Railroad baron Charles Crocker came to the rescue, donating $10,000 for its restoration. It miraculously survived the 1906 and 1989 earthquakes and greets visitors now as it has for more than a century.

Crossing the hothouse threshold is like stepping into the tropics. The most striking specimen is the towering plant that fills the central dome. With its three-foot-long leaves, it appears to be a rain-forest giant. In fact, it's one of the most common house plants, a philodendron, more than a century old.

Strolling through this indoor garden, you'll discover delicate orchids, sweetly scented hibiscus and flower shows, like the splendid tuberous begonias in summer. An old-fashioned gazebo invites visitors to rest a spell, surrounded by the flourishing green, and enjoy this beautiful legacy of our Victorian past.

Japanese Tea Garden
Next to the Asian Art Museum, Golden Gate Park
415/752-1171
Open daily 9-6:30 Mar.-Sept.; 8:30-6 Oct.-Feb.
Tea House open daily 10:30-5:30
$2 Adults; $1 Seniors 65 and over and ages 6-12
First and last half-hour free.
($2 additional for tea and cookies)

The Conservatory
Kennedy Drive, Golden Gate Park
415/666-7017
Open daily 9-5 (until 6 during
Daylight Savings Time)
$1.50 Adults;
$.75 Seniors 65 and over and ages 6-12

🌸 *Hakone Gardens*

Deep in the woods of Saratoga, just southwest of San Jose, a surprising slice of old Japan invites you to enjoy peaceful harmony with nature. This is Hakone Japanese Gardens, a 75-year-old canvas of sculpted trees, splashing waterfalls and still reflecting ponds, punctuated with traditional Japanese houses.

This land was part of the 16-acre summer estate of Oliver and Isabel Stine of San Francisco. In 1917, Mrs. Stine spent six months in Japan to follow her artistic bent. She was captivated with Japanese gardens and the Fuji-Hakone National Park.

Upon her return to California, Stine hired an Imperial gardener to create her Hakone Gardens. It is patterned after a traditional 17th-century Zen garden. A Japanese architect designed her home and the Upper House to harmonize with the landscape.

The main gate, or Mon, was added in 1932 by Major Charles Lee Tilden, who owned the gardens at that time. The City of Saratoga purchased it in 1966 for all to enjoy, hiring a Japanese specialist to ensure the garden's continued authenticity.

A sense of timelessness prevails in Hakone. Visitors in the early 1900s were as equally entranced as today's tourists. The Mon is still a magic threshold from modern world to ancient orient.

A medley of splashing water draws you to the hill and pond garden. A wooden bridge arches over one side of the reflecting pond. Below, bright gold and white carp, or koi, swim gracefully through the water. The shaded wooden Wisteria Pavilion on the opposite bank is an inviting respite on a sunny day.

Your gaze is drawn up the hillside to the Upper House, with its simple lines and pagoda-style roof. This is the Moon Viewing House, designed by a Japanese master craftsman in 1917. It was built in the traditional samurai style, without nails. Its exterior was treated to lend the proper look of age.

You're welcome to stroll onto the verandah, or engawa, which wraps around three sides of the house. It offers one of the finest views of the hill and pond garden below. Peer through the windows to see the traditional tatami mats placed neatly on the floor of this one open, uncluttered room.

A Wisteria-entwined arborway leads to the Upper Pavilion, another inviting spot to contemplate the gardens. Paths wind across the hillside to one of Hakone's newest additions, the Kizuna-En, or Bamboo Garden.

Not long ago, this 2-acre garden was a tangled jungle of brush and trees. Now it is a sea of delicate greens, with the swirl of a white pebble pathway and precisely placed stones. This is a joint effort between Saratoga and their Japanese sister city, Muko-shi. It symbolizes their international partnership. The white gravel area represents the Pacific ocean, with 5 large stones as the local Council members and 26 field stones as the Japanese Council members.

Bamboo, which is a giant grass, grows in South and Central America, the Far East and eastern U.S. and Mexico. Almost all the specimens here are found in Japan. Golden Bamboo, Black Stemmed Bamboo, Striped Sasa and Palmata are a sample of the more than 1,000 varieties of this diverse plant.

Tea and snacks are served on weekend afternoons from April through September near the garden's Lower House. Stine built this house in 1922 as the family' summer home. In front of this home is a Zen or Dry Garden, a simple arrangement of five large stones, a Shrine lantern, black pine and gravel, which is raked into patterns.

You can enjoy a picnic below Hakone's new Cultural Exchange Center, a shady spot to contemplate the timelessness of a garden.

Hakone Gardens & Cultural Center
21000 Big Basin Way, Saratoga
408/741-4994
Mon.-Fri. 10-5; Sat. & Sun. 11-5
Parking Fee: $5 on weekends, $3 on weekdays
Free on Tuesdays

❧ *Saso Herb Gardens*

"Sometimes the things we step on can be those that are most helpful," said Louis Saso on a tour of his beloved herb garden.

Louis and his wife, Virginia, grow one of the largest collections of culinary, medicinal and ornamental herbs on the west coast, all in compact beds surrounding their home in Saratoga. Herbs are more than beautiful to look at and delicious to smell. The benefits of these plants range from curing migraine headaches to spicing up sausage.

You can stop by the gardens and gift shop during their open hours. To get the most out of your visit, call ahead to make sure someone will be available to show you around and answer questions.

Even better, come for a free guided tour, generally offered once a month. Although the Saso's have semi-retired from the nursery business, they are always enthusiastic about sharing their love of herbs. Included are plantings based on the signs of the Zodiac, Chinese medicinal herbs and ornamental oreganos. They're happy to answer questions about growing particular herbs and how they are used for cooking or healing.

The Saso's have been growing herbs for more than 30 years. It started when Louis was working in the wholesale produce business. He became intrigued by the small potted herbs that sold along with his vegetables and fruits.

He began growing herbs as a hobby. With the resurgence of herbs in cooking and healing in the 1960s, Louis grew even more involved. Virginia became adept at culinary herbal use and creating dry flower arrangements with ornamental herbs. By 1974, they started their own retail herb business.

Today, they share their expertise with visitors on a tour for all five senses. You begin with a free sample of herbal tea, while relaxing in the shade of a sprawling 400-year-old oak tree. As you walk around, Virginia cuts pieces of herbs and passes them among the group to feel, smell or taste. Tips cover growing, harvesting and how the herb is used.

Several beds are devoted to oregano. "It's more than just for pizza," Virginia said. Many of these are ornamental, perfect for dried flower arrangements. "The best oreganos for eating are Italian and Greek," she said, snipping off pieces for visitors to try.

There's good reason why many herbs are traditional favorites with certain foods. Sage, for example, helps in digesting fats, which is why it tastes so good in sausage and turkey stuffing.

Looking over all this herbal abundance is a carved wooden statue of St. Fiacre, standing in the hub of the Zodiac beds. A bishop offered Fiacre all the land he could till in one day. With his guardian angel's help, Fiacre tilled a great expanse of land. People came to him and were miraculously cured by the herbs Fiacre grew.

Herbal cures aren't limited to miracle-workers. One migraine sufferer tried every medical procedure available without success. Then he tried feverfew. Each day, he'd eat three leaves. Within two months, he noticed a difference. Today, he is virtually cured. He doesn't even have to eat the pungent-tasting feverfew leaves anymore to prevent the headaches.

Some herbs are natural pesticides. Garlic chives keep aphids away from roses. Pots of basil are used in France at sidewalk cafes to repel flies. Others attract hummingbirds to your garden, including the ornamental varieties of Saso's 50 sages.

In the Saso's gift shop, you can admire Virginia's dried flower wreaths, ornaments and bouquets and choose a favorite to purchase.

Saso Herb Gardens
14625 Fruitvale Ave., Saratoga
408/867-2135
Call for open hours and tour times
Free, donations appreciated

❦ *UC Berkeley Botanical Garden*

The 33-acre University of California Botanical Garden encompasses more than 20,000 species and varieties of plants from every continent except Antarctica. Tucked into the Berkeley hills well off the beaten path, this is the fifth largest collection of plants in the United States.

Since they are arranged according to their native region, from Australia to the Mediterranean, the garden is a microcosm of the Earth, itself. You can walk through a New World Desert, where some of the cacti tower above your head, then skip over a stream gurgling through a redwood forest, see insect-eating tropical plants in the fern house, then discover how roses are hybridized.

The garden's roots trail as far back as the 1890s. Six hundred types of California native trees and shrubs were collected and planted in the area of campus that is now the Moffitt Undergraduate Library. All were drought tolerant since no irrigation system was in place.

By 1895, the garden blossomed to seven acres and 1,500 species. It was transplanted to its present location in Strawberry Canyon in the 1920s, but still clings to its roots—about a third of the garden is devoted to California native plants, including several rare and endangered species.

One unusual plant community in the California section is a compact patch of a pygmy forest. Like Paul Bunyan, you can look down to the tops of trees that are 50 years old. The display explains how a unique geology creates these naturally miniaturized forests. Other California native plant communities range from fresh water marsh to chaparral.

One of the oldest and most striking sections of the garden is the New World Desert with plantings dating back to the 1930s. Cacti from North and

Central America and the Andes grow here. Some are ten feet high.

In sharp contrast is the lush forest directly downhill, where the path crosses over the babbling Strawberry Creek. On one end of the creek, a waterfall cascades gracefully to the serene Japanese pool. Follow the creek down to the palms and cycads. Here you can cross the threshold into the tropics in the hot, humid greenhouse. Plants include taro from tropical Asia, African violets from Tanzania, a prayer plant from Brazil and Arabian coffee from east Africa.

Man's use of plants is best seen in the Asia Garden nearby. In the medicinal herb section, markers, in both English and Asian characters, describe how the plant is used. Coriander induces perspiration and relieves chicken pox and measles. Ginger helps alleviate the common cold, nausea and seafood poisoning. There's even an opium poppy growing here.

Most of these plants are "wild-collected." Botanists actually obtained the seeds and cuttings from the plant's native area. Data on location, habitat, collector and date of collection is kept for each specimen. If you come from one of the United States, you might see a wildflower from your county planted in the North American section.

The "Garden of Plants for Mankind" reminds you you're in Berkeley. If you climb up the steep hill beyond that, you'll be rewarded with an informative display on selective breeding and hybridization of old roses. On a clear day, you can glimpse the Bay and the Golden Gate Bridge on the horizon.

UC Berkeley Botanical Garden
Centennial Dr., above Berkeley campus
510/642-3343
Open daily 9-4:45
(Wed. until 7 PM Memorial Day-Labor Day)
Closed Christmas
Free, contributions appreciated

🌺 *Luther Burbank & California Carnivores*

Sonoma County attracts some of the most creative gardeners anywhere, from the bountiful creations of Luther Burbank in Santa Rosa to the bizarre California Carnivores in nearby Forestville.

The Luther Burbank Home and Gardens is a unique tribute to one of our nation's most prolific horticulturists. He introduced more than 800 new varieties of plants into the world, including over 200 varieties of fruits alone, many vegetables, nuts and grains and hundreds of ornamental flowers.

Two of his most famous creations are the Shasta Daisy, with pure white petals, and the kiwi fruit. As you explore the garden, you'll find many of the plants that grow on this earth thanks to Burbank, including Burbank potatoes and the spineless cactus. From April through October, you also can tour the home where Burbank lived from 1884 to 1906.

Burbank dedicated himself to improving the quality of plants to increase the world's food supply. On this site and in nearby Sebastopol, his work gained world renown. Today, a 50-foot, pictorial tile wall in the hub of the garden tells the story of Burbank's life and work.

Plantings include Shasta daisies, raised beds with vegetables and fruits from Burbank's experiments, a Paradox walnut tree and his plumcot, which is a cross between an apricot and a plum. Signs highlight some of his accomplishments. When Burbank died in 1926, he was buried in this garden in an unmarked grave, surrounded by his enduring creations.

To see some of the most unusual plants in the world, without sloshing through a bog, try California Carnivores. It is one of the largest private collections of carnivorous plants in the world on display to the public. Over 400 varieties add to the jungle-like feel of this compact greenhouse.

Grower Peter D'Amato has been cultivating carnivorous plants since he was 12 and general manager Marilee Maertz is equally devoted. They delight in showing visitors their unusual specimens.

Carnivorous plants have been cultivated for almost 300 years. In 1875, Charles Darwin first proved that certain plants do eat insects and small animals. Some prey is microscopic. Large carnivores in the jungle have been known to consume rats—but never a man.

The plants at California Carnivores range from bizarre to beautiful. Butterworts are pretty, delicate plants with vibrant flowers, much like small orchid blooms. Their flat, sticky leaves catch tiny prey, like whiteflies, digested for their mineral content.

Another attractive variety is the American Pitcher Plant. These make excellent flycatchers. You can place purple pitchers on a sunny windowsill or the slender trumpet species on your patio. The growers once counted 22 flies caught in one hour by a white trumpet on a sunny spring morning.

You can buy many of the different varieties of carnivorous plants to beautify and help de-bug your home and patio. Prices range from $5 to $50.

California Carnivores shares its lovely hilltop site with Mark West Vineyards, which offers wine tasting and a delightful picnic area.

Luther Burbank Home & Gardens
corner Santa Rosa Ave. & Sonoma Ave, Santa Rosa
707/524-5445
Garden open daily, during daylight hours
Home open April-Oct., Wed.-Sun. 10-3:30
Garden Free; House Tour $2 Adults, under 12 Free

California Carnivores
at Mark West Vineyards, Forestville; from River Rd,
turn north on Healdsburg-Trenton Rd.
707/838-1630
Open daily 10-4; call ahead Dec.-Mar.
Free

Mendocino Coast Botanical Gardens

The Mendocino Coast Botanical Gardens is a surprising oasis of more than 3,000 varieties of native and cultivated plants in over 20 plant collections. You can stroll through a formal perennial garden, meander along a gurgling stream hemmed with fern-covered hills, study the strange growths near the bog and even discover a pioneer grave deep in the forest.

During the whale watching months of December and March, the Gardens offers an added plus— secluded benches perched along the cliffs overlooking the crashing surf and restless Pacific. Whales have been spotted as close as 100 yards off-shore.

Even if you don't see any behemoths of the deep, this is a spectacular setting. You can see fishing boats bobbing in the waves, smell the briny scent of sea water and listen for the mournful call of a foghorn above the roar of the surf.

The Mendocino Coast Botanical Gardens are planted and maintained by almost 100 dedicated volunteers. They rely exclusively on the financial support from admissions, donations, memberships and plant and garden store sales. Recently, the California State Coastal Conservancy voted unanimously to purchase a 35-acre parcel which will nearly quadruple the size of the Gardens from 12 to 47 acres.

Open year-round, this is truly "a garden for all seasons." In early spring, camellias, daffodils and magnolias welcome you. The Gardens are famous for their Rhododendrons, which explode with color, reaching their peak about May 1. More than 1,200 species of Rhododendron are known worldwide, exhibiting pink, white, mauve and yellow flowers.

In the late summer and early fall, the perennial garden bursts with color. From March through October, a different plant collection is highlighted each month in the display area.

Even in the midst of winter, you'll find colorful blooms and ornamental leaves in both the formal plantings and natural areas of the preserve. The Heath collection is a palette of pastels. The cactus and succulent garden seem otherworldly in this rich, forested region.

At the end of the Canyon Rim Trail, a small sign directs you to the Pioneer Grave Site. Deep in an evergreen grove is a tiny, turn-of-the-century cemetery. Picket fences, once white but now weatherworn, enclose the graves. Anonymous wooden crosses mark the tombs.

One gravesite is hardly bigger than a cradle. On another grave marker, the crude lettering reads, "In Memory of Irene Parrish. Born Dec 24, 1900. Died Nov 12, 1902. Aged 1 yr 10 mo 19 days." The tidy cemetery is a pleasant but poignant reminder to take time to smell the roses.

If you're inspired to beautify your own Eden, the retail nursery and garden shop offer a fine selection of tools, books and more.

Mendocino Coast Botanical Gardens
West side of Highway 1,
two miles south of Fort Bragg
707/964-4352
Open daily 9-4, Nov.-Feb.; 9-5 rest of year
Closed Thanksgiving and Dec. 25
$5 Adults; $4 Seniors over 60;
$3 ages 13-17; under 12 Free

Notes

*Historic
Haunts*

Ω *Alcatraz*

They were the worst of the worst, the incorrigibles, the prisoners that other prisons couldn't handle. Infamous criminals like Al Capone, Machine Gun Kelly and Robert "the Birdman" Stroud did time on "the Rock." Their legends still attract thousands of visitors to Alcatraz each year— these days for a more temporary stay.

This fascinating excursion begins with a fun 10-minute ferry ride on the Red & White Fleet from San Francisco's Pier 41 to Alcatraz island. You can relax inside, protected from the elements, or brave the bracing breeze to take in the panoramic view of the city skyline, Golden Gate Bridge and Alcatraz island.

Once you reach Alcatraz, you're welcome to wander past the guards' residences, around the prison grounds and through the ghostly cell house, where displays capture the stories of the prison's most notorious inmates. Exhibit rooms illustrate the history of the island, the myths and reality of its years as a prison and the prisons of today.

Although it's best known for its prison years, the history of La Isla de las Alcatraces, the island of the pelicans, dates to the late 1840s. The gold rush brought a boom in commerce on the Bay. Ships needed protection from natural hazards and pirates, particularly confederates hoping to finance the Civil War. The Alcatraz lighthouse was completed in 1854 and Fort Alcatraz became the most heavily armed fortification on the west coast.

The fort's natural isolation was ideal for housing military prisoners. By the early 1930s gangster era, it evolved into the ultimate federal penitentiary. Prisoners generally did not begin nor end their incarceration here. They were sent here only when proven too unruly for other jails and returned to other prisons when deemed manageable again.

Al Capone arrived with the first group of prisoners at the new Alcatraz federal penitentiary. Once he arrived, he was just another number. Capone and Machine Gun Kelly became altar boys.

Many cells suffer the ravages of time and vandalism. Others are restored. They had little more than a small table and chair that folded down from the wall, a cot and a toilet. Step into a cell and imagine spending 18 hours a day behind bars for many hopeless years. On the superb cellhouse audiocassette tour, you hear the Alcatraz story first-hand from the prisoners and guards who lived here.

One cell recreates the "Escape from Alcatraz" immortalized in the Clint Eastwood movie. Brothers Clarence and John Anglin and Frank Morris chiseled holes through their cell walls into a utility corridor. To fool the guard, they created dummy heads with art supplies and hair from the barber shop, then tucked them into blankets as if they were sleeping.

The escapees made it to the roof, down the outside of the cell house and into the water. They were never seen again. Most believe they drowned in the Bay's freezing water and strong tides.

In the dining room, you can see tear gas canisters on the wall, to be used in case of a riot. The menu still shows the last meal served in Alcatraz before it was closed in 1963.

Frank Heaney, author of *Inside the Walls of Alcatraz*, was the prison's youngest correctional officer. The island was "thick with animosity, dread and despair," he recalled. Worst of all, inmates could see vibrant San Francisco as they walked from the recreation yard to prison jobs. "It was like holding water out to a thirsty man," said Heaney.

Alcatraz Island
Golden Gate National Recreation Area
415/546-2700 (ferry information)
415/556-0560 (park information)
Frequent daily departures; Schedule varies by season
Advance reservations strongly recommended
Without Cell House audio tour: $5.75 Adults;
$4.75 Seniors 62 and over; $3.25 ages 5-11
Audio Tour: $3 Adults; $1 ages 5-11

☖ *Mission San Francisco de Asis*

With towering skyscrapers, perpetual traffic and more than 3 million people, it's hard to imagine the San Francisco area as wilderness. The Mission San Francisco de Asis, located in the heart of the city, is one of the few remnants of that era.

Popularly known as the Mission Dolores, this is the oldest intact building in San Francisco. It was completed in 1791. At the time, this was a remote outpost, the sixth mission established by Father Junipero Serra. The village of Yerba Buena, later called San Francisco, was not even founded until 44 years later.

You enter immediately into the cool, cavernous chapel, 114 feet long by 22 wide. Its four-foot-thick adobe walls effectively cut off the outside heat, sunlight and 20th-century noises.

The wooden confessional doors are to the left as you enter. Men stood or knelt in front of the priest for confession while women entered a side closet to confess through the opening.

The ceiling is unusual for a chapel, painted entirely in a type of Bargello-striped pattern with Native American dyes. The vegetable dyes created dark, rich hues of brown, tawny mauve and gray. The altar, too, features darker colors, a marbled gray-green and dark mauve highlighted with gold. The altar and its statues came from Mexico in the early 1800s and, besides the gold being renewed, have remained unchanged for almost two centuries.

Just outside the chapel, historical prints depict mission life in the 1800s—undeveloped hills, few people. One scene captures an 1842 bullfight at the Spanish mission. Another display illustrates the damage sustained by the 1906 quake.

In back of the chapel, a small museum showcases artifacts from the mission and San

Francisco's first settlers. The original A-frame roof truss hangs on one wall. Immense pieces of timber are lashed together with rawhide, not nailed. In 1918, these wood trusses were reinforced with steel to protect against earthquake damage. A window cut from the wall plaster reveals the adobe brick structure.

This room was once used as the mission's school. Artifacts include an 1860s slate scratched with barely legible chalk letters, a far cry from today's computers. Another case encloses an intricate silver ciboria, monstrance and missal stand. Unfortunately some of these are replicas. The originals were stolen in 1982 and never recovered.

The small, peaceful cemetery borders one side of the chapel. Originally, the cemetery was much larger, as the faithful have been buried here since the mission's earliest days. Their graves were marked with simple wooden crosses that deteriorated with time. In consolidating the cemetery, the unidentified bodies were placed in a common grave.

Many of the existing markers are from those who died in the years following the gold rush. San Francisco was growing rapidly, from a village of fewer than 100 to a metropolis of well over 10,000. You may recognize some of the names, such as Don Luis Antonio Arguello, the first governor of Alta California under Mexican rule, and the Castro's. City streets have been named after these pioneers who were laid to rest at this church, the birthplace of San Francisco.

Mission San Francisco de Asis
16th and Dolores Sts., San Francisco
415/621-8203
Open daily 9-4
$1 contribution

◘ *Peralta Adobe & Fallon House*

One is a simple, two-room adobe with rough, wooden furniture and animal hide rugs. The other is a magnificent, 15-room Victorian, lavishly decorated with gilded mirrors, a horsehair parlor set, even a sewing room complete with ball gown. Yet these neighboring homes reflect decorative styles separated by less than two decades—and the gold rush.

This quiet street in San Jose is, perhaps, the best place in the state to discover the extraordinary contrast between pre- and post-gold rush California. Although these homes have been landmarks for years, they've only recently been fully refurbished and opened for tours by the San Jose Historical Museum Association.

Built in 1797, the Peralta Adobe is one of California's oldest existing homes. It is furnished to reflect the 1800s and 1840s, during the Spanish & Mexican Colonial eras.

Peralta, who bought the adobe in 1807, was a prominent community leader, the "Comisionado" of San Jose. He was one of only twenty to receive land grants that comprised the whole of California.

Although his estate was worth some $1,380,000 when he died in 1851, his soldier's lifestyle was simple, not sumptuous. Traditionally, their money went into their horses, saddles, clothing and jewelry, not their homes.

Furnishings are sparse but significant in the 1840s living room. A desk topped with quill pen and inkwell illustrates Peralta's literacy, unusual at the time. A felt hat and Spanish-style scarves hang from a peg rack. A sampling of embroidered pieces showcases the Mexican woman's forte. A large wooden table is set for preparing food. The small 1840 American Empire table shows the influence of expanded trade.

The pictures of the Virgin of Guadalupe and St. Joseph are copies of the originals that hung in the

Peraltas' living room. Occasionally, the priest celebrated mass here. A kneeler is topped with candles and crucifix.

In the 1800s bedroom, a whale vertebrae chair illustrates how early Californians were masters at using found materials. A cradle hangs from the ceiling by the parents' bed so they could simply reach out to rock it. You'll see a replica of "leather jacket" armor, so thick it could repel most arrows, and a formal, brass-buttoned military coat.

Walk across the street to the 1855 Fallon House and a new era in California culture. Through the grand, wooden doors you'll find a beautifully refurbished Victorian.

Fifteen-foot ceilings rise above the parlors. One has a horsehair parlor set, with the original upholstery. The front room's carpets not only follow a Victorian design, but were woven on period looms.

In the back parlor, or "smoking room," stogies sit in the ash tray, as if the men had just taken a break from politics and brandy. In the dining room, a gilded mirror hangs above the marble hearth.

Upstairs, you'll find more elaborate furnishings, like the grand, carved wooden bed in the master bedroom or the pint-sized rocking chair and table in the children's room.

An extraordinary 1861 ball gown, displayed in the sewing room, has a hoop 31 feet around and weighs about 20 pounds.

If the Fallon House inspires you to add some Victorian touches to your home, you'll find a splendid selection of decorative ware, papergoods, historical books and unique souvenirs in The City Store Gift Shop next door.

Fallon House & Peralta Adobe
175 W. St. John St., one block west of Market St.
San Jose
408/993-8182
Th.-Sun. 11-4:30
(Pre-arranged group tours available on Wed.)
$6 Adults; $5 Seniors 65 and older; $3 ages 6-18

♪   *San Jose*
 Historical   Museum

During a sunny midweek day, ladies in long skirts and wide-brimmed hats stroll past Victorian homes, peek into the doctor's office and drop by the imposing Empire Firehouse, where horse-drawn hook and ladder trucks await the next disaster. Most lead a boisterous brood of children, like old-fashioned schoolmarms on a class outing.

This is San Jose Historical Museum, a village of late 19th-century buildings relocated or reconstructed here from around the city, saved from the crush of ever-expanding development. Far removed from skyscrapers and silicon, the 25-acre museum is on the southern end of verdant Kelley Park, which also has a small zoo and Japanese Friendship Garden.

Clustered in this small town are the grand Pacific Hotel, founded in 1880, the 1862 Coyote Post Office and Dashaway Stables with its collection of high-toned riding carriages.

A favorite stop is O'Brien's Candy Store, once acclaimed as "the prettiest and most attractive candy store on the Pacific Coast." Founded in 1868 by an Irish immigrant, it was the first place to serve ice cream and sodas west of Detroit. Today, you can enjoy a sundae in its old-fashioned soda shop.

This is one of the shops on the ground floor of the Pacific Hotel. The hotel flourished in the late 19th century, advertised as "the most convenient house on the coast." For $1 to $1.50 per day for room and board, guests enjoyed a bar, bath, reading rooms, billiard halls and hardy German food.

The oddest structure in this village is a scaled-down replica of San Jose's Electric Light Tower. The idea was to turn night into day downtown with one high and immense light.

On December 13, 1881, the 237-foot tower straddling Santa Clara and Market Streets was lighted, but the 24,000 candlepower beam proved a not-so-brilliant innovation. It didn't sufficiently light the area. By 1915, already damaged by a windstorm, the tower collapsed into the street.

The Umbarger and Chiechi Houses reflect the traditional family life of old San Jose. In the Umbarger's cozy, one-story gingerbread house, furnishings reveal the day-to-day lifestyle of the Victorian period—upright and refined.

The Chiechi House, which belonged to prominent orchardists, is furnished to reflect a later era. Children's games clutter the living room, a no-no in Victorian times. The kitchen features many newfangled electrical appliances, including a toaster, beaters and an ice box with a motor on top.

A peek into the dentist's office reveals why many people fear this profession. A nasty-looking drill hangs over the dentist's chair. Cuffs on the chair's arms kept squirming patients strapped in tight.

A replica of the 1888 Ng Shing Gung temple includes an original altar, carved and gilded in China, and exhibits on the history of San Jose's Chinese community.

The rambling Stevens Ranch Fruit Barn recalls the area's major industry from the 1870s to 1940s. Orchards of prunes, apricots, plums and pears earned Santa Clara Valley the reputation as an international fruit production center. Once used for fruit drying, the barn now exhibits an excellent collection of historical photographs, antique fruit sorting bins and other artifacts.

Antique firefighting equipment is housed in the Empire Firehouse. The collection includes an 1808 hose truck with hand pump and the trampoline-style life saving system used to catch jumpers from tall buildings. A small park nearby offers a pleasant place to sit among San Jose's pioneer buildings.

San Jose Historical Museum
Kelley Park, at Senter and Phelan, San Jose
408/287-2290
Mon.-Fri. 10-4:30; Sat. & Sun. 12-4:30
$4 Adults; $3 Seniors 65 and over; $2 ages 6-17

♫ *Carmel Mission*

More than two centuries ago, Father Junipero Serra raised a cross in the wilderness that we now call Carmel.

Today, a rough wooden cross stands in the very spot where the original was erected on August 24, 1771. Behind it rises the Mission San Carlos Borromeo del Rio Carmel, one of the most beautifully restored California missions.

Here you can see the graceful catenary arch of the chapel, the Moorish-style bell tower, period rooms depicting California's first library, a primitive kitchen and Serra's spartan bedroom as well as mission artifacts, richly embroidered vestments and the simple graveyard where Serra is buried.

The mission began as a crude log structure, a place to preach the word of Christ to the Indians. Wood buildings were replaced with more permanent adobe as Serra continued his journey along the California coast, founding nine more missions.

Serra would never see the present stone church that is the prize of the Carmel Mission. He died in 1784, nine years before its construction began. But near his quiet burial plot, his successor, Padre Lausen, fulfilled Serra's vision.

A colorful, Spanish-style garden leads to the graceful facade of the church. Two towers, one topped with a dome and a cross, frame its large wooden doors. Above the doors, a star-shaped window serves as focal point for the design.

This is actually a reconstruction of the original church. After Carmel was secularized in 1834, the mission was gradually abandoned and fell into decay and ruin. Photos just inside the entrance reveal the disastrous state of the mission. Complete restoration began in 1931, bringing the church and its environs back to their original state.

Built of native sandstone, the church's interior walls curve inward forming a graceful seamless arch overhead. The altar is painted in rich burgundy and deep sea green tones. On the rear balcony, a large pipe organ reaches for the ceiling.

Allow time to wander through the smaller adobe rooms of the mission. One display shines with intricate gold and silver altar pieces Serra brought from Mexico in the 1770s. Another room holds richly embroidered vestments from the 1780s to 1800s. The finely crafted white lace was made by Indian girls who were taught by the Spanish soldiers' wives.

The Carmel Mission was home to California's first library. It began with 30 volumes acquired from Mexico City's Apostolic College in 1778. One period room recreates the small library. Worn leather volumes crowd the shelves surrounding a sturdy desk topped with a candle and hourglass.

In contrast with Serra's elaborate sarcophagus are his spartan sleeping quarters, furnished with little more than a crude bed. Another room recreates the mission's kitchen complete with beehive oven and cords of garlic dangling from the ceiling.

The courtyard is the most peaceful place in the mission, with soft Wisteria hanging from its walls and a pleasant fountain splashing in its center. A smaller courtyard encompasses graves outlined with abalone shells and marked with small wooden crosses.

One gravestone commemorates "Old Gabriel," who died on March 14, 1890, "Aged 151 years." Church records show that Gabriel was not so long-lived, however, leaving this life at a spry 119 years old.

Take your time wandering through the Carmel Mission to enjoy its tranquil gardens and get a feel for this slice of old California and life at one of its most graceful missions.

Carmel Mission
Rio Rd. and Lausen Dr., Carmel
408/624-3600
Mon.-Sat. 9:30-4:30; Sun. 10:30-4:30
$1 Donation requested

♤ *Wilder Ranch*
State Park

In 1896 the local paper called Wilder Ranch "the cream dairy of the county and one of the finest in California." In its extra long cow barn, 206 cows were milked twice a day. The Victorian horse barn sported four different types of shingles and five colors of paint. The farmhouse was not only one of the first in the county to get electricity, but it had innovative lights that turned on automatically when the closet door was opened.

This is a time capsule of a turn-of-the-century California dairy farm. The milking barn, horse barn, Victorian farmhouses, machine shops and eight other ranch buildings have been preserved as Wilder Ranch State Park. A small herd of cattle and pair of draft horses echo the sounds and scents of the past. On weekends, costumed docents demonstrate traditional ranchwork, such as blacksmithing, baking or butter churning.

The oldest building on the ranch is the weathered, circa 1839 Bolcoff Adobe. Bolcoff, a Russian sailor who jumped ship in Monterey and later married a wealthy Mexican woman, first started a butter and cheese dairy here.

By the 1850s, a man named Moses Meder owned the ranch. Meder had been a ship's carpenter and it's believed that he built the east coast Gothic-style Victorian farmhouse himself. It is the fanciest building on the ranch even today.

The farm grew into a major dairy operation 20 years later under a new owner, Levi K. Baldwin, a dairyman from Marin, and his partner, Deloss D. Wilder. Each day, they churned 300 pounds of butter by horsepower and shipped it north to San Francisco.

Wilder introduced a major innovation to his dairy business by installing Pelton water wheels. Turned by water pressure and connected by belts and pulleys to various machines, these wheels powered saws, drills, lathes, even a coffee grinder. Today, with a turn of a faucet, docents put the actual Pelton wheel back to work in the machine shop.

The other large farmhouse on the property was built for Deloss' son, Melvin D. Wilder, the engineer of the family. The home has been authentically renovated to reflect that era. The kitchen holds the original massive cast iron stove. Redwood paneling has been false-grained to look like oak, a popular style at the time.

When you open the dining room closet door, Melvin's inventive light automatically turns on and you discover the Wilder family's growth chart on the back of the door. In the living room fireplace hearth is a tile bearing the likeness of former president McKinley. Melvin was a staunch Republican.

You also can explore the garage, with its 1930 Model A Ford and 1916 Dodge Brothers touring sedan. In the horse barn, innovative shoots sent hay directly from the loft to each stall. The visitor center tells the story of the ranch with historical photographs, newspaper clippings and dairy farm artifacts.

When you stroll around Wilder Ranch State Park, you easily can imagine that you're visiting a dairy farm of 100 years past. Twenty-eight miles of trails, some leading to the ocean, are open to hikers, bicyclists and horseback riders from sunrise to sunset.

Wilder Ranch State Park
Along Highway 1, two miles north of Santa Cruz
408/426-0505
Visitor Center and Book Store open Wed.-Sun. 10-4
(Call first. Hours may vary.)
$6 per vehicle day use parking fee;
$5 if senior is in car
Includes same-day admission
to other state parks and beaches

☖ *Ardenwood Historic Farm*

There are few places where you actually relive history. Ardenwood Historic Farm is one of them. You can help harvest wheat and other crops using vintage tools, ride on a horse-powered railroad, tour a Victorian farm house, taste home-made jam with biscuits baked in an old-fashioned oven, watch a blacksmith work and much more.

This 205-acre treasure is located just east of the Dumbarton Bridge in Fremont. Follow the signs down a narrow country lane. As you drive by the bountiful vegetable fields, you head further into the past until you reach Ardenwood and the late 1800s.

A graceful, gleaming white Victorian is the hub of the farm. This was the home of George and Clara Patterson. Patterson came west in 1849 to join the gold rush, but a year and a half of mining left him ill and broke. He realized the real fortune lay in what he knew best—farming.

After working for farmers near Mission San Jose, he was able to acquire nearly 6,000 acres of land, becoming one of the wealthiest men in the area.

The elaborate Queen Anne addition of this house was built in 1889 by renowned architect Samuel Newsom. It features a two-story turret, arched porticos and stained glass windows.

Exotic woods highlight the interior. In the double foyers, sycamore archways echo a Turkish influence in vogue at the time. The mantel in the guest parlor is carved mahogany. The pocket door has a veneer of burled redwood.

Period furnishings set the mood throughout the home. Upstairs, you can feel the unusual horsehair mattress on George and Clara's elaborate wood bed. The kitchen is full of gadgets from the early 1900s, including a vintage butter churner, bread kneader, cherry pitter, hot water heater and 1911 stove still used today.

Patterson fought an ongoing battle with the railroad, who wanted a right-of-way across his land. When he returned from his honeymoon, he found that the railroad had laid the track in his absence. After he successfully sued, the railroad had to stop on demand for the Pattersons. They had their own private depot.

Today, you can ride on a horse-powered railroad around Ardenwood. There's also a haywagon pulled by a brother and sister team of 2,000-pound Belgian draft horses. It winds past crops that Patterson grew here 100 years ago.

Special programs offered throughout the seasons include jam-making, storytelling and animal feeding. During wheat harvest in mid- to late summer, volunteers are handed old-fashioned wooden pitchforks to heave bundles of wheat onto the wagon. Then, you watch as the 1920s thresher separates the wheat berry from the chaff. The berries are then ground into flour. You can taste foods cooked the old-fashioned way in the wood-fueled oven.

Kids especially enjoy visiting the sheep, goats, pigs, turkeys and chickens. They'll also surprise you by wanting to do the laundry, using a hand-powered agitator and wringer. The General Store sells old-fashioned toys, cookbooks and other gifts.

Come to Ardenwood early. The Patterson House tours are offered on a first-come, first served basis and can sell out. Children under 6 are not allowed on the House tours, but there is plenty of fun here for the whole family.

Ardenwood Historic Farm
34600 Ardenwood Blvd., Fremont
510/796-0663 (recording)
Open April-Nov., Th.-Sun. 10-5
Also open Labor Day, Memorial Day, July 4
and first weekend in Dec.
$6 Adults; $4 Seniors 62 and over; $3.50 ages 4-17
(includes haywagon and railway rides, house tour
and special programs)

♩ *Camron-Stanford House*

Lifestyles of the rich and famous—in Oakland? Yes, in the 1870s. Lake Merritt was the playground of the Victorian elite. The Camron-Stanford house, overlooking the water, is a living reminder of that era, an intimate look at Oakland's heyday.

At one time, several stately Victorian homes ringed the lake. Each sported a carriage house, a boathouse and a boat.

Built in 1876, the Camron-Stanford House was not the grandest, largest nor most expensive. Nevertheless, it boasts an elaborate exterior and interior, which has been lovingly restored by historic-minded preservationists.

The home is a large four-story structure, its ground floor patterned with arched Italianate windows. As in most Victorian homes, it is highlighted with graceful and intricate details. Columns topped with lotus-motif capitals frame the front door. A delicate pattern is wheel-cut into the door's glass panels. On the side door, one wheel-cut glass panel is a century old, the other a reproduction, but even close inspection won't reveal the difference.

Much of the home had to be restored after its long and varied history. In addition to Josiah Stanford, the man who introduced the champagne grape to California and the older brother to railroad baron Leland, four other families lived here. In 1907, the City of Oakland purchased the house and, after remodeling, used it as the Oakland Public Museum until 1967 when the new museum was built.

The Camron-Stanford House Preservation Association rallied to save the house from demolition. Using diaries, letters and newspaper accounts, they restored the home to the time when the David Hewes family lived here, from 1877 to 1881. Hewes was the man who gave the Golden Spike that joined the trans-continental railroad.

The best way to start your tour is by watching "Living In a House." This award-winning slide show relates the history of three generations by combining vintage photographs with the colorful letters of Franklina Gray Bartlett, Hewes' stepdaughter. It is a telling illustration of how changing lifestyles are reflected in home furnishings and decorations.

In the hall, there is a pump organ and an ornate statuary cabinet patterned with inlaid wood. Some of the elaborate flower arrangements, sea-shell picture frames and other crafts were created by the lady of the house, which not only showed artistic talent but that they were wealthy enough to have the leisure to do it.

In the formal parlor, the center table is covered with a soft paisley cloth, very chic at the time. Many of the tables in the home are covered—the Victorians didn't like bareness in anything.

The gas chandelier, or "gasolier," is one of two still working in Oakland. Lighting determined the arrangement of furniture. The table is in the center of the room to take advantage of the gasolier's light. When wall fixtures came into vogue, reading chairs and small tables were moved to a room's perimeter.

Throughout the house, patterns decorate the wall borders, carpets and ceiling medallions. Whether you look up, down or around, you will see flowing geometric shapes and unusual colors.

The Crafts Revival Show, downstairs, illustrates the stages of restoration through photographs, tools and cutaways of plaster and wood. You'll come away with a full appreciation of the energy Victorians devoted to their homes, and of the restorers who brought it back to life.

Camron-Stanford House
Oak and 14th Sts., Oakland
510/836-1976
Wed. 11-4; Sun. 1-5
$2 Adults; $1 Seniors 65 and over, under 12 free

♫ *Shadelands Ranch*

If you want to see what the East Bay was like before high-tech office buildings, shopping malls and traffic congestion, visit the Shadelands Ranch Historical Museum in Walnut Creek. It is a provocative glimpse into the hard-working farm life of the early 20th century.

Completed in 1903, this two-story Colonial Revival house was the home of Hiram Penniman, his wife, Carrie, and his unmarried daughter, Mary. At the time, it was surrounded by 320 acres of farmland, where Penniman raised pears, prunes and three different types of walnuts.

Originally from New York, Penniman came west for the gold rush, but he didn't pursue that for long. Like a lot of prospectors, he discovered the real gold was in agriculture. In 1854, Penniman and his brother-in-law squatted on this land. They eventually purchased it, creating the Shadelands Ranch.

Don't expect a frilly Victorian. The Shadelands home was a sturdy, practical farmhouse, something you might see in the midwest, with sunny bay windows and a wrap-around verandah. Even the door is exceptionally wide and solid-looking. Some say the extra width was the ultimate practicality—it accommodated caskets. At the time, the deceased were viewed in people's parlors. Another story claims that the extra wide door allowed for the Pennimans' heavy wood furniture.

Almost all of the furniture in the Shadelands Museum was in the home when the Pennimans lived here nearly 90 years ago. A true time capsule of that era, even the books, china and tablecloths belonged to the Pennimans.

In the dining room, the table is set with white china with gold leaf trim. An ornate wooden sideboard, featuring a carved wooden buck's head, holds odd pieces, including a pretty serving plate and an oblong teapot with a blue windmills and fishermen design from about the 1840s.

The parlor's wooden furniture includes an octagonal table and a heavy, gracefully carved writing desk. The unusual texture in these rooms' fireplaces are from "clinker bricks." These bricks are seconds, off-sized and mis-shaped.

A wide oak staircase rises majestically through the center of the house. On the landing, a window seat stretches beneath a row of sunny windows that once overlooked acres of walnuts.

Upstairs, the master bedroom has been transformed into the "History Room." Here, the Walnut Creek Historical Society preserves old maps, records and photographs of the area. On the wall, an aerial photograph shows how the town looked on September 13, 1928, one of the archives' estimated 1,000 pictures.

The second bedroom belonged to Mary, Penniman's unwed daughter. Many believe that Penniman, thinking Mary would remain a spinster, built this house for her.

A hall closet holds Bessie's wedding dress, Penniman's daughter from his second marriage. Bessie stayed in the third bedroom when she visited. Like the other bedrooms, it has its own closet and washroom with pumped water. The Shadelands had several modern amenities, including central heat.

The guest bedroom now showcases kitchen memorabilia from the Pennimans' time here, offering a homespun look at everyday life in the early 1900s. The collection includes a two-burner kerosene stove, a wooden icebox, tin bread and cake boxes, a large wicker baby carriage, an unusual hand-powered vacuum and more.

Shadelands Ranch Historical Museum
2660 Ygnacio Valley Rd., Walnut Creek
5 miles east of I-680
510/935-7871
Wed.-Th. 11:30-4; Sun. 1-4
$2 Adults; $1 Seniors; Children under 12 Free

♫ *Treasure Island*

When San Francisco hosted the west coast's 1939 World's Fair, we celebrated on a grand scale. This was an 18-month jubilee of new deals, broadened horizons and futuristic technology—the Golden Gate International Exposition.

Even with economic depression, labor unrest and impending world war, nothing seemed far from the grasp of modern man. Travelers flew across the vast Pacific to Honolulu in an amazing 18 hours. Two grand bridges now spanned the San Francisco Bay.

Not just any stretch of land would do for the Exposition. From the depths of the San Francisco Bay, we created an island. It would stand near the center of the spanking new Bay Bridge. As legend has it, when the dredges scooped up decades of soil washed into the Bay from Sierra mines, flecks of gold gave the new land its name—Treasure Island.

Today, it is a quiet Navy base, far removed from the time when hundreds of thousand of visitors filled its shores. Although thousands of motorists speed by the island on their way to and from San Francisco, few stop to see what it's all about.

Those who do veer off the sharp Treasure Island exit will find a quiet, palm-lined island, one of the best and most easily accessible views of the San Francisco skyline and a small museum that capsules the fabulous Exposition days, the building of the Bay Bridge, our nation's military at sea and more.

The Treasure Island Museum is in one of the few original buildings from the exposition. It is "Streamlined Moderne" style, a horse-shoe shaped structure with art deco details. The only other exposition-era structures are two hangars inaccessible to the general public, as is the rest of the island. The glory of the Exposition is long gone.

But imagine for a moment one of the museum building's original purposes. It was the West Coast China Clipper Terminal for Pan-American Airways, the take-off point for destinations in the Far East. Twice a week during the exposition years, these propeller-driven "flying boats" landed in the water here. Fashionable ladies and adventurers embarked for exotic Asia. The setting has remained so authentic that Hollywood used it as the Berlin Airport in "Indiana Jones and the Last Crusade."

The palms are what remains of the more than 4,000 trees lifted from California gardens and planted here, along with 800,000 annuals, 400,000 perennials and 250,000 tulips.

During its heyday, parades, cavalcades, pole-balancing acts, motorcycle cowgirls, comedians, presidents and maharajahs filled Treasure Island with an unmatched exuberance. Shows ranged from wholesome puppet theater to nude follies. Exhibits boasted of the transparent "phone of the future," robots and diesel automobile engines.

The museum's excellent "Jewels of the Bay" gallery showcases a fun, nostalgic collection of Exposition memorabilia. Photographs, souvenirs, posters, even a shiny model of a China Clipper bring back the island's past, when visitors envisioned a exhilarating future.

But the Exposition closed its doors on September 29, 1940. Soon naval buildings replaced the Tower of the Sun and Triumphal Arch. The celebration of the Pacific Basin fell to the War in the Pacific.

The museum's 251-foot-long, 26-foot-high mural depicts some key chapters in naval history. Exhibit highlights include period uniforms, ship models and paintings. One exhibit highlights Navajo "Code-Talkers." Their language was so foreign to the Japanese that they never broke the code. There is an immense, working, circa-1854 Fresnel lighthouse lens from the Farallon Islands and much more.

Next time you're speeding by Treasure Island, take a quick detour to discover this island in history.

Treasure Island Museum
Treasure Island
415/395-5067
Open daily 10-3:30
Free

☖ *Petaluma Adobe*

A rooster crows as the morning light shines on the whitewashed adobe walls. The burro and small herd of sheep shake off the night chill. Beehive ovens stand ready for the baker. A huge iron cauldron awaits the candle-maker.

This is a typical day on the rancho of the 1830s and '40s recreated with period furniture, a menagerie of livestock and authentic details at the Petaluma Adobe State Historic Park, one of the largest and best restored of California's Mexican-era adobes.

This immense fortress of an adobe was once the center of activity for Mariano Guadalupe Vallejo's Petaluma Rancho, a sprawling 66,000-acre, 100-square-mile agricultural empire. The existing west wing alone is more than half a football field long.

Now it forms one side of a giant horseshoe-shaped, two-story building, with wide wooden verandahs and balconies stretching completely around the structure. In its prime, it was twice as large, forming a quadrangle where more than 2,000 Indians worked.

The workers would feel right at home if they returned today. Whitewashed beehive ovens wait in the courtyard. The crude wooden oxcart is one of only three authentically recreated, working "carretas" in the state.

As you wander around, you will find a fully stocked indoor kitchen and a weaving room with looms, spinning wheels and brightly colored finished cloth hanging from the rafters. Further along, you'll see the fancy living quarters of Vallejo, the simple room of the rancho's majordomo and the comfortable guest room. Across the courtyard are a workshop and warehouse for the hide and tallow trade and more.

Hides and tallow, which was rendered from cattle fat to make soap and candles, were the rancho's main industry. They were traded for goods from the European, American and other foreign ships that plied the California coast. Some of these international goods are represented in Vallejo's parlor, including a marble-topped table, crystal stemware and fine wood writing desk.

The rancho's farms raised an abundance of wheat, barley, corn, beans and vegetables. Its weavers manufactured enough cloth and blankets for 2,000 Indians. Blacksmiths and tanneries were mini-factories, turning out finished nails, tools and ready-made leather for saddles. Vallejo became one of the richest men in California.

The empire fell to a sudden end when the Bear Flag Revolt of 1846 claimed California for America. The Indian workers ran away and looters and squatters cleaned out the rancho's holdings. In 1880, at 72 years old, Vallejo returned to look at his adobe, now in ruins. "I compare the old relic with myself," he wrote to his son. "Then Youth, strength, and riches; now Age, weakness and poverty."

Petaluma Adobe State Historic Park
Adobe Rd., Petaluma
707/762-4871
Open daily 10-5
$2 Adults; $1 ages 6-17

Extra Tip...If you're planning to spend the day visiting the area's historic sites, $2 covers same-day admission to Vallejo's home in Sonoma, the Sonoma Mission (see "Sonoma" in the "Towns to Explore" chapter) and the Sonoma barracks museum.

△ *China Camp State Park*

It is more than a century old, the last of the bay's Chinese fishing villages. In the 1880s, China Camp was a bustling town of 500, with a schoolteacher, barber, two gardeners, a doctor and three general stores.

Today one man, Frank Quan, carries on the heritage of his ancestors. You can catch a glimpse of what their life was like by visiting China Camp State Park's historic village and museum.

Just north of the Richmond/San Rafael Bridge in Marin County, China Camp is an easy, sunny getaway. Hikers explore forested hills. Birdwatchers flock to the emerald-hued wetlands. Picnickers enjoy the tables overlooking the bay and the sandy beaches.

A winding road along the bay's shore leads to the weathered wooden buildings of China Camp. Only a few structures remain, including Frank Quan's simple home, a shrimp drying platform and a long pier jutting into the water. A decayed fishing boat rests on the beach.

One of the buildings has been converted to a nostalgic beach food stand. Another houses a small museum that tells the story of the bay's Chinese fishing villages through artifacts and historical photos.

Lured to California by gold, the Chinese found success in a more familiar endeavor—shrimp fishing. In the late 19th century, as many as 30 Chinese fishing villages, with their fishing junks and sampans, dotted the San Francisco and San Pablo Bays. The immigrants found peace from prejudice in their isolated communities, where they maintained their Chinese culture and spoke their native language.

The museum's small aquarium showcases the tiny shrimp that the Chinese caught in these waters. Most of the shrimp were dried and exported to China, up to one million pounds in a good year. In season, the hillsides were covered with drying shrimp.

One of the museum's wooden artifacts includes a five-foot-tall fan mill. Following a 2,000-year-old Chinese design, this mill crushed the dried shrimp and separated the shells from the meat. Other artifacts include barrels, nets and china rice bowls and soup spoons found on the site.

The Chinese shrimp export industry thrived until the late 1800s, when racial hostility heightened. In 1905, the export of dried shrimp was banned. In 1910, the season was closed during the best shrimping months. In 1911, a law prohibited bag nets and the possession of dried shrimp.

These laws effectively cut off any hope of the Chinese continuing their shrimp fishing. The villages slowly died out. By the 1930s, China Camp was the last of the Chinese fishing villages on the bay, operated by a sole family, the Quan's.

Frank Quan still fishes here. Most of his shrimp catch is sold as bait, but depending on the catch you may still be able to purchase fresh grass shrimp at the snack bar on weekends. It is said to be one of the tastiest shrimp in the world.

China Camp State Park
North of Richmond/San Rafael Bridge, Marin
Exit N. San Pedro Rd. off 101 North,
head east on N. San Pedro Rd. to park.
State Park open daily 8 A.M.-Sunset
Museum open daily 10-5
415/456-0766
$3 Parking Fee (inside village)

♫ *Fort Ross* *State Historic Park*

Long before most American pioneers headed west to tame a new frontier, the Russians journeyed east to become some of California's first white settlers. Fort Ross is dedicated to preserving that fascinating, if short-lived, Russian pioneer era.

Perched on a rocky bluff above the Pacific coast north of Jenner, this is an authentic recreation of the original fort that stood on this site from 1812 to 1841. You can venture into an octagonal blockhouse complete with cannons and an armory with barrels of gun powder and rows of muskets. Imagine the fort's past in the officials' quarters, with its well-stocked kitchen, and the Russian Orthodox chapel.

Begin your tour of Fort Ross in the visitor center. Take time to review the exhibits that illustrate the history of the area. They present an intriguing picture of the peoples that lived here.

The Kashaya Pomo Indians had inhabited the area for centuries, living off the land and sea. The Russian founder of the fort, Ivan Alexandrovich Kuskov, arrived in 1812 with 25 fellow countrymen and 80 native Alaskans. They constructed a fort with the traditional stockade, blockhouses and log buildings like those in Siberia and Alaska.

The Russians came to hunt sea otter, a prized pelt in their cold homeland. The Alaskans, skilled hunters and expert fishermen, brought 40 baidarkas with them for hunting. An example of these swift, maneuverable kayaks is on display.

Before long, the supply of sea otters along this coast was exhausted. The managers of Fort Ross tried to establish a new industry in agriculture to supply Russian outposts in Alaska. This, too, proved unsuccessful. Despite developing such industries as brickmaking, timber products, milling, tanning, metalworking and three inland ranches, Fort Ross was losing money consistently.

In 1841, the Russians decided to abandon their colony on North America's western frontier. They sold the land to John Sutter, who moved the livestock, equipment and armaments to his fort of New Helvetia, which later became Sacramento.

Today, Fort Ross stands as though the Russians still live and work here. A tall, hand-hewn fence encircles the fort, with blockhouses—one eight-sided, one seven-sided—towering above opposite corners. You can climb up to the blockhouse's second story and peek out past the cannons to a scene little changed over the years.

The Rotchev House is the only structure with original Russian materials. Although it is empty now, records show that this home of Fort Ross' last manager once held a "choice library, a piano, and a score of Mozart."

Spartan but adequate furnishings decorate the rooms of the officials' quarters. Its iron workers' and carpenters' shops contain a small forge, tools and finished goods. The pantry is filled with a large brass samovar, barrels of peaches and potatoes and unplucked chickens hanging from hooks.

The armory in the Kuskov House is well-stocked with barrels of powder and muskets. Other storerooms contain barrels marked in Russian, teapots, boots and fabrics. Upstairs, a scientist's lab has small animal skulls and a primitive microscope.

The chapel is the most graceful building in the fort. The original was built in the mid-1820s and was the first Russian Orthodox structure on this continent outside Alaska.

After touring Fort Ross, you can walk out to the windy bluff and look back on what was once one of the loneliest settlements on the coast.

Fort Ross State Historic Park
Highway 1, 13 miles north of Jenner
707/847-3286
Open daily 10-4:30
$5 per car day use fee; $4 if senior is in car
Living History Day: last Sat. in July, $2 extra

♫ *Sutter's Fort*

Who first cultivated California's central valley on a commercial scale? Whose enterprise led to the discovery of gold in the Sierra? Whose fledgling pioneer settlement evolved into our state capitol?

The answer is John Sutter. With little more than a dream, he set out to build an empire. He acquired 150,000 acres of land, herds of cattle and shipping, tanning and fishery industries. Ironically, his own logging operation would make his dream a nightmare, when it led to the discovery of gold.

Sutter's Fort State Historic Park in Sacramento recreates life in California before the gold rush and preserves Sutter's pioneering spirit. In the summer months, docents in period dress demonstrate the crafts of Sutter's time.

The year is 1846. Sutter's dream is at its height. Whitewashed, 18-foot-tall adobe walls enclose an independent, self-contained community. As you walk around Sutter's Fort you will see a cooperage, textile mill, blacksmith, distillery, gunshop, bakery, trade store and living quarters.

Be sure to pick up a sound wand before you start your tour. Through it, you can hear the story of Sutter's Fort told through Sutter's diaries.

One exhibit room illustrates the history of the fort. The most striking display encases the doll that belonged to eight-year-old Patty Reed of the ill-fated Donner party. Originally headed for Sutter's Fort, the Donner party was trapped in the Sierra's winter snows. Many died; the others turned to cannibalism to survive.

Sutter welcomed all travelers to his fort and was well-known for his hospitality. Living quarters were spartan but adequate. One room in the fort recreates the Richie family's quarters, with a simple bed, cradle, spinning wheel and one small luxury, a pendant clock on the mantel.

In the blanket factory, massive, authentically recreated looms and spinning wheels hint at the extent of this industry.

The kitchen, well-stocked with fireplaces and large iron pots, could feed up to 200 people a day. Usually about 50 were fed here. At least one or two steers were killed every day; during harvest, five or six were killed. Bread was baked in the beehive ovens in the courtyard.

You'll find period tools in the carpenter's shop. Almost everything, from doors and windows to cannon mounts, depended on craftsmen who knew how to use and shape different types of wood.

Lumber mills that provided this wood were an important facet of Sutter's empire. In 1847, he commissioned James Marshall to build a sawmill on land Sutter leased from the Coloma Indians. While building that mill, on January 24, 1848, Marshall discovered gold.

Sutter tried keeping the discovery a secret, but word leaked out. By May, many of Sutter's workers joined the rush. Skilled craftsmen left. Two-thirds of his wheat crop went unharvested.

Sutter could not protect his empire until the U.S. government officially recognized his Mexican land grants. By the time they did, in 1855, the squatters had settled in and could not be removed.

Ten years later, Sutter moved to Pennsylvania, leaving California and his dream behind. He traveled frequently to Washington, DC hoping to gain compensation for his lost land from the U.S. government. After 14 years of fruitlessly struggling for retribution, Sutter died in a Washington hotel room on June 18, 1880.

Sutter's Fort State Historic Park
L St., between 26th & 28th, Sacramento
916/445-4422
Open daily 10-5,
except Thanksgiving, Dec. 25 & Jan. 1
$2 Adults; $1 ages 6-12
Memorial Day-Labor Day: $5 Adults; $2 ages 6-12
Mountain Man Trader's Fair in May

♤ Columbia
State Historic Park

Columbia is the best preserved gold rush town in California, a highlight of anyone's journey to the Mother Lode. Almost all the buildings in this 12-block section of town have been restored or authentically reconstructed. You can peek into a miner's cabin, enjoy a sarsaparilla in the saloon or buy gold panning supplies at the general store.

Costumed docents people the village, playing the roles of their counterparts from 140 years ago. The only mode of transportation is the stagecoach—modern-day contraptions like the automobile are not allowed in this time capsule town.

The only sounds are the clip-clop of horses, the clang of the blacksmith's hammer and, perhaps, the tune of an old-time fiddler playing in the street on weekends.

Columbia was once the second largest town in California. It boasted four banks, eight hotels, 53 stores, three churches, 40 saloons and one of the largest gambling halls in gold country. Like other Mother Lode towns , it was all built around gold.

A member of Dr. Thaddeus Hildreth's party first found the precious yellow mineral here in March of 1850. Within a month, 5,000 miners turned "Hildreth's Diggin's" into a boomtown of tents and shanties.

Buildings sprang up to house businesses serving the miners. And wealth started pouring in. An intricate water system, including a 60-mile-long aqueduct, was built to supply water for the placer mines. It's still used today.

People called Columbia "the Gem of the Southern Mines." The area yielded more than 150,000 pounds of gold. Today, you can see the scale that weighed $55 million of that fortune in the Wells Fargo office. This elegant scale is so precise it can measure the weight of a signature on a piece of paper.

For a few dollars, you can relive the past with a ride on an authentic stagecoach. It comes thundering up to the Wells Fargo depot to let off and pick up passengers just like in the old west. You can even ride "shotgun" on the top of the stage next to the driver.

As you stroll down Main Street, you'll notice that many of the buildings, like the 1858 Wells Fargo office, are brick with iron shutters. Fire was always a problem in gold rush towns, and Columbia wasn't spared. An 1854 fire destroyed nearly the entire town. An 1857 fire burnt down all the wooden buildings. From then on, most buildings were made of brick with iron shutters as protection from fire.

Take a left down State Street to find Firehouse #1. Columbia's pride and joy is here—"Papeete," a bright red, gold-embossed, hand-pumped fire truck. Legend says that Papeete was originally made in Boston for the king of the Society Islands. (Papeete is the capital of Tahiti.) The machine arrived in San Francisco by sail, but the ship's crew rushed to the gold mines and abandoned it. Columbia bought it in 1859. Today, Papeete still shows off its stuff in the annual Fireman's Muster, held in May.

Many of the buildings house fun stores where you can buy antiques, toys or souvenirs. Peek into the City Hotel. Opened in 1856, it is restored to reflect its elegant heyday. Don't miss the museum with its excellent collection of gold rush artifacts.

For $3 to $5, you can even pan for gold in Columbia. Matlock Cabin, diagonally across from Wells Fargo, has a water trough seeded with real gold. Even if you don't strike it rich, you'll come home with golden memories of Columbia.

Columbia State Historic Park
Box 151, Columbia, CA 95310
209/532-4301
Open daily 10-4 year-round
Closed Thanksgiving & Dec. 25
Free

◠ *Donner Memorial*
State Park

It is a story of courage, tragedy, survival and just plain bad luck. Ninety pioneers attempted to cross the Sierra Nevada mountains to California in 1846, but became trapped in one of the worst winters on record. Only 48 made it to the promised land, surviving on boiled ox hides, bones once thrown away as scraps and, ultimately, the bodies of those who succumbed.

At the Donner Memorial State Park near Truckee, a monument to these pioneers tells their story in more than words. The pedestal of the monument, four times taller than the average person, marks the depth of the snow that winter. It is 22 feet high.

In the visitor center, you can learn more about the pioneers' journey in a provoking slide show. The center also features displays and artifacts that recount the history of our nation's westward emigration, from trailblazer Jebediah Smith to railroad baron Leland Stanford.

A self-guiding nature trail leads to the boulder that served as the back wall of the Murphy cabin. A plaque here lists the members of the ill-fated wagon train. Seven of the Donner family are listed under "Perished." The remaining seven Donners, mostly orphaned children, "Survived."

Like most pioneers, the Donners began their journey with high hopes of a new life in a bountiful land called California. A prosperous Illinois farm family, they started west with $10,000 sewn into a quilt and a few worldly goods in a covered wagon.

In Wyoming, an explorer, Lansford Hastings, recommended they try a new shortcut that would slice 350 miles off their route. The Donners, along with the Reeds, Murphys and several other families, decided to break away from the main wagon train and follow Hastings' directions.

That was their first mistake. Following the "shortcut," they had to hack a road out of 36 miles of wilderness, then cross 80 miles of desert, where they lost most of their oxen and cattle. By the time they rejoined the traditional route, they were three weeks behind the main wagon train.

Then they made their second mistake. Warned of a rough mountain crossing ahead, they rested near what is now Reno for a week. It was late October and snow started falling in the mountains, but they pushed on. They made it to Donner Lake, but could go no further through the ever-deepening snow drifts. Three attempts to cross the pass ended in snowbound defeat.

Trapped for the winter, they built shelters, but food was scarce. One by one, they died from starvation. The survivors resorted to eating the bodies of the deceased. The struggle continued for three cold months, until a rescue party reached them in late February.

The Donners' story is the most tragic of the pioneers' journeys, but the trail west led to hardship and endurance for all who traveled it. In the visitor center, a full-size covered wagon, with cooking pots, a simple prairie dress and water barrels, illustrates the crude lifestyle of the trail.

One display shows how wagons were dismantled and hauled with ropes up the steep, almost impassable hillsides. In another display, broken china pieces and beloved family heirlooms represent those left behind in desert sand after the oxen died and wagons were abandoned.

These are symbolic of the pioneers' battles, but Patty Reed, who was 8 years old when trapped here in 1846, told the lesson best: "Never take no cut-offs and hurry along as fast as you can."

Donner Memorial State Park
Off Highway 80, west of Truckee
916/582-7892
Open daily 10-4
$2 Adults; $1 ages 6-12

☁ *Pioneer Yosemite History Center*

In the late 1800s, people came from throughout the west to see the natural marvels of what is now Yosemite National Park. Some decided to stay here. They were homesteaders, painters, cavalrymen, blacksmiths and bakers. Each carved out their place in Yosemite and in the Park's history.

The Pioneer Yosemite History Center in Wawona is a living tribute to the Park's pioneers. Century-old log buildings belonging to its first settlers were relocated here from around the Park in the 1950s and 1960s. More than a "village," it is a chronology of events illustrating the Park system's development.

The buildings aren't open year-round, but you can peek into windows to see their rugged furnishings as you wander among them during the quieter off-season. During the summer, costumed docents enact the roles of Yosemite's pioneers.

A covered bridge reminiscent of Vermont is the gateway to this village-like setting. The bridge was built in 1857 by Galen Clark, Yosemite's first guardian.

The artist's cabin is a tribute to those who first inspired others to travel here. Another building was George Anderson's home, when he wasn't on the trail. One of Yosemite's original tourist guides, Anderson was the first to climb Half Dome in 1875.

Homesteaders claimed their piece of Yosemite. The home here was built in 1879 by the Hodgdons, ranchers from the San Joaquin Valley. Originally, this 2-story log building was located in Aspen Valley, near Crane Flat, where the Hodgdon's grazed cattle in the summer.

Damage caused by cattle and sheep grazing spurred John Muir and other preservationists to petition the government demanding protection of the land. Yosemite National Park was established in 1890, ending grazing in the high country.

The name Degnan is still seen on many of Yosemite's food services. In this bakery building, Bridget Degnan began selling bread in the 1880s at 12 1/2 cents per loaf. As travel to Yosemite increased, the demand for her bread grew. An oven capable of baking 50 loaves a day was used until 1900, when the permanent brick oven, taking up nearly half of this building, was installed.

At the turn of the century, visitors traveled by horseback and horse-drawn stage to the Valley. The trip from Wawona took 8 hours and stages had to change their 4-horse teams four times during the strenuous journey. Blacksmith shops, like the one here, were located throughout the park. Today, for a few dollars, you can still experience a short stage coach ride from the Wells Fargo office here.

The influx of visitors created the need for more security. In the early years, the U.S. Cavalry handled the job. Each summer, 150 troopers from San Francisco patrolled trails, fought fires, stocked fish and enforced the no grazing and hunting regulations.

By 1914, the cavalry was replaced by Rangers, who had a new problem to deal with—automobiles. Buildings such as this Ranger Patrol station were used as automobile checkpoints. Drivers stopped to pay the Park fee—$5 in 1915, the same as today.

While in the Wawona area, hardy hikers will enjoy the trail to Chilnualna Falls—one of Yosemite's prettiest cascades. To reach the trail head, follow Chilnualna Falls Road. Just before the pavement ends, bear left. The trail begins immediately on your right. This is a steep path but the waterfall is not very far. The trail continues to climb through picturesque woods to splendid views.

Pioneer Yosemite History Center
Wawona, Yosemite National Park
209/372-0563 or 209/372-0265
Center open daily year-round;
Buildings open late June-Labor Day
Free with $5 per car Yosemite National Park fee

Notes

The Great Outdoors

♠ *Marin Headlands*

San Francisco is one of the few metropolitan areas in the country that is blessed with the stunning beauty of places like Marin Headlands. With the San Francisco skyline glimmering across the water, nature rules here with its rugged cliffs, mighty surf and soaring hawks.

In this surprising park, you can hike scenic trails, explore World War II batteries, visit a NIKE missile site, see a lonesome lighthouse, see marine mammals being nursed back to health, search for agates on the beach, even stay overnight in a hostel. Be sure to call ahead for special ranger-led tours of the restricted areas, such as the lighthouse and missile site.

The Marin Headlands, an extension of the Golden Gate National Recreation Area, lies just northwest of the Golden Gate Bridge. The road along the shore offers an unbeatable close-up view of the graceful Golden Gate Bridge, but it is not for the faint of heart. Heading west, it becomes one-way, with steep curves and fatal drop-offs.

As you near the open Pacific, military relics become more prevalent. The tunnel-like Battery Wallace was first used in 1919 as an open firing platform. The 12-inch guns here could duel with ships 17 miles out to sea. During World War II, the battery was covered with an earth shelter for fear of aerial attacks. By 1948, it was obsolete and shut down.

Displays along the road explain how the headlands was used for several generations of defense, from the Spanish-American to the Cold Wars, from mortars to disappearing guns. On certain days, you can visit the only NIKE missile site still preserved in the United States. It's usually open the first weekend of every month, but a "Park Events" brochure prints an updated schedule every three months.

Point Bonita and its lonesome lighthouse stand on the western tip of the headlands, the threshold of the slim channel of water called the Golden Gate. Until 1775, explorers sailed past and missed this narrow opening to the San Francisco Bay. From the open ocean, it appears as a continuous coastline and the area was frequently obscured by fog.

During the gold rush of 1849, 775 vessels sailed through the Golden Gate. An historic photo on the display near the lighthouse shows San Francisco Bay as a forest of masts. But the rugged coastline became a graveyard of ships.

The Point Bonita Lighthouse was installed in 1855 to help guide vessels through the merciless waters. The original glass Fresnel lens has been in continuous use since then.

You can visit injured elephant seals, sea lions and harbor seals being nursed back to health at the Marine Mammal Center (tel. 415/289-SEAL). The Headlands also is one of the best spots in the Bay Area to watch hawks. The migration begins in late August and peaks with several hundred sightings a day in late September. The best viewing point is the aptly named Hawk Hill.

Enjoy a day on the seashore at Rodeo Beach or search for agates at nearby Rodeo Lagoon. And if you don't want to rush home at night, you can stay in the Golden Gate Hostel (tel. 415/331-2777). Dormitory accommodations are available to guests of any age at $10 per night. Also ask about the availability of couple and family rooms. The spacious hostel has a complete kitchen (you bring your own food), comfortable living room with fireplace, ping pong and pool tables and company from all over the world with whom you can share your day's experience.

Marin Headlands
Northwest of the Golden Gate Bridge
From 101 North, take the Alexander Ave. exit
From 101 South, take the last Sausalito exit
Open 24 hours daily
415/331-1540
Free

♣ *Muir Woods National Monument*

Coast Redwoods are the tallest living things known to man. There is only one place on Earth where these trees grow—in scattered groves along just 500 miles of the Pacific coast from southern Oregon to San Luis Obispo County, California.

People from around the world journey to Muir Woods National Monument to walk among these awe-inspiring giants. This is one of the most magnificent and accessible of the Coast Redwood groves, located just a half-hour's scenic drive north of the Golden Gate bridge.

Coast Redwoods in this forest tower more than 25 stories into the sky. Although this park is popular, crowds appear subdued next to these massive trees.

Paved, easy loop trails meander along Redwood Creek past several of Muir Woods' most spectacular groves. Hardy hikers can find solitude in the forest by following the steeper paths up the wooded canyon. Several trails eventually connect to Mt. Tamalpais State Park offering hours of quiet hiking.

As you enter Muir Woods National Monument, take a look at the cross-section of a Redwood trunk. It reveals hundreds of tree rings—one for each year of the tree's life. Dates are marked on certain rings to show how the tree grew silently and steadily upward while the civilization of man developed in the far corners of the world.

Most of the mature trees in Muir Woods are between 600 and 800 years old. The grove's oldest redwood is at least 1,000 years old. Until the 1800s, Coast Redwoods like these covered many northern California coastal valleys. Many of them fell to the logger's ax.

The grove at Muir Woods was spared because it was in a deep canyon that hampered accessibility. In

1905, recognizing that it was one of the Bay Area's last uncut stands of old-growth redwood, Congressman William Kent bought 295 acres and donated the land to the federal government. In 1908 President Theodore Roosevelt declared it a national monument. Kent requested it be named after famous conservationist John Muir.

The tallest trees in Muir Woods today are in the Cathedral and Bohemian Groves, easily reached by the paved, wheelchair- and stroller-accessible trail along the stream. The tallest tree here stretches 254 feet high; the thickest is nearly 13 feet in diameter.

The redwood bark alone is six to 12 inches thick. It insulates the tree against fire. Still, repeated fires can burn through the bark, exposing heartwood to dry rot. Subsequent fires blacken the cavities that you see at the base of many trees in Muir Woods.

For 150 years, fires were suppressed to protect the forest. Now it's known that fire is essential to the forest's ecosystem. One benefit is that it clears the forest floor so that redwood seeds have a chance to reach soil and sprout.

Most of the redwoods reproduce by burl sprouting. The tight clusters of trees you see probably began as sprouts on the burl at the base of an established tree. As you walk through the woods, you can see these burl sprouts at different stages of development.

Coast Redwoods aren't the only living things you'll see here. Other trees include the Douglas fir, maple, oak and laurel. Often deer forage near Redwood Creek in the early morning or at dusk. A popular bird with the kids is the bright blue Stellar's jay. The forest floor is carpeted with ferns and Redwood sorrel. Each season offers something special so if you haven't been to Muir Woods, go now. If you have visited, go again.

Muir Woods National Monument
Hwy 1/Muir Woods exit off 101, Marin County
415/388-2595 (recording)
Open daily 8 A.M.-Sunset
Free, donations appreciated

♠ *Point Reyes National Seashore*

It exploded with the force of 15,000,000 tons of TNT. It destroyed an entire city. And you are standing where it all began, at the 1906 earthquake's epicenter, when you walk along the self-guiding Earthquake Trail at Point Reyes National Seashore, about an hour's drive north of San Francisco.

This half-mile, wheelchair-accessible loop that teeters on the San Andreas Fault illustrates the history and future of a land in motion—the California coast. You can learn first-hand when to expect The Big One and still have plenty of time to explore the Point Reyes peninsula before it becomes an island.

Begin at the Bear Valley Visitor Center. It has excellent dioramas of sea and land animals in their natural habitats, Miwok Indian artifacts, displays focusing on settlers and shipwrecks and a superb selection of books on the area. Near the seismographs, records of recent earthquakes, marked with their epicenters and strengths on the Richter scale, are evidence of the land's instability.

If you're still willing to walk along the active San Andreas Fault, cross the Bear Valley picnic area to the start of the Earthquake Trail, just to the left of the restrooms.

Along the trail, a line of blue posts marks the exact position of the San Andreas Fault. You are now standing on land that lurched 16 feet northward on April 18, 1906. The barn to your left moved along with the land, splitting from its foundation. Legend claims that this was near the spot where an unfortunate cow named Matilda met her demise. According to one story of the fateful day in 1906, the earth yawned open and swallowed her whole.

As you follow the trail, the line of blue posts bisects a fence. Here, it's easy to visualize the theory of plate tectonics explained in the trail's displays. The fence is split 16 feet apart. Half stands on one side of the Fault, on the Pacific plate; the other half stands on the other side of the Fault, on the North American plate.

If you could remain in one spot in front of the visitor center for millions of years, you could see the land in motion. In an estimated half-million years, the Center becomes waterfront property as the Point Reyes peninsula, along with Los Angeles, breaks from the continental U.S. and drifts northward. In about 13 million years, the Center becomes a Los Angeles suburb . In about 40 million years, Point Reyes slides into the Aleutian Trench near Alaska.

Back in the 1990s, you have the rest of the day to explore Point Reyes. Near the Visitor Center, a recreation of a Miwok Indian Village presents a picture of the area before the white man. You can peek into the teepee-like Kotcha huts. The village also features an underground Lamma, or ceremonial house. Every detail is authentic.

A 45-minute drive takes you over rolling, pastoral countryside and past dairy farms to the ocean. A half-mile walk further will bring you to the historic Point Reyes Lighthouse, which first guided ships in 1870 and was in service for more than a century before being retired.

The Seashore also encompasses many hiking trails, backpacking camps and excellent bird-watching spots. In the northern end of the park, you'll find an historic dairy farm and may catch a glimpse of the Seashore's free-roaming herd of tule elk near the more remote trails. Plan on spending a full day to explore Point Reyes. You only have half a million years before it breaks off and drifts away.

Point Reyes National Seashore
Off Highway 1, Marin County
415/663-1092
Seashore open 24 hours daily
Visitor Center open daily 9-5,
weekends and holidays 8-5; closed Christmas
Lighthouse open Th.-Mon. 10-4:30
Free, donations appreciated

♠ *Richardson Bay Audubon Center*

Just outside of Tiburon, the 900-acre Richardson Bay Audubon Center and Sanctuary showcases Marin's natural beauty, before condominiums conquered these quiet shores. It is an ideal spot for a short country walk, especially for bird watchers. The demonstration hummingbird garden and bird feeding station are just two of the Center's delights.

From October through April, migrating birds settle for the winter in the gentle waters and grassy hilltops of the Sanctuary. Autumn leaves carpet the path by the pond. The graceful Lyford house, an 1876 Victorian, is open for public tours on Sunday afternoons from November through April.

The Lyford House is perched on a small, tree-shaded bluff, just above the lapping waves of Richardson Bay with a view of the San Francisco skyline on the far horizon.

The house seems custom-made for this setting, but it was not built here. It originally stood on Strawberry Point, a half-mile across Richardson Bay, where Dr. Benjamin Lyford operated an "ultra-hygienic" dairy farm. Some thought Lyford was obsessed with cleanliness for advocating such ideas as chemical septic tanks and city sewage systems. By employing these healthful living theories at the dairy, Lyford could claim that his Jersey cows produced the healthiest milk.

Lyford died in 1906. His wife, Hilarita, passed on two years later, leaving no heirs. The Victorian home stood empty and abandoned. Suffering from years of neglect, it was scheduled for demolition in 1957 to make way for new development.

Rosie "the goat lady" Verrall came to its rescue. Since the age of three, Verrall lived on what is now the nature preserve. For years, her goats grazed on the lower slopes of the hills. To protect it from encroaching development, Verrall deeded this prime piece of real estate as a wildlife sanctuary. The Lyford House was loaded in one piece onto a barge and towed across the bay to its present location.

The 1/3-mile, self-guided nature trail begins just beyond the Lyford House. Be sure to borrow the booklet describing the plant life and habitats along the trail. With it, you can distinguish a Laurel from a Live Oak and learn how Native Americans used the Soap Root plant to stupefy fish.

A gentle, uphill climb winds beneath three of California's most common trees: Coastal Live Oak, with prickly-edged leaves, California Bay, which emits a pungent odor when you rub its leaves, and Toyon, or California Holly, with bright red berries.

The top of the hill offers a lofty view of the area framing the San Francisco and Richardson Bays, including Angel Island, San Francisco, Sausalito and the coastal mountains.

The trail circles down the back of the hill. Ignore the freeway buzz in the distance and listen as the breeze whispers through the native bunch grasses. Near the bottom of the hill, you will hear shorebirds as they float and fly across the inlet.

Walk along the back of the hill to find another distinct habitat in this small sanctuary. Woodland trees arch over the trail, providing cool shade. Relax for a moment in the redwood grove's sitting area.

Veer off the main trail to the wooden bridge to your left. It crosses a small pond which attracts woodland and aquatic birds. This sidetrip also takes you to the compact garden devoted to California's native plants, a short walk from the parking lot.

Allow time to browse in the bookshop before you leave. It offers a beautiful selection of books and gifts for bird and nature lovers.

Richardson Bay Audubon Center
376 Greenwood Beach Rd., Tiburon
415/388-2524
Sanctuary open Wed.-Sun. 9-5 year-round
Lyford House open Sun. 1-4,
first weekend in Nov.-end of April,
$2 Adults; $1 ages 12 & under

🌲 *Pinnacles National Monument*

Wild pigs, pitch dark caves, towering rock spires, tarantulas—you don't have to travel far, or be Indiana Jones, to explore the exotic animal life and geologic formations of Pinnacles National Monument. This natural anomaly is located about three hours drive south of San Francisco, off Route 25 out of Gilroy and Hollister.

The east entrance to Pinnacles is the most popular starting point. Here, a visitor center features exhibits on the history of the park, its animal life and geological heritage.

The most striking aspect of Pinnacles is its sharp contrast to the land surrounding it. Rolling farmland suddenly gives way to craggy castles of rock, appearing like a strange island of stone towers.

This was once the insides of an 8,000-foot volcano. Twenty-three million years ago, this volcano lay 195 miles further south, east of what is now Los Angeles. Centered on the San Andreas rift zone, half the volcano lay on the Pacific Plate, the other half on the North American Plate.

The Pacific Plate migrated northward, carrying the west side of the immense volcano with it. Over the years, wind and rain eroded the rock into the turrets, peaks, spires and monuments that we now call the Pinnacles.

Pick up the 50-cent Moses Spring Self-guiding Trail brochure at the visitor center before embarking on this short, easy trail. It highlights the details that make Pinnacles unique. Without it, you might miss the gnarled red trunk of a manzanita, the lime green patches of lichens and the fertile oasis of chain ferns. Look for the Digger Pine's root which snakes through 26 feet of rock in its search for moisture.

You most likely will not miss the most pervasive wildlife in Pinnacles—rock climbers. With neon-colored ropes and the clang of carabiners, they seem to be scrambling up every rock tower along this trail. Almost everyone stops momentarily to watch them.

The Bear Gulch Caves are a favorite spot. Bring a flashlight and be aware that the caves are not for the claustrophobic. This is a narrow passage, completely cut off from outside light in several stretches, but a safe adventure for kids and adults.

The High Peaks Trail is one of the most exciting trails in the park. A steep, winding climb brings you into, around and on top of the pinnacles. The trail is a legacy of the 1930s Civilian Conservation Corps. You can scramble up narrow steps carved out of sheer rock, then sidle beneath stony overhangs, the closest thing to rock climbing without a rope. Remember, always carry water with you on Pinnacles' hot, dry trails.

If you want to stay the night, a nicely landscaped, privately run campground is just outside the Pinnacles east entrance. Camping costs $6 per person per night, with a maximum of $24 charged per campsite. Facilities include a convenience store, swimming pool, showers, electrical hook-ups and group sites. For campground information, call 408/389-4462. There also is a small, walk-in campground located in Pinnacles on the west side of the park.

Pinnacles National Monument
101 to Gilroy, to Route 25 south,
to Route 146 west
408/389-4485
Park open 24 hours as a day-use area
Visitor Center open daily 9-5
Walk-in Campground open daily Memorial Day-mid-Feb.; open Mon.-Thurs., mid-Feb.-Memorial Day;
$4 per vehicle, pass good for 7 days

♠ Point Lobos State Reserve

It's been called "the greatest meeting of land and water in the world." This extravagant claim is close to the truth. Point Lobos preserves the best of California's coastline.

Short, easy trails lead to groves of Monterey Cypress, a colony of barking sea lions, otters cavorting in kelp beds, crashing waves and lively tide pools. The reserve is off Highway 1 just four miles south of Carmel.

Begin your visit at Whalers Cove. This is a popular launch point for SCUBA divers. These waters were declared the first underwater reserve in the U.S. in 1960 and access is strictly limited to protect the environment. From the parking lot, walk back up the road to Whaler's Cabin.

This weather-worn cabin was built around 1851, home to a family of Chinese fishermen. Today it is a museum which encapsulates the cove's history through photographs and fascinating artifacts.

Wooden buttons, a ceramic rice bowl and clay marbles were found when excavating the original dirt floor of the cabin. The wood floor that exists now was built near the turn of the century. A window cut into the floor planks reveals its unique support—a whale vertebra.

Whaling was the cove's main industry from 1862 to 1882. On the beach below this cabin, the Portuguese Whaling Company hauled in their harvest to render oil from the blubber.

An abalone cannery operated here from 1902 to 1933. The museum's two-man pump, resembling a railroad handcar, was used to pump air to the brave souls who worked underwater as helmet divers for abalone. A mannequin models the complete diver's suit, from helmet to the heavy lead boots that held them to the bottom.

Another display shows a Monterey Jack cheese press and tells the story of the dairy on this land from 1903 to 1954. The cabin was used by the military during WW II when the cove was a training site for amphibious landing craft. Hollywood also discovered Point Lobos, shooting 45 films in this area, the first in the early 1900s.

Today, Point Lobos is reserved for the natural treasure of land meeting sea. A number of trails explore the shoreline. Not far from the Whaler's Cabin, the Granite Point Trail winds around the cove far above the water.

Keep an eye out for harbor seals sunning themselves on the rocks below. Seals grow to about six feet long, are often gray or tan and usually sun on rocks close to the water.

To see and hear their larger cousins, the sea lions, drive to the Sea Lion Point parking lot. Follow the barking sounds down the reserve's most popular trail to the jut of land overlooking Sea Lion rocks. Point Lobos is named after these barking animals, a shortened version of its original description, "Punta de los Lobos Marinos," translated as "Point of the Sea Wolves."

Walk down one side of the overlook to the tidal pools near the crashing waves. Stay still for a moment and crabs and hermit crabs will appear from their rocky hiding places. Bright purple sea urchins squeeze into crevices.

Climb the trail to the point above the kelp beds. Look closely for sea otters in the kelp. From here, they resemble small logs. You may hear them "clapping" a shellfish open or see them looping in and out of the water.

After exploring Point Lobos, you may agree that it is "the greatest meeting of land and water in the world."

Point Lobos State Reserve
Off Highway 1; Three miles south of Carmel
408/624-4909
Open daily 9-7, May-Sept.; 9-5 Oct.-April
$6 per car day use fee; $5 per car if senior is present

🌲 *Mariposa Grove of Big Trees*

They are not the oldest living things on earth. That distinction belongs to the bristle cone pine. They aren't even the tallest living things on earth. Those are the coastal redwoods. But Sequoiadendron giganteum, the giant Sequoia trees, are the largest living things, in sheer volume.

The Mariposa Grove of Big Trees is an awe-inspiring forest of giants. The Sequoias are thousands of years old and hundreds of feet tall. To get a feel for the size of these trees, here is an easy comparison. Take a friend who is 6 feet tall. Near his toe, place a twig that is 2 inches tall. The friend is the Sequoia. The twig is you.

This is just one of the comparisons that the park ranger may offer on an intriguing tour of this magnificent grove. Anyone who hasn't seen these trees might find it hard to believe. They wouldn't be alone.

In 1852, Mr. Dowd, a professional bear hunter, first stumbled upon the nearby Calaveras Big Trees. When he returned to camp with his stories of the immense forest, people figured it was simply a tall tale. He had to connive them into visiting the area by claiming he needed five men to help carry back the grizzly he shot.

Once the word was out, loggers came to this gold mine of lumber. They were soon disappointed. The Sequoias produced a brittle wood, often splintering when the tree fell. About 75% of the trees felled by the early loggers are still lying in the Mariposa Grove. The other 25% were made into vineyard stakes, shingles and matchsticks.

In 1864, congress set aside Mariposa Grove as a state reserve. Eventually, it became part of Yosemite National Park.

The granddaddy of all the Sequoias in this grove is the Grizzly Giant. It's one of the oldest and largest living things in Yosemite. This massive tree is 209 feet tall and 32 feet in diameter. Its age is estimated at 2,700 years. One of its limbs alone is almost 7 feet in diameter, larger than the trunk of any non-Sequoia in the grove.

It all began with a seed the size of an oat flake. These seeds are found in the Sequoia's cones, which are hardly bigger than a golf ball. Each cone contains about 250 to 300 seeds and each tree has as many as 10,000 cones. Some cones stay on the trees for years. You can count their rings just as in tree trunks. But please remember everything in Yosemite is protected, so cones do not make good souvenirs.

Fire is essential to the growth of new Sequoias. Flames clear the forest floor of undergrowth creating a bed for the seeds. Cones on the ground are burnt, allowing the seeds, which are protected by a natural fire retardant, to disperse.

The Chickaree squirrel helps, too. When gathering food for the winter, the squirrel can bite 286 cones off the tree in 18 minutes. He eats the fleshy part of the cone, leaving the seeds to grow.

As the Sequoia grows taller, its roots spread outward, not deeper. During the growing season, they suck up about 1,000 gallons of water each day. Their roots are usually no deeper than 6 feet, but fan out to more than 150 feet, creating a stable base for the towering tree.

Still, many Sequoias have fallen in this grove. When the tunnel tree fell, it could be felt in Fish Camp, five miles away. The immense trunks stretching across the forest floor provide another unique perspective on the world's largest living things.

Mariposa Grove of Big Trees
Yosemite National Park
209/372-0563
Open daily year-round, weather permitting
Free with $5 per car Yosemite National Park fee

🌲 *Yosemite Camera Walk & Other Freebies*

"It's not the camera that takes the picture. It's the photographer," our guide remarked as he led a group of amateur shutterbugs into Yosemite's meadows. "If there's one thing I'm going to teach you today, it's how to recognize a good photographic situation."

These free 90-minute camera walks, run by Yosemite Concession Services, are one of the Valley's best bargains. They offer insights for visitors with pocket-sized, point-and-shoot cameras as well as enthusiasts with the three Nikons, a tripod and complete filter set. Group size may be limited, so sign up in advance at the front desk of the Yosemite Lodge, Curry Village (summer only) or the Ahwahnee.

Many photos of Yosemite share a common scene—and a common mistake. Friends and family pose in front of sun-soaked waterfalls and cliffs—except the people in the photo are too dark and the background is washed out. The camera, even an automatic, didn't know which exposure to use.

One solution is to make sure the people in your pictures are not in the shade. Another is to use a flash, even outdoors. If your camera only has an automatic flash, cover the flash's electric eye to fool the camera into thinking it needs to use the flash.

Our guide covered the basics, such as making sure the person in your photo doesn't have a lamp post coming out of his head, and pointed out photographic opportunities that many may have missed. A good picture doesn't have to take in Yosemite's powerful falls or majestic cliffs. It can be as simple as early morning frost on a weed or sunlight refracting through pine branches.

Our guide delved into more advanced photographic lessons, from film speeds to filters. He set up his tripod near the Merced River to photograph the reflection of Half Dome. He then used a polarizer filter, a warming filter, a graduated filter and a special focusing procedure to get the shot he envisioned. The group looked through the lens to see how the filters enhanced the image. Each camera walk is different, depending on the instructor and the location visited.

In the evening, you can see how other photographers have captured Yosemite's geology, wildlife and history. These free programs are listed in the Yosemite Guide, which you can pick up free at entrances and visitor centers.

Another way to bring home creative images of Yosemite is to participate in the Art Activity Center workshops. These free mid-day classes are taught by professional, often well-known, artists in watercolor, etching, drawing and other mediums. Programs are offered from late March through early October. These are for adults and younger students with an earnest interest in art. Classes are held outdoors at inspiring spots, depending on the weather. Bring your own materials or purchase the basics for about $10. Register at the Center.

In the summer, Junior & Senior Rangers (ages 8-12) are free naturalist activities led by a park ranger. Parents are welcome to accompany their children or drop them off for the day's activities. Kids earn a patch for accomplishing an assigned task.

At Happy Isles Nature Center, the family can borrow free Explorer Packs ($25-$50 return deposit) to help identify birds, rocks and the small delights of summer. For park ranger activities, phone 209/372-0265 or 209/372-0299 (Visitor Center) or 209/372-0287 (Happy Isles Nature Center).

Yosemite Camera Walk
Yosemite Valley
209/372-1129
Daily, 8:30 A.M.
Free

Notes

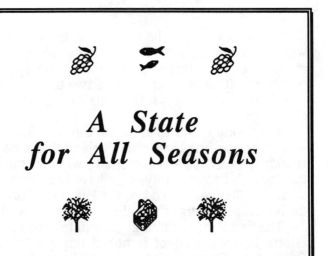

Gloria Ferrer Champagne Caves

Cheers! Will you be toasting in the new year with a bottle of bubbly? There is a good reason why many of us save this tingling libation for special occasions. It takes a minimum of two to four years and eight major steps to transform grapes to champagne.

The Gloria Ferrer Champagne Caves in Sonoma will show you first hand what's behind that glass of sparkling wine. This is one of five wineries run by the Spanish Ferrer family, who have been creating wines for 700 years. Today, the Ferrers are one of the largest producers of sparkling wine in the world.

The first thing the tour guide will tell you is that Gloria Ferrer's product is not champagne at all. Officially, "Champagne" can only be made from grapes grown in the Champagne region of France. Gloria Ferrer produces "sparkling wine" using the methode champenoise.

Methode champenoise means the champagne is created, fermented and sold in the same bottle. Less expensive sparkling wines are fermented in large steel tanks, then transferred to bottles for distribution.

At Gloria Ferrer you learn the basics of champagne-making through their display of antique equipment. The exhibit is strategically placed on a balcony overlooking their state-of-the-art winemaking operation. Although the methode champenoise has evolved into a delicate art enhanced by high technology, it still follows the same basic steps.

Champagne grapes, about 80% Pinot Noir and 20% Chardonnay, are harvested a month before still wine grapes. All are hand-picked and pressed gently. A yeast culture is added and the juice ferments in large steel tanks until the next spring.

The winemaker then creates a unique cuvee, or blend of juices, and adds sugar and yeast for the second fermentation, this time in its own bottle. The bottles are placed on their side on racks in Ferrer's subterranean caves and left to age from 18 months to four years.

After aging, two workers riddle, or quarter turn, 30,000 bottles a day for a month. More than 50,000 more bottles are riddled by immense machines. Riddling coaxes the yeast sediment to the neck of the bottle. Then the liquid in the neck is frozen and disgorged with the sediment.

Each bottle is topped off with a dosage, or sweetener made with a sugar solution in still wine. The bottle is corked tightly. A wire basket is added to protect the cork from popping under the champagne's pressure. The "punt," or hollow in the bottom of the bottle, also adds strength to protect it from bursting.

Now it's your turn. Champagne used to be reserved for cocktail hour, but now is served throughout a meal and with meat, poultry or fish. It should be consumed within five years after purchase and should always be served chilled.

In selecting champagne, remember that Brut means dry, Dry means sweeter than Brut and Extra Dry is even sweeter. To open champagne, remove the foil. Place a towel over the neck, loosen the wire hood and tilt the bottle slightly, keeping firm hold on the cork. Don't pop the cork. Instead, grasp the bottom of the bottle and slowly twist the bottle out of the cork, not the cork out of the bottle. Enjoy!

Gloria Ferrer Champagne Caves
Highway 121, Sonoma
707/996-7256
Tastings 10:30-5:30 daily; Tours on the hour 11-4
Closed major holidays
Samples $2.75 and up per glass
Tours Free

Whale Watching

There's something reassuring about a creature so large and yet so peaceful, who lives in perfect harmony with its own kind and its environment. Perhaps this is why people flock to the coast to see the annual migration of these mighty mammals.

Several spots along the California coast offer excellent vantage points to watch the gray whales and a free and comfortable alternative to whale watching cruises. All you need is the four P's: a warm parka, a picnic lunch, a pair of binoculars and patience.

The peak season for gray whale watching begins in mid-December and January, when the winter cold ices over their Arctic feeding grounds. They head south for warmer waters and shallow, protected lagoons to bear their young.

Pregnant females are the first to head south, usually alone. Courting females and males are next, traveling in groups, or "pods," of two to three. They move at about five miles per hour, covering 70 to 80 miles each day.

Even though gray whales weigh between 20 to 40 tons and are 35 to 50 feet long, they still can be hard to spot. It's best to watch for them with your naked eye. The first sign you'll most likely see is the telltale spout. Once you've spotted the spout, use binoculars for a better view.

Gray whales breathe through a blowhole, actually two nostrils, on top of their heads. When they dive, these nostrils automatically close. The gray whales surface every three to six minutes to breathe, releasing their warm, humid breath as a 10 to 15-foot-high spout. The whale usually spouts three to five times, with more than a minute in between, before diving again.

The gray whale is named for its color. You may see the whale's mottled and barnacle-encrusted back as it arches through the water. Another distinguishing feature is that the gray whale has a low hump on its back rather than a dorsal fin.

If you're lucky, you may see the whale raise its head out of the water to look around. One theory speculates that this "spy hopping" is one way the whale can get its bearings. Other theories say gray whales also use solar navigation and remember the contours of the ocean bottom.

After spending the winter off the coast of Baja, Mexico, the gray whales head back north to their Arctic feeding grounds. You can see some returning along the coast from mid-February through May. This annual migration is one of the longest of any mammal, about 10,000 to 12,000 miles round-trip.

On the coast north of San Francisco, the Mendocino Coast Botanical Gardens offers a scenic site for whale watching. At Fort Ross State Historic Park, paths lead through a recreation of the old Russian settlement to the rugged coast.

Point Reyes National Seashore is one of the best spots on the coast for whale watching, especially at the Lighthouse. It's best to come in the morning when it's less crowded and generally less windy, making it easier to spot the spouts. You can watch for whales from the upper patio or walk down the 300-plus steps to the lighthouse for a better view (but remember you'll have to climb back up!).

Prime viewing spots south of San Francisco include the Point Montara Lighthouse and Pigeon Point Lighthouse, where whales sometimes come within 50 yards from shore. Near Monterey, Point Lobos State Park also is a prime whale watching point, as well as a stunning natural setting.

Whale Watching
Mendocino Coast Botanical Gardens (see Gardens)
Fort Ross State Historic Park (see Historic Haunts)
Point Reyes Seashore (see The Great Outdoors)
Point Montara (off Hwy. 1, 25 mi. S of SF)
Pigeon Point (off Hwy. 1, Pescadero)
Point Lobos (see The Great Outdoors)
Dec.-Jan. & mid-February-May
Free

Strybing Arboretum

New Zealand may be half-way around the world, but you can see a piece of it right here in San Francisco. The exotic flora of this island nation, and of China, Australia, Japan, Chile and many more are just part of the Strybing Arboretum's "museum of plants."

Located in Golden Gate Park near the de Young Museum, the Strybing offers a compact trip around the world along with insights into the plants that make California unique. It's a delightful sojourn any time of year, especially in spring. It may be the best spot anywhere to celebrate Arbor Day in April.

Maps of the Arboretum, available at the book store and gift shop, entice you to stroll and discover the breadth of the plantings.

The 70-acre Arboretum holds many surprises—the aromatic Garden of Fragrance, the New World Cloud forest, the Mediterranean Cape Province Garden, the Moon-viewing Garden and a dusky grove of towering redwoods to name a few. These are interspersed with spacious lawns, trickling streams and a delightful pond with ducks and a graceful black swan.

It all began in 1937 with a $100,000 bequest from San Francisco flower enthusiast Helen Strybing, along with aid from the city and the federal Works Progress Administration. Today it is home to more than 6,000 species from around the world.

The Garden of Fragrance is a favorite in the Arboretum. You'll know you've found it by the sweet and pungent scents. With plant markings in English and Braille, it's enjoyed equally by the visually impaired.

Here you'll find French, Spanish and English lavender, peppermint and lemon balm. One patch is medicinal herbs. Another is culinary herbs including the fragrant winter savory, pineapple sage and French sorrel. The plants are in raised stone beds to entice you to stop and smell the flowers and herbs. You're welcome to feel the texture and press a leaf to release the plant's aromas, but be careful not to damage it.

Nearby is the Biblical Garden, devoted to plants mentioned in the Bible, like citron and table grape.

The Cape Province Garden represents a Mediterranean climate, with winter rains and summer droughts, the same climate as the Bay Area. Displays explain how plants adapt to the difficult growing weather.

Succulents, like ice plants, store water in their leaves and stems. Their shallow roots quickly absorb large quantities of water from short rains. Annuals, like some daisies, avoid drought by setting seed before drying out. Perennials have succulent leaves or leaves with hair to reflect sunlight.

In the compact California Garden, tour the state's varied habitats, from dry rock garden, to meadow, arroyo, pond and chaparral. Displays explain how plants have adapted to the climate and how man has adapted plants to fit his needs. The exhibit illustrates how Native Americans used Coast Live Oak acorns for food and meadow grass for baskets.

The Redwood Trail is a sharp contrast to the rolling lawns and rock gardens. It is a dark, cool forest of 90-year-old redwoods, giant chain ferns and the clover-leafed redwood sorrel ground cover. In the exotic New World Cloud Forest, plants flourish on the bare branch of a tree.

Allow at least an hour to see the Strybing Arboretum, or, like many visitors, relax for an afternoon on the lawn and benches and enjoy this garden of the world. To get even more out of your visit, join one of the free guided tours, and be sure to ask about their special plant sales.

Strybing Arboretum
Golden Gate Park, San Francisco
415/661-1316
Open Mon.-Fri. 8-4:30, weekends 10-5
Guided Tours daily 1:30; weekends 10:30 & 1:30
Free, donations appreciated

East Bay Parks

If you're looking for a place to stretch your legs and soak up some spring sunshine after the long winter rains, try the East Bay. These three diverse parks are perfect for a nearby getaway, romantic retreat or family outing.

Along with scenic trails, Black Diamond Mines Regional Park in Antioch is the setting for California's intriguing coal mining history.

Briones Regional Park in central Contra Costa County encompasses more than 5,800 acres of rolling ranchland, panoramic views, forested trails and picnic grounds.

Point Pinole Regional Shoreline is a surprising oasis hidden amidst the industrial development along San Pablo Bay.

Black Diamond Mines is the furthest east of these parks. Begin at the Visitor Center, where you can learn the park's story through historic photos and video, meet a gopher snake or browse through their selection of books on natural and human history.

While you walk along the quiet trails of this more than 4,000-acre park today, it's hard to imagine that a thriving community once existed here.

From the 1860s to the turn of the century, this area boasted the largest coal mining operation in California. Nearly four million tons of "black diamonds" were removed. They supplied the pivotal fuel as the state moved from an agrarian economy through the Industrial Revolution.

By the 1920s, the coal mining operations had shut down due to rising production costs and the use of new energy sources. Over the next 30 years, 1,800,000 tons of sand were mined here. It was made into glass in Oakland and used for steel casting in Pittsburg, until these industries closed down.

Today, you can see a remnant of the area's history at the Rose Hill Cemetery, a short walk from the Somersville Road entrance. Weathered stones mark the graves of children who died in epidemics, women who died in childbirth and men who died in mining disasters. Some are marked in Welsh, the native country of many of the miners. From here, 34 miles of hiking trails wander past grassland, foothill woodland, chaparral and stream vegetation.

Briones Regional Park harkens back to the Mexican era when Felipe Briones had a cattle ranch here in 1829. Today, cattle still graze in the meadows of Briones. The park also is popular with horseback riders, mountain bikers and picnickers.

Trails follow streams and climb up past bay laurel and buckeye trees to panoramic views of the surrounding area. This expansive park has entrances on all four sides, making it a nearby getaway from Lafayette, Pleasant Hill, Martinez and Berkeley.

Point Pinole Regional Shoreline is a hidden gem on the San Pablo Bay shore. Picnic tables and a play area are perched on a bluff above the water, a short walk from the parking lot. From here, trails lead to salt marshes, grassland and eucalyptus woodland.

For $1 round trip ($.50 for kids 6-11, free for seniors and disabled), a shuttle van carries fishermen and picnickers to the 1,225-foot pier in the northern section of the park. From here you can dangle a line or just sit and watch the freight ships, tankers and sailboats cruise by.

Black Diamond Mines Regional Preserve
South end of Somersville Rd., Antioch
510/757-2620
Park open daily 8 A.M.-dusk
Visitor Center open daily 8-5
Free

Briones Regional Park
Central Contra Costa County
510/229-3020
Open daily 8 A.M.-10 P.M.
$3 Parking Fee on weekends and holidays

Point Pinole Regional Shoreline
From San Pablo Ave., follow Atlas Rd. to water
510/237-6896
Open daily 7 A.M.-sunset
$3 Parking Fee on weekends and holidays

🎲 *Bocce, Baseball & Birdwatching*

If you're looking for something new to do on a lazy summer day, try the Martinez Regional Shoreline. Bocce, baseball, birdwatching, boating and a whole lot of summer fun that doesn't start with a "B" awaits you here. This 343-acre park has soccer fields, a playground, a duck pond, horse arena, marina, fishing pier, exercise course and quiet trails through a salt marsh. And, for those coming from out of town without a car, it's an easy walk from the Amtrak station.

Bocce is one of the most popular sports at the Shoreline. The Martinez Bocce Federation is one of the largest Bocce organizations west of the Mississippi. More than 1,700 Bocce aficionados play in Martinez on 130 teams. Several national bocce champions hail from Martinez. The Northern California Open Bocce Championship is held on these courts, usually in July.

No longer reserved for old Italian men, Bocce Ball is a fun, social sport for the whole family. Men, women and children play almost every day of the week at this shoreline park.

Here you can practice the sport of Bocce on no less than 12 regulation-size, clay and ground oyster-shell courts. If you don't have your own set of balls, you can rent them for $10 per weekend from the Martinez Leisure Services Department (tel. 510/313-0930). It's a good idea to reserve ahead as they only have two sets and be prepared to leave a $55 returnable deposit.

If you're not sure of the rules, these are the highlights. There are traditionally two teams of four players each, eight Bocce balls and one pallino, or target ball. The game starts with one player rolling the pallino, a lemon-sized ball, down the court. Then she rolls a Bocce ball, about the size of a grapefruit, as near to the pallino as possible.

The opposing team member tries to roll his Bocce ball closer to the pallino than his opponent's. He also might knock hers out of the way or knock the pallino away. His team continues to roll until one of their balls is closer or all four of his team's balls are rolled.

The team with the Bocce ball nearest the pallino scores a point for that Bocce ball and for each of their Bocce balls that are closer to the pallino than their opponents' nearest ball. It is possible to score four points in one round. The game is played to 12 points. Three games are played for each match.

Some players in Martinez play by the "International" rules, using brass balls that can be tossed through the air rather than rolled as in the more popular "Open" rules.

If all this sounds confusing, don't worry. There's usually an avid player nearby to explain the scoring and offer tips on how to aim and roll the balls. Picnic tables between the courts offer spectators comfortable seats and a place for refreshments.

Kids also will enjoy playing catch on the Joe DiMaggio ball fields, named after the Martinez native who became famous playing for the New York Yankees. Kite flying and picnicking also are fun activities on the park's lawns.

Down by the shoreline, visit the quacking ducks and honking geese at the duck pond. A walk to the end of the old-fashioned wooden fishing pier offers a view of the massive steel Carquinez bridge. For the quieter side of this family park, follow the paths west along the shoreline through the marsh.

To top off your day, save time to explore Martinez' downtown. The many antique stores are brimming with fun and unusual knick knacks.

Martinez Regional Shoreline
Follow signs from downtown Martinez
510/313-0930 (City Recreation Office-
for bocce, baseball and boating questions)
510/228-0112 (Park Office-for marsh questions)
Open daily
Free

Delta Drive

The Sacramento River delta is ideal for an old-fashioned Sunday drive, especially on a warm summer afternoon. Fishermen, houseboaters, water-skiers and windsurfers are all out to enjoy the cool waters of this slow-poke river.

If you've only got a day to get away from it all, this scenic loop winds along the river, takes in two old-fashioned ferry rides and stops at historic small towns. It begins as you cross the bridge from Antioch on Route 160 into Delta country.

This is Sherman Island. It doesn't look like much today—a flat, green expanse—but it looked like even less in the past. Like other islands that make up Delta Country, this was once mosquito-infested swampland. The first Spanish explorers passed it off as a treacherous everglade.

About 30,000 Native Americans called it home, enjoying the bounty of edible wild plants, tule elk, beaver, salmon and waterfowl. Then came the trappers. From 1830 to 1845 they commandeered the area, selling beaver, otter and mink pelts to the Hudson Bay Company. By the 1840s, farmers also recognized the potential of the Delta's rich soil.

In 1848, the sleepy delta was thrust awake by cries of Gold! Paddlewheel steamers were some of the more than 250 delta vessels that ferried fortune-seekers to the Mother Lode. Before long, the less jubilant miners returned. Some settled on the delta to farm. The formation of levees, islands and arable farmland, a process called reclamation, began.

If you plan to camp or picnic on the Delta, stop just across the next bridge at Brannan Island State Recreation Area. This preserve offers shaded tent sites, group picnic areas, tables and barbecues near the river, and a small beach with calm water for swimming.

At the next bridge, take a left onto Route 12 and follow the signs to Rio Vista. Foster's Big Horn

Saloon, at 143 Main Street, is the most intriguing spot in town. Great White Hunter William Foster collected more than 300 animal trophies from around the world at a time when it was considered a fashionable adventure. On the walls you'll see lions, antelope, an African elephant and more, as well as pictures showing Foster in the field with his kills.

For a touch of modern-day nostalgia, stroll to the waterfront to see a marble monument dedicated to none other than wayward Humphrey the Humpback Whale, who played in the waters here in 1985.

Follow the riverfront north to the Ryer Island ferry landing and our first ferry ride on the diesel-powered "Real McCoy." It's small, transporting just a few cars at a time across to the island. Like all Delta ferries, it is free and runs continuously, with short breaks at lunch and dinner. At one time, ferries were the only way to "island hop" in the Delta. Now, drawbridges have replaced all but a few.

Take a right off the Real McCoy and circle the outer edge of Ryer Island to the Grand Island ferry. This vessel pulls itself along a cable strung across the water. When not in use, the cable rests on the bottom so boats can pass. Take a left off the ferry, along the shore of Grand Island to the graceful Grand Island Mansion on the right. This stately, plantation-style home with the cypress-lined circular drive was built in 1917. It is open to the public on Sunday for an elegant brunch.

Backtrack to just past the ferry landing, turning left on Walker Landing Road. This cross-island roads deposits you at the pink Grand Island Inn, an art deco lovers delight. Here, you can relax with a soda in prohibition-era surroundings and plan a sidetrip to the nearby, weatherworn town of Locke (see Towns to Explore chapter) or simply sit and watch the slow-poke Delta waters flow by.

Walnut Grove Area Chamber of Commerce
P.O. Box 100
Walnut Grove, CA 95690
916/776-1442 (recording)

Monarch Butterflies

It's like walking into a storybook. Bright orange and black Monarch butterflies—thousands of them— flutter like a kaleidoscope around you, cling to the sweet-smelling eucalyptus and prance on tangled berry bushes.

This is Natural Bridges State Park in Santa Cruz, winter home to the Monarch, the queen of butterflies. Just how many of these regal winged creatures will visit in an average year? One thousand? Ten thousand? Keep counting. Each year, as many as 160,000 Monarch butterflies spend the colder months in this compact eucalyptus grove. They begin to appear in mid-October and leave again in February.

A raised wooden walkway brings you down the hill, into the forest and to a patio in the midst of butterfly country. The best time to come is mid-day, when the warm sun beams into the shady canyon and the butterflies are most active. Monarchs can't fly at temperatures lower than 55 degrees and are unable to move at all when the mercury sinks below 40 degrees.

The Monarchs come from as far away as Idaho, Colorado, Montana and British Columbia, wending their way over mountains, cities, fields and lakes. But these are not the same Monarchs that stayed here last winter. Three to five generational cycles— mating, laying eggs, the new caterpillar transforming to an adult butterfly, the parent butterfly's death— have passed. Yet the great, great grandchildren of those who wintered in Santa Cruz know to head for the coast and warmer climes when the days start getting shorter. How do they find their way?

"The navigation aspects of Monarch biology are the most intriguing and least understood," said John Lane, a Santa Cruz biologist who has been studying butterflies for more than 30 years. Some believe that Monarchs have an inborn sun compass, which directs them according to the position of the sun. They are also tuned in to the Earth's magnetic pole. Lane compares their double-edged navigational systems to "a high-quality jetliner."

Many of the Monarchs you see in this grove will be hanging in clusters from the drooping eucalyptus branches. At first, with their folded wings, they appear almost like leaves, layered one on top of the other similar to shingles on a roof. This is a form of group protection. They not only stay warmer, but the rain slides off more easily and the weight of the many butterflies prevents the branch from swaying in the wind.

In spring they start a new year of migration. The Monarchs mate while migrating and egg-laden females must fly in search of milkweed plants to deposit their eggs. Some head north; others south to New Mexico and Arizona. Generations of monarchs continue to migrate and spread their population to the north and east until autumn urges the butterflies to return.

Inside the visitor center, informative displays tell the story of the Monarch and migration. You can touch a delicate butterfly wing or feel the soft fur of an otter in the exhibit focusing on the park's other natural highlights.

There's more to do at Natural Bridges than visit butterflies. Take a walk along the beach to the rock arch that gave the park its name. Have a picnic. Build a sand castle. Watch the wind-surfers. Or explore the mussels and anemones in the tidal pools at low tide. Like the Monarchs, you, too, can enjoy a cool weather day in the seashore town of Santa Cruz.

Natural Bridges State Park
West Cliff Dr., Santa Cruz
Open daily 8 A.M.-sunset
408/423-4609
$6 per car, includes same-day admission
to other state parks and beaches

Salmon Run Taylor Creek

What's at the end of the Rainbow Trail? Follow the path through shimmering aspens, over trickling streams, around a grassy meadow and you will find a nature-lover's dream—an underwater view of a pool full of brown, rainbow and brook trout.

The pool is especially colorful in October, when Kokanee Salmon, which are dwarf, land-locked sockeye salmon, spawn here. These fascinating fish have blue backs and silvery sides except in mating, when both sexes turn a brilliant red and males develop hooked jaws and humped backs. The salmon return to spawn in the stream of their births, lay eggs, and die.

These are just some of the intriguing facts you'll find on the displays along the trails at the Forest Service Taylor Creek Area near South Lake Tahoe. The Lake of the Sky Trail lends new perspectives on the land around you as seen through the eyes of those who first experienced it. Another trail circles turn-of-the-century mansions at Tallac Historic Site. The Visitor Center, where the trails begin, is just north of Camp Richardson along Route 89.

Children and adults enjoy the short, level Rainbow Trail to the Stream Profile Chamber. Markers along the way point out the natural diversity of this compact area. The trail starts out through dry, sparse land, then slopes downward through a small aspen grove, then winds through a wet meadow. You can conduct experiments, such as measuring the water flow of a stream with a gallon can, to better understand the importance of water here.

The most popular stop along the Trail is the underground viewing chamber. A wall of windows reveals the Rainbow Pool and its fishy residents. In addition to the salmon displays, others illustrate how fish see two things at once and how their scales can be used like tree rings to determine age. Small aquariums contain crawdads, tadpoles and minnows.

The short Lake of the Sky Trail leads past a wildlife viewing platform overlooking Taylor Marsh to the lake shore. Along the way, you'll share in the impressions of the first to experience this magical lake. Displays relay quotes from a Washoe Indian, explorer John Fremont, Mark Twain, John Muir, even "Lucky" Baldwin, who brings you into Lake Tahoe's turn of the century era of sprawling estates created by wealthy San Franciscans.

This is Tallac Historic Site, a collection of rustic mansions used as summer homes by the city's elite. You'll see the 1920 Baldwin-McGonagle estate and the 1923 Valhalla, built by San Francisco broker, Walter Heller.

The 1894 Pope House was purchased by George Pope in 1923. This mansion has four bedrooms, four baths, 13 closets, two fireplaces, an entry hall and a butlers pantry. Pope referred to it as the "Vatican Lodge." But that's just the beginning.

The estate's buildings include a dairy, ice house, laundry and kitchen. The family and guests played on polo fields and tennis courts nearby. An idyllic, wooded garden with an arched footbridge and rock waterfall is reminiscent of a Monet painting.

Even if you can't come during the salmon spawning season, Taylor Creek is worth a visit at any time of year. Although the underground viewing chamber is closed in the colder months, the trails are ideal for hiking and cross-country skiing.

Forest Service Taylor Creek Area
Route 89 near South Lake Tahoe
(1/2-mi. north of Camp Richardson)
916/573-2674
Stream Profile Chamber and Visitor Center
open daily 8-5:30 Memorial Day-Labor Day;
Sat. & Sun. 9-4 in October
Free

Notes

Where It's At

These spotting maps and brief descriptions of the 101 excursions will help you plan your afternoon, daytrip or weekend getaway. You may want to see more than one excursion in an area or enjoy a new experience in a familiar destination. There's plenty to see, do and learn. Remember, it's all affordable!

Symbols Used

 Behind the Scenes

 For Kids of All Ages

 We Got Culture

 Towns to Explore

 Literary Landmarks

 Gardens

 Historic Haunts

 The Great Outdoors

 A State for All Seasons

R   **Restrooms**
F   **Food sold on premises**
P   **Free parking in vicinity**

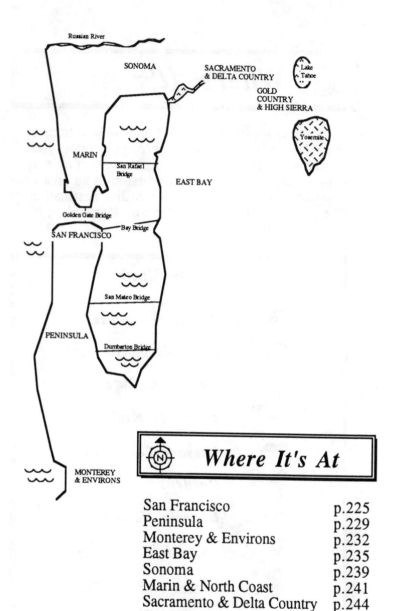

Russian River

SONOMA

SACRAMENTO
& DELTA COUNTRY

Lake
Tahoe

GOLD
COUNTRY
& HIGH SIERRA

Yosemite

MARIN

San Rafael
Bridge

EAST BAY

Golden Gate Bridge

Bay Bridge

SAN FRANCISCO

San Mateo Bridge

PENINSULA

Dumbarton Bridge

MONTEREY
& ENVIRONS

Where It's At

San Francisco	p.225
Peninsula	p.229
Monterey & Environs	p.232
East Bay	p.235
Sonoma	p.239
Marin & North Coast	p.241
Sacramento & Delta Country	p.244
Gold Country & High Sierra	p.247

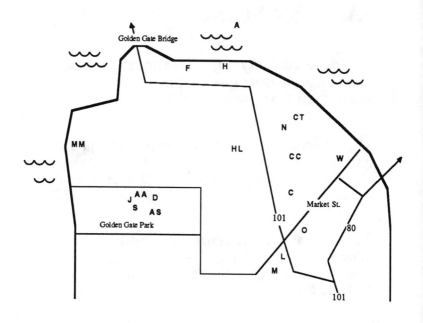

San Francisco

A S	Academy of Sciences
A	Alcatraz
A A	Asian Art Museum
C C	Cable Car Barn Museum
C	Chinese Historical Society
C T	Coit Tower
D	de Young Museum
F	Fort Mason Ethnic Museums
HL	Haas-Lilienthal House
H	Hyde Street Pier
J	Japanese Tea & The Conservatory
L	Levi Strauss Factory
M	Mission San Francisco de Asis
MM	Musée Mécanique & Cliff House
N	North Beach
O	Old Mint & Ansel Adams Center
S	Strybing Arboretum
W	Walking Tours

SAN FRANCISCO

Academy of Sciences. Journey back in time, to outer space and to the depths of the ocean in this fun museum. **R F P** - **30**

Alcatraz. The prison within the prison system. Legendary inmates include Al Capone, Machine Gun Kelly and Robert "The Birdman" Stroud. **R** - **152**

Asian Art Museum. The world's largest collection of Asian Art outside Asia. Cost includes same-day admission to the de Young Museum next door. **R F P** - **62**

Cable Car Barn Museum. See the inner workings of our nation's only moving National Historic Landmark. **R** - **32**

Chinese Historical Society. The story of San Francisco's Chinese heritage, just a few blocks from Chinatown. - **64**

Coit Tower. Recently refurbished social realist murals, painted in the 1930s. Ride the elevator to the top of the tower for one of the city's best views. **R P** - **66**

de Young Museum. A journey through American culture through art. Free docent tours. Museum price includes same-day admission to the Asian Art Museum next door. **R F P** - **68**

SAN FRANCISCO (continued)

☼ *Fort Mason Ethnic Museums.*
Museums devoted to folk and contemporary art from
America, Africa, Italy & Mexico. Gift shops with
fun folk art for sale. **R F** (vegetarian) **P**   **- 70**

☼ *Haas-Lilienthal House.* Step back to
the Victorian era during a tour of this 1886 home.
Many original furnishings. **R P**   **- 72**

🚂 *Hyde Street Pier.* Welcome aboard
this fine collection of historic ships, located right
across from The Cannery. **R**   **- 34**

🌷 *Japanese Tea & The Conservatory.*
Stroll past a bonsai forest, 200-year-old Buddha,
carp ponds and pagodas. See orchids and tropical
plants in The Conservatory, a Victorian-era "crystal
palace" greenhouse. **R F** (tea & cookies) **P**   **- 138**

👁 *Levi Strauss.* A behind-the-scenes look at
how the original 501 blue jean is stitched together.
Film. Small museum with nostalgic Levi's. **R** **- 4**

🔔 *Mission San Francisco de Asis.* The
oldest intact building in San Francisco. Restored
1791 mission established by Father Junipero Serra
R P   **- 154**

SAN FRANCISCO (continued)

Musée Mécanique. One of the world's largest private collections of antique amusements, located at the Cliff House. **R F P - 36**

North Beach. Taste a slice of Italy and learn about the area's Italian heritage in North Beach. Walking tour and museum. **F P**   **- 74**

Old Mint & Ansel Adams Center. See the Old Mint's finely crafted proof sets and create a commemorative medal. Vintage photographs and contemporary works displayed at the Ansel Adams Center. **R**   **- 76**

Strybing Arboretum. Celebrate spring at this "museum of plants" and its collection of flora from around the world. **R P**   **- 210**

Walking Tours. See San Francisco's hidden history on these free City Guides tours. More than a dozen tours offered year-round.   **- 6**

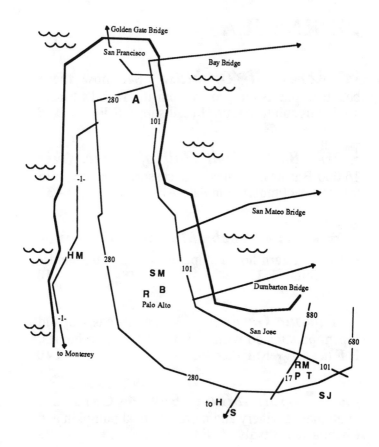

Peninsula

A	Acres of Orchids
B	Barbie Doll Hall of Fame
H	Hakone Gardens & Cultural Center
HM	Half Moon Bay
R	Rodin Sculpture Garden
RM	Rosicrucian Egyptian Museum
P	Peralta Adobe & Fallon House
SJ	San Jose Historical Museum
S	Saso Herb Gardens
SM	Sunset Magazine
T	The Tech Museum of Innovation

PENINSULA

👁 *Acres of Orchids.* See how these beautiful plants are grown from the world's tiniest seed. Greenhouse tour. Retail shop. **R P**   **- 8**

🚂 *Barbie Doll Hall of Fame.* Over 16,000 Barbies, clothes & accessories packed into this compact museum in Palo Alto. **R P**   **- 38**

🚂 *The Tech Museum of Innovation.* Learn how computers work. Fun hands-on exhibits. **R F**   **- 40**

🌸 *Hakone Gardens.* A tranquil oasis of old Japan, punctuated with traditional Japanese homes. **R F** (tea & sweets) **P** (free Tuesdays)   **- 140**

👣 💬 *Half Moon Bay.* Gardens, boutiques, a winery and more. Annual pumpkin and Chamarita festivals. **R F P**   **- 98**

🔔 *Peralta Adobe & Fallon House.* Tour one of California's oldest adobes and the lavishly refurbished Victorian next door. **R P - 156**

☀ *Rodin Sculpture Garden.* Selection of masterpieces from world's 2nd largest collection of Rodin. Includes Gates of Hell.   **- 78**

☀ *Rosicrucian Egyptian Museum.* Artifacts from ancient Egypt, including life-size tomb, mummies, stone tablets. **R P**   **- 80**

PENINSULA (continued)

🔔 *San Jose Historical Museum.*
Century-old buildings, village setting.
R F(ice cream) **P**   **- 158**

🌹*Saso Herb Gardens.* Family-run herb
garden. Tours. **P**   **- 142**

👁*Sunset Magazine.* Tour offices & gardens
of the Magazine of Western Living. **R P**   **- 10**

Symbols Used

👁	*Behind the Scenes*
🚂	*For Kids of All Ages*
☀	*We Got Culture*
👣	*Towns to Explore*
📖	*Literary Landmarks*
🌹	*Gardens*
🔔	*Historic Haunts*
🌲	*The Great Outdoors*
💎	*A State for All Seasons*

R   **Restrooms**
F   **Food sold on premises**
P   **Free parking in vicinity**

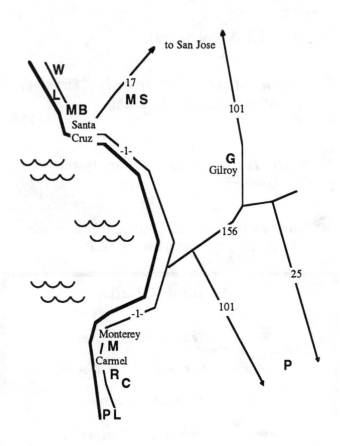

Monterey & Environs

C	Carmel Mission
G	Gilroy & Environs
L	Long Marine Laboratory
MB	Monarch Butterflies
M	Monterey
MS	Mystery Spot
P	Pinnacles National Monument
PL	Point Lobos State Reserve
R	Robinson Jeffers' Tor House
W	Wilder Ranch State Park

MONTEREY & ENVIRONS

🔔 *Carmel Mission.* Restored 200-year-old mission, California's first library, Father Junipero Serra's tomb. **R P**   **- 160**

👣 *Gilroy & Environs.* Driving tour to wineries, outlet stores, San Juan Bautista Historic Park and Mission. **R F P**   **- 100**

👁 *Long Marine Laboratory.* A behind-the-scenes look at marine research. Blue whale skeleton. Aquarium with touch tank. **R P**   **- 12**

🦋 *Monarch Butterflies..* See 160,000 butterflies in one compact eucalyptus grove. Peak season is October through February. **R**   **- 218**

👣 *Monterey.* Walking tour on Monterey's Path of History. Custom House, Monterey's first theater, nostalgic general store, site where state's first constitution was written. **R F**   **- 102**

🚂 *The Mystery Spot.* See a golf ball roll uphill and people shrink and grow in this fun, mysterious site near Santa Cruz. **R P**   **- 42**

🌲 *Pinnacles National Monument.* Hike below, around and above odd rock spires. Explore dark caves with a flashlight. Watch rock climbers. See tarantulas and wild pigs. **R**   **- 196**

MONTEREY & ENVIRONS (continued)

🌲 *Point Lobos State Reserve.* Called the "greatest meeting of land and water in the world." Rugged coastline, small historic museum, sea lion rocks, tide pools. **R** 		 **- 198**

🛶 *Robinson Jeffers' Tor House.* An oasis of old Carmel at this poet's residence. Romantic Hawk Tower built of stone by Jeffers. Guided tours enhanced by Jeffers' poems. **P - 124**

🔔 *Wilder Ranch State Park.* Restored turn-of-the-century dairy farm. Costumed docents perform traditional chores on weekends. Two miles north of Santa Cruz. **R** 		 **- 162**

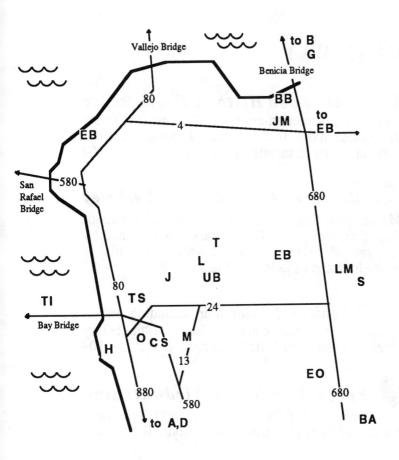

East Bay

A	Ardenwood Historic Farm	**J**	Judah L. Magnes Museum
B A	Behring Auto & UC Museum	**L**	Lawrence Hall of Science
B	Benicia	**LM**	Lindsay Museum
B B	Bocce, Baseball, Birdwatching	**M**	Mormon Temple
C S	Camron-Stanford House	**O**	Oakland Museum
D	Dreyer's Ice Cream	**S**	Shadelands Ranch
EB	East Bay Parks	**TS**	Takara Sake
EO	Eugene O'Neill's Tao House	**T**	Tilden Regional Park
G	Glass Blowers of Benicia	**TI**	Treasure Island
H	Heinhold's Saloon	**U B**	UC Berkeley Botanical Garden
JM	John Muir Historic Site		

EAST BAY

Ardenwood Historic Farm. Relive history on a Victorian-era farm. Harvest crops with traditional hand tools. Ride a horse-powered railroad. Visit farm animals. **R F P** - **164**

Behring Auto & UC Berkeley Museums. One of the world's best collections of classic automobiles. Dream cars, autos owned by Hollywood celebrities and royalty. Fossils of mastodons and camels found nearby. **R P** - **82**

Benicia. Walking tour, including one of California's first state capitol buildings, 19th-century hotel, fun shops, historic buildings. **R F P** - **104**

Bocce, Baseball & Birdwatching Bocce courts, Joe DiMaggio ball field, salt water marsh and more at Martinez waterfront. **R P** - **214**

Camron-Stanford House. Guided tours of restored, furnished 1876 Victorian mansion. Exhibit room on restoration process. - **166**

Dreyer's Ice Cream Factory. Be an official "ice cream taster for the day." Factory tour. Free tasting. **R P F** (ice cream) - **14**

East Bay Parks. Includes Black Diamond Mines in Antioch, Briones in central Contra Costa County and Point Pinole along San Pablo Bay. **R** (outhouses) **P** (free at Black Diamond) - **212**

EAST BAY (continued)

Eugene O'Neill's Tao House.
Home where playwright lived and wrote "The
Iceman Cometh, "Hughie," "Moon for the
Misbegotten" and more. **P**   **- 126**

Glass Blowers of Benicia. See molten
glass transformed into delicate vases, perfume
bottles and stemware. **P**   **- 16**

**Heinhold's First and Last Chance
Saloon.** Jack London studied here as a child and
overheard sea-faring tales recounted later in his
books. Historic photos, memorabilia. **R**   **- 128**

John Muir Historic Site. Muir's
Victorian home and fruit ranch.   Writings on
conservation from his "scribble den" here initiated
preservation of many national parks. **R P**   **- 130**

Judah L. Magnes Museum. Third
largest Jewish museum in the US.   Exhibits on the
Sabbath, Jewish history, holidays. Judaica library.
R P (limited, on street)   **- 84**

Lawrence Hall of Science. Fun
hands-on exhibits on holography, lasers, the brain
and more. Weekend workshops, star-gazing.
R F P   **- 44**

Lindsay Museum. Learn more about
the wild creatures in our own backyard. Permanent
family with bobcat, raccoon and owls.   Visitor-
animal interaction. **R P**   **- 46**

EAST BAY (continued)

☀ *Mormon Temple.* Guided tours of grounds and Inter-Stake center at this landmark temple high in the Oakland hills. Introduction to Mormon religion. Genealogical library. **R P** - **86**

☀ *Oakland Museum.* Three floors of superb exhibits focusing on California's natural history, heritage, culture and art. **R F** - **88**

◮ *Shadelands Ranch.* 1903 Colonial Revival home, with original furnishings, reflects farm life of early 20th century. **R P** - **168**

👁 *Takara Sake.* Behind-the-scenes look into Bay Area's most unusual "winery." Free tasting. **R P** (on street) - **18**

🚂 *Tilden Regional Park.* Fun for the whole family. Wilderness trails. Miniature steam train. Little Farm with pigs, sheep. Botanic Garden. Antique carousel. **R**(Lake Anza, Merry-go-round) **P** - **48**

◮ *Treasure Island.* Former site of the 1939 Golden Gate International Exposition. Now a military base. Museum with military and exposition memorabilia. View of San Francisco. **R P** - **170**

🌹 *UC Berkeley Botanical Garden.* Encompasses more than 12,000 species and varieties of plants from around the world. California natives, tropicals, Oriental medicinal herbs. **R P** - **144**

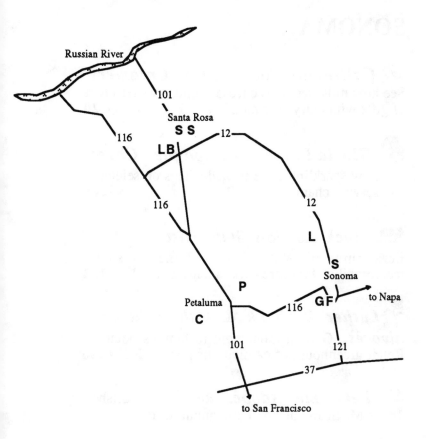

Sonoma

C	California Cooperative Creamery
GF	Gloria Ferrer Champagne Caves
L	Jack London State Historic Park
LB	Luther Burbank & California Carnivores
P	Petaluma Adobe
S S	Snoopy & Skating
S	Sonoma Plaza

SONOMA

👁 *California Cooperative Creamery*.
See how milk becomes cheese. Extensive selection
of gifts with dairy cow motif. **R F P**   **- 20**

🍇 *Gloria Ferrer Champagne Caves*.
See how sparkling wine is made. Tips on selecting
and serving champagne. **R P**   **- 206**

📖 *Jack London State Historic Park*.
Eerie ruins of Wolf House.   London's study,
memorabilia. 800-acre park. Picnic area. **R - 132**

🌸 *Luther Burbank & California Carnivores*. Garden monument to famous botanist.
Retail greenhouse of carnivorous plants. **R P - 146**

🔔 *Petaluma Adobe*.   Restored, furnished
1830s Mexican rancho. Farm animals. **R P   - 172**

🚂 *Snoopy & Skating*.   Original Peanuts
cartoons, memorabilia. World's largest collection of
Peanuts gifts. Ice arena. **R F P**   **- 50**

👣 *Sonoma*. Walking tour of Plaza. Historic
buildings, mission, fun shops. **R F P**   **- 106**

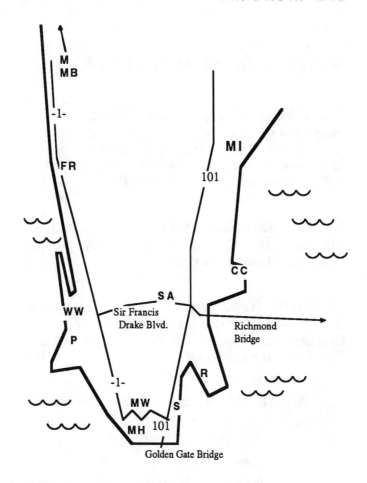

Marin & North Coast

CC	China Camp State Park
FR	Fort Ross State Historic Park
MH	Marin Headlands
MI	Marin Museum of the American Indian
M	Mendocino
MB	Mendocino Botanical Gardens
MW	Muir Woods National Monument
P	Point Reyes National Seashore
R	Richardson Bay Audubon Center
S A	San Anselmo
S	Sausalito
WW	Whale Watching

MARIN & NORTH COAST

△ *China Camp State Park.* Last remnant of Chinese fishing villages that once dotted coast of San Pablo Bay. Small museum. Picnic grounds with water views. Hiking. Birdwatching. **R F** (snack bar open on busy weekends) **P** - **174**

△ *Fort Ross State Historic Park.* Restored wooden fort. One of Russia's early pioneer outposts. Visitor Center. **R** - **176**

🌲 *Marin Headlands.* Explore hiking trails, World War II batteries, lighthouse, beaches. Excellent views of Golden Gate Bridge and San Francisco. **R**(outhouses) **P** - **188**

☼ *Marin Museum of the American Indian.* Diorama, artifacts and informative displays illustrate Miwok culture. **R P** - **90**

👣 *Mendocino.* Walking tour of historic side of Mendocino. Museum. Victorians. Kwan Ti Temple. "Murder, She Wrote" house. **R F P** - **112**

🌷 *Mendocino Coast Botanical Gardens.* More than 3,000 varieties of native and cultivated plants in over 20 plant communities. Hidden pioneer cemetery. Superb views of Pacific. Whale watching in season. **R P** - **148**

MARIN & NORTH COAST (continued)

🌲 *Muir Woods National Monument.*
Walk among the world's tallest living things.
Redwoods, wildflowers, deer. **R F P** **- 190**

🌲 *Point Reyes National Seashore.*
Earthquake Trail along San Andreas Fault.
Wilderness hikes to secluded beaches. Miwok
Indian Village. Historic Lighthouse. **R P** **- 192**

🌲 *Richardson Bay Audubon Center.*
A 900-acre sanctuary, just outside of Tiburon. 1876
restored Victorian. Nature trail. Peak bird migration
is October through April. **P** **- 194**

👣 *San Anselmo.* More than 130 antique
dealers within half a mile. **R F P** **- 108**

👣 *Sausalito.* A sunny getaway just north of
Golden Gate Bridge. Walking tour explores back
roads and historic sites of town. **R F** **- 110**

🐋 *Whale Watching.* The best coastal sites to
watch for whales. Tips on how to locate whales and
why they migrate. Peak season is mid-December
through January and mid-February through May.
R P(depending on site) **- 208**

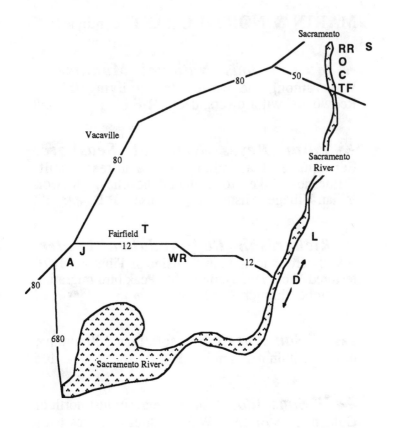

Sacramento & Delta Country

A	Anheuser Busch Beer Brewery
C	Crocker Art Museum
D	Delta Drive
J	Jelly Belly Factory
L	Locke
O	Old Sacramento
RR	California State Railroad Museum
S	Sutter's Fort
TF	Towe Ford Museum
T	Travis Air Force Museum
WR	Western Railway Museum

SACRAMENTO & DELTA COUNTRY

👁 *Anheuser Busch Beer Brewery.*
See how the King of Beers is aged, bottled and packaged in the world's largest brewery. **R P - 22**

☼ *Crocker Art Museum.* Oldest public art museum in the west, housed in a magnificent 1871 mansion. Works by Californian and European masters. **R P**   **- 92**

🪨 *Delta Drive.* An old-fashioned driving tour for a sunny summer afternoon. Free ferry boat rides, houseboats, art deco hotel. **R F P**   **- 216**

👁 *Jelly Belly Factory.* Watch jelly belly jelly beans being created. Free samples on tour. Candy gift shop. **R F**(candy) **P**   **- 24**

👣 *Locke.* Only rural town in U.S. built entirely by Chinese. Gambling house museum. Weathered buildings. Import shops. **R F P**   **- 114**

👣 *Old Sacramento.* Five fun history museums. See $1 million in gold. Send a telegraph to a friend. Visit 1870s railroad depot. **R F - 116**

🚂 *California State Railroad Museum.* Explore above, on board and below 21 beautifully restored locomotives and railroad cars. One of the finest museums of its kind. **R**   **- 52**

SACRAMENTO
& DELTA COUNTRY (continued)

◊ *Sutter's Fort.* Restored, furnished 1846 fort. One of first settlements in California. Exhibit rooms. Sound wand narrates history. **R   - 178**

☼ *Towe Ford Museum.* World's most complete collection of antique Fords. More than 170 cars on display. Near Old Sacramento. **R P   - 94**

🚂 *Travis Air Force Museum.* More than 20 aircraft on display, including helicopters, immense transport planes, bombers and jets. Air Force and NASA exhibits. **R P   - 54**

🚂 *Western Railway Museum.* Ride on an antique trolley car. See antique passenger cars, cabooses, unusual railroad cars. **R P   - 56**

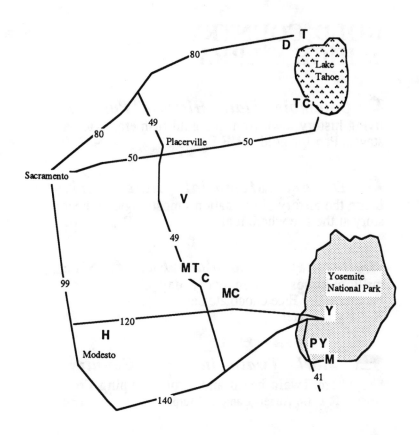

Gold Country & High Sierra

C	Columbia State Historic Park
D	Donner Memorial State Park
H	Hershey's Chocolate Factory
MT	Mark Twain in Gold Country
M	Mariposa Grove of Big Trees
MC	Mercer Caverns
PY	Pioneer Yosemite History Center
TC	Salmon Run, Taylor Creek
T	Truckee
V	Volcano
Y	Yosemite Camera Walk

GOLD COUNTRY
& HIGH SIERRA

🔔 *Columbia State Historic Park.* A living history town from the gold rush era. Ride a stage. Pan for gold. **R F P**   **- 180**

🔔 *Donner Memorial State Park.* Learn the history of our nation's most tragic pioneer story at the site where it all happened. **R P**   **- 182**

👁 *Hershey's Chocolate Factory.* Nine million kisses created every day at this plant. Factory tour. Free chocolate bar.
R P F (chocolate)   **- 26**

🛶 *Mark Twain in Gold Country.* See where Twain heard and wrote Jumping Frog story. **R F** (in Angels Camp & Murphy's) **P**   **- 134**

🌲 *Mariposa Grove of Big Trees.* Walk among world's largest living things. **R P**   **- 200**

🚂 *Mercer Caverns.* Explore nature's underground art in stalagmites, stalactites and "iron flowers." Picnic area. **R F** (snacks) **P**   **- 58**

🔔 *Pioneer Yosemite History Center.* Century-old buildings in village setting. Costumed docents in summer. **P**   **- 184**

GOLD COUNTRY
& HIGH SIERRA (continued)

Salmon Run, Taylor Creek. Nature trails. Underwater view of pond with trout, salmon. Peak salmon run is Oct. **R F P**   **- 220**

Truckee. History of railroad town. Fun shops. **R F P**   **- 118**

Volcano. The gold country town that tourism forgot. **R F P**   **- 120**

Yosemite Camera Walk. Free camera walks, art workshops, more. **R F P**   **- 202**

For Your Information

If you plan to explore one of our regions more in-depth, or extend your day trip for a weekend or longer, the following sources provide information on activities, restaurants, lodging and more—all free for the asking. Just write or call in advance of your trip.

California

California Office of Tourism. 801 K St., Suite 1600, Sacramento 95814-3520, tel. 800/TO-CALIF (for Visitors Guide, map, events calendar or other printed material) or 916/322-2881 (for specific information).

San Francisco

San Francisco Convention and Visitors Bureau. 201 Third St., Suite 900, San Francisco 94103, tel. 415/974-6900.

San Francisco Visitor Information Center. Hallidie Plaza, Lower Level, 900 Market St., Box 429097, San Francisco 94142-9097, tel. 415/391-2000.

Bay Area Rapid Transit (BART). 415/992-BART.

San Francisco Municipal Railway System (MUNI). 415/673-MUNI.

Peninsula

Half Moon Bay/Coastside Chamber of Commerce. 520 Kelly Ave., Half Moon Bay 94019, tel. 415/726-5202 or 415/726-8380.

San Jose Visitor Information Center. McEnery Convention Center Lobby, 150 W. San Carlos St., San Jose 95110, tel. 800/SAN-JOSE ext. 141 or 408/283-8833.

Saratoga Chamber of Commerce. 20460 Saratoga-Los Gatos Rd., Saratoga 95070, tel. 408/867-0753.

Monterey & Environs

Carmel Valley Chamber of Commerce. 71 W. Carmel Valley Rd., Suite 206, Box 288, Carmel Valley 93924, tel. 800/543-8343 or 408/659-4000.

Gilroy Visitors Bureau. 7780 Monterey St., Gilroy 95020, tel. 408/842-6436.

Monterey Peninsula Visitors and Convention Bureau. 380 Alvarado St., Box 1770, Monterey 93942, tel. 408/649-1770.

Pacific Grove Chamber of Commerce. Forest and Central Avenues, Box 167, Pacific Grove 93950, tel. 408/373-3304.

San Juan Bautista Chamber of Commerce. 402A Third St., Box 1037, San Juan Bautista 95045, tel. 408/623-2454.

Santa Cruz County Conference and Visitors Council. 701 Front St., Santa Cruz 95060, tel. 800/833-3494 or 408/425-1234.

East Bay

Benicia Chamber of Commerce. 601 First St., Benicia 94510, tel. 707/745-2120.

Berkeley Convention and Visitors Bureau. 1834 University Ave., 1st Flr., Berkeley 94703, tel. 800/847-4823 or 510/549-7040.

Martinez Area Chamber of Commerce. 620 Las Juntas St., Martinez 94553, tel. 510/228-2345.

Oakland Convention & Visitors Bureau. 1000 Broadway, Suite 200, Oakland 94607, tel. 800/2-OAKLAND or 510/839-9000.

Walnut Creek Chamber of Commerce. 1501 N. Broadway, #110, Walnut Creek 94596, tel. 510/934-2007.

Sonoma

Petaluma Area Chamber of Commerce. 779 Baywood Dr., Suite 3, Petaluma 94954, tel. 707/762-2785.

Russian River Chamber of Commerce. 16200 First St., Box 331, Guerneville 95446, tel. 707/869-9000.

Sonoma County Convention and Visitors Bureau. 5000 Roberts Lake Rd., Suite A, Rohnert Park 94928, tel. 800/326-7666 or 707/586-8100.

Sonoma Valley Visitors Bureau. 453 First Street East (on the Plaza), Sonoma 95476, tel. 707/996-1090.

Sonoma County Farm Trails. Send self-addressed, stamped envelope with 52 cents postage for area map of locally owned farm stands and tree farms. Box 6032, Santa Rosa 95406, tel. 707/996-2154.

Marin & North Coast

Fort Bragg-Mendocino Coast Chamber of Commerce. 332 N. Main St., Fort Bragg 95437, tel. 800/726-2780 or 707/961-6300.

Marin County Chamber of Commerce and Visitors Bureau. 30 N. San Pedro Rd., Suite 150, San Rafael 94903, tel. 415/472-7470.

Redwood Empire Association. 785 Market St., 15th Flr, San Francisco 94103-2022, tel. 415/543-8334. (Visitor information for entire North Coast region; $3 postage and handling for their 48-page guide.)

San Anselmo Chamber of Commerce. Box 2844, San Anselmo 94979, tel. 415/454-2510.

Sausalito Chamber of Commerce. 333 Caledonia St., Box 566, Sausalito 94966, tel. 415/332-0505.

West Marin Chamber of Commerce. 11431 State Route 1, The Creamery Building, #15, Point Reyes Station 94956, tel. 415/663-9232.

West Marin Network. (lodging information) Box 834, Point Reyes Station 94956, tel. 415/663-9543.

Golden Gate Ferry. Crosses bay from Ferry Building in San Francisco to Sausalito, tel. 415/332-6600.

Red and White Fleet. From San Francisco's Pier 43½ at Fisherman's Wharf to Sausalito and Tiburon, tel. 415/546-2700.

Sacramento

Sacramento Convention & Visitors Bureau. 1421 K St., Sacramento 95814, tel. 916/264-7777.

Sacramento Visitor Information Center. 1104 Front St., Old Sacramento 95814, tel. 916/442-7644.

Gold Country & High Sierra

Amador County Chamber of Commerce. 125 Peck St., Jackson 95642, tel. 800/649-4988 or 209/223-0350.

Calaveras County Lodging and Visitors Center. 1211 S. Main St., Box 637, Angels Camp 95222, Tel. 800/225-3764 or 209/736-0049.

Lake Tahoe Visitors Authority. 1156 Ski Run Blvd., South Lake Tahoe 96150, tel. 800/AT-TAHOE or 916/544-5050.

Tahoe North Visitors and Convention Bureau. 950 N. Lake Blvd., Suite 3, Box 5578, Tahoe City 96145, tel. 800/824-6348 or 916/583-3494.

Truckee-Donner Chamber of Commerce and Visitors Bureau. 12036 Donner Pass Rd., Box 2757, Truckee 96160, tel. 800/548-8388 or 916/587-2757.

National Park Service Information Office. Box 577, Yosemite National Park 95389, tel. 209/372-0265 Mon.-Fri. 9-5; 209/372-0200 (24-hour recording with touch-tone connection to recorded information, including road conditions and weather).

Yosemite Concessions Services Corporation. For lodging reservations in the park. Yosemite National Park 95389, tel. 209/252-4848.

MISTIX. For Yosemite camping reservations. Tel. 800/365-2267.

Index

Page references in italics refer to entries in the Where It's At and For Your Information chapters

Academy of Sciences 30-31,*226*
Acres of Orchids 8-9,*230*
Airplanes 54-55
Alcatraz 152-3,*226*
Amador County Information *254*
Angels Camp 134-5
Anheuser Busch Brewery 22-23,*245*
Ansel Adams 77,202
Anti-aircraft gun (Iraqi) 54
Antioch 213,216
Antique Amusements 36
Antique Cable Cars 33
Antique Cars 34,82-83,94-95,163
Antique Trolley and Railway Cars 56-57
Antiques 105,107,108-9,115,215
Aquariums 12-13,30,47
Ardenwood Historic Farm 164-5,*236*
Art Classes 203
Art Galleries/Studios 16-17, 75,99
Asian Art Museum 62-63, 226
Atomic Bomb 54

Balclutha 35
Barbie Doll Hall of Fame 38-39,*230*
BART (Bay Area Rapid Transit) *250*
Beaches 48,99,174,189, 193,216,219
Bear Flag Revolt 106,173
Beer Tasting 22-23

Behring Auto & UC Berkeley Museums 82-83,*236*
Benicia 16-17,104-5,*236* *252*
Berkeley 19,45,49, 85,145,*252*
Bicycle Design 41
Bicycling 163,214
Bird Watching 174,193, 194,214-5
Birds, gifts and books on 195
Black Diamond Mines 212
Blackhawk 83
Blue Whale 12
Boating and Sailing 214
Bobcat 46
Bocce, Baseball & Birdwatching 214-5,*236*
Brannan Island State Rec Area 216
Briones Regional Park 212-3

C.A. Thayer 34
Cable Car Barn Museum 32-33,*226*
Calaveras County Information *254*
California Cooperative Creamery 20-21,*240*
California Office of Tourism *250*
California State Railroad Museum 52-53,*245*
Camron-Stanford House 166-7,*236*
Carmel 125,161,199,*251*
Carmel Mission 160-161,*233*
Carousels 49

Caves 58-59,197
Central Pacific Railroad
    Depot 53, 116
Cheesemaking 20-21
China Camp State Park
174-5,*242*
Chinatown 65
Chinese Historical Society
64-65,*226*
Chinese in CA 52,64-65,
75,114-5,119,174-5
Cliff House 37
Coit Tower 66-67,*226*
Columbia State Historic Park
180-181,*248*
Commemorative Medals 76
Computer , designing on 40
Conservatory 138
Crocker Art Museum 92-93,
245
Custom House 102

Danville 127
de Young Museum 68-69,
226
Delta Drive 216-217,*245*
Designing Bicycles 41
Dinosaur 31
Dolls 38-39
Dolphins 12-13,30
Donner Memorial State Park
182-3,*248*
Dreyer's Ice Cream 14-15,
236

Earthquake 7,30,76,79,
128,154,192-3
East Bay Parks 212-3,*236*
Egyptian Tombs 80
Eugene O'Neill's Tao House
126-7,*237*
Eureka Ferry Ship 34
Evolution Exhibit 31
Explorer Packs 203

Factory Tours 5,8,14-15,
20-27

Fairfield 23,25,55
Farm Trails, Sonoma *252*
Ferries, Delta 217
Festivals 98,100
Films 53,55,86,88
Fish Roundabout 30
Fishing Piers 213,215
Fords, vintage 94-95
Forestville 147
Fort Bragg 149,*253*
Fort Mason Ethnic Museums
70-71,*227*
Fort Ross State Historic Park
176-7,*242*
Fremont 165

Garden Stores 9,11,143,147,
148,210
Gardenia 8
Gardening Advice 11,143
Gardens/Greenhouses 8,9,11,
48,100,158,210-1 see also
    Gardens Chapter
Garlic 100
Genealogical Library 87
Gift Shops see also Garden
    Stores
        Anheuser-Busch 22
        City Store (San Jose) 157
        Coins & Medals 76
        Creamery 20-21
        Glassware 16-17
        Hershey's 26
        Jelly Belly 25
        Museum 41,70,84
        Nature Lovers 195
        Peanuts 50-51
        Sunset Magazine 11
        Toys 49
        Winery 107
Gilroy & Environs 100-101,
197,*233*,*251*
Glass Blowers of Benicia 16-
17,*237*
Glen Ellen 133
Gloria Ferrer Champagne Caves
206-7,*240*

Gold Panning 116-7,181
Gold Rush 6-7,120,134,
155,156,180
Golden Gate Ferry *253*
Golden Gate National
    Recreation Area 188
Golden Gate Park 30,62,69,
138,210
Goldsmith Seeds 100
Grand Island 217
Guided Tours see also
    Factory Tours &
    Walking Tours
        Alcatraz 153
        Caverns 58-59
        Champagne Winery 206
        Churches 86-87,105
        Gardens 142,211
        Houses 73,125,127
        Magazine 10-11
        Mystery Spot 42-43
        Nursery 8-9
        Old Mint 77

Haas-Lilienthal House
72-73,*227*
Haight Ashbury 6
Hakone Gardens 140-1,*230*
Half Moon Bay 98-99,
230,251
Harvesting Wheat 165
Heinhold's Saloon 128-9,
237
Herman Goelitz Company
24
Hershey Chocolate Factory
26-27,*248*
Hiking 49,163,174,185,188,
190,193,197,199,212-3,220
Hill, Thomas 10
Historic Ships 34-35
Horseback Riding 163
Hostels 189
Hyde Street Pier 34-35,*227*

Ice cream 14-15
Ice Skating 50

Italians in CA 70,75

Jack London State Historic
Park 132-133,*240*
Japanese Friendship Garden
158
Japanese Tea House & The
    Conservatory 138-9,*227*
Jeffers, Robinson 124-5
Jelly Belly Factory 24-25,*245*
Jenner 177
Joaquin Miller Park 87
John Muir Historic Site
130-1,*237*
Judah L. Magnes Museum
84-85,*237*
Judaica Library 84
Junior & Senior Rangers 203

Kasaya Pomo 176
Koi/Carp 138,140

Laboratories 5,9,12-13
Lawrence Hall of Science 44-
45,*237*
Levi Strauss 4,*227*
Levi's 4-5
Lighthouses 189,193,209
Lindsay Museum 46-47,*237*
Little Farm 49
Locke 114-115,217,*245*
London, Jack 105,128-9,132-3
Long Marine Laboratory 12-
13,*233*
Luther Burbank & California
    Carnivores 146-7,*240*

Maharajah's car 83
Marin County Information *253*
Marin Headlands 188,*242*
Marin Museum of the
American Indian 90-91,*242*
Marine Mammal Center 189
Mariposa Grove of Big Trees
200-201,*248*
Maritime Store 35

Mark Twain in Gold Country
134-135,*248*
Market Street, Historic,
    San Francisco 6
Martinez 131,215,*252*
Martinez Adobe 131
Martinez Regional Shoreline
214-215
Memorial Church 79
Mendocino 112-3,148,
242,253
Mendocino Botanical Gardens
148-9,*242*
Menlo Park 11
Mercer Caverns 58-59,*248*
Mission San Francisco de
    Asis 154-5,*227*
Missions 101,106,154-5,
160-1
MISTIX *254*
Miwok Indian Village
90,193
Monarch Butterflies 218-9,
233
Monterey 102-3,*233,251*
Mormon Temple 86-87,*238*
Muir Woods National
Monument 190-191,*243*
Muir, John 130-1,184,191
MUNI (Buses) *250*
Murals 66-7,79,171
Murphy's 59,135
Musée Mécanique and
    Cliff House 36-37,*228*
Museum Tours 35,68,77,79
Museums
        African American 70
        American Indian 90-91
        Art 62-63,68-69,83,
        88-89,92-93
        Auto 82-83,94-95
        Balclutha 35
        Barbie Doll 38-39
        Cable Car 32
        Camel Barn 105
        Chinese 64,75
        Computer 40-41

Museums, cont.
        Constitutional 103
        Craft & Folk Art 70
        Egyptian 80-81
        Ethnic 70-71,75
        Gold Rush 181
        Historical 88-89,112,
        114-5,116-7,155,158-9,
        168,174,198
        Italian 70,75
        Jack London 132-3
        Jewish 84-85
        Marine Lab 12
        Maritime 103
        Mechanical 36-37
        Mexican 71
        Military 54
        Natural History 30,46,
        83,88,113
        Old Mint 77
        Photography 77
        Railroad & Railway
        52-53,56-57
        Technology 40-41
        Treasure Island 170
Mystery Spot 42-43,*233*

Natural Bridges 12,218-219
Nature Trails 195,196,220
Nelson, Baby Face 110,119
NIKE Missile Site 188
North Beach 66,74-75,*228*
Nourot Glass 16-17
Novato 91

O'Neill, Eugene 126-127
Oakdale 27
Oakland 87,89,129,167,*252*
Oakland Museum of California
88-89,*238*
Old Mint and Ansel Adams
    Center 76-77,*228*
Old Sacramento 116-7,*245*
Opossum 47
Orchids 8-9,
Otters 12,176,199
Outlet Stores 101,118

Pacific Grove *251*
Pacific Heights 6
Palo Alto 39
Pampanito 35
Peanuts Cartoon 50
Peralta Adobe & Fallon
   House 156-7,*230*
Pescadero 209
Petaluma 21,173,*252*
Petaluma Adobe 172-3,*240*
Pigeon Point 209
Pinnacles National Monu
   ment 101,196-7,*233*
Pioneer Yosemite History
   Center 184-5,*248*
Planetarium 45,81
Point Lobos State Reserve
198-9,*233*
Point Montara 209
Point Pinole Regional Park
213
Point Reyes National
   Seashore 192-3,*243*
Pony Express 7, 105
Pumpkins 98

Railroad Bookstore 57
Railroad/Railway 52-53,56-
57,116
Red & White Fleet *253*
Redwood Empire *253*
Redwoods 190-191
Richardson Bay Audubon
Center 194-5,*243*
Robinson Jeffers' Tor House
124-5,*233*
Rock Climbing 196-197
Rodin Sculpture Garden 78-
79,*230*
Rosicrucian Egyptian
Museum 80-81,*230*
Russian River *252*
Russians in CA 176-177

Sacramento 53,93,95,117,
179,*253*
Sailing ships 6,34-35,71

Sake 18-19
Salmon Run, Taylor Creek
220-1,*248*
San Andreas Fault 192
San Anselmo 108-9,*243,253*
San Francisco 5,7,31,33,35,37,
63,65,67,69,71,73,75,77,139,
155,211,*250*
San Francisco City Hall 6
San Francisco Theological 109
San Jose 41,81,157,159,*251*
San Jose Historical Museum
158-9,*231*
San Juan Bautista 101,*251*
Santa Cruz 13,43,163,219,*251*
Santa Rosa 51,147
Saratoga 141,143,*251*
Saso Herb Gardens 142-3,*231*
Sausalito 110-1,*243,253*
Schulz, Charles 50
Sculpture 78-79
Sea Lions 12-13,37,189,199
Seals 13,31,189,199
Sequoias 200-201
Serra, Fr. Junipero 102,154,
160
Shadelands Ranch 168-9,*238*
Sharks 30
Shopping see Antiques, Garden
   Stores, Gift Stores, Outlets
Showrooms, Glass 16-17
Smyers' Glass 16-17
Snakes 46
Snoopy and Skating 50-51,*240*
Sonoma 106-107,207,*252*
Sonoma Plaza 106-107,*240*
South Lake Tahoe 221
South San Francisco 9
Spacecraft 54
St. Paul's Episcopal Church
104-5
Stagecoach Rides 181
Stanford University 78-79
State Capitol, Benicia 104
State Historical Parks
101,104,106,132,176,178
Steam Train 48

Steinhart Aquarium 30-31
Stevenson, Robert Louis
6-7,128
Storytellers 63,71
Strybing Arboretum 210-1,
228
Sunset Magazine 10-11,*231*
Sutro Baths 37
Sutter's Fort 178-9,*246*
Sutter, John 105,177,178-9

Tahoe Area Information *254*
Takara Sake 18-19,*238*
Tea House 138
The Tech Museum of
   Innovation 40-41,*230*
Tiburon 195
Tiger-hunting Car 83
Tilden Regional Park 48-49,
238
Tomales Bay 10
Towe Ford Museum 94-95,
246
Travis Air Force Museum
54-55,*246*
Treasure Island 170-1,*238*
Trolley Rides 56
Truckee 118-9,183,*248,254*
Twain, Mark 6-7,135-135

UC Berkeley 45,83,145
UC Berkeley Botanical
   Garden 144-5,*238*
Underwater Reserve 198
Union City 15

Vallejo, Mariano 106,172-3
Victorian Farm 162,164-5
Victorian Homes 72-73,92,
104,112,130,156-7,166-7, 194
Videos 20,25,32,82
Volcano 120-1,*248*

Walking Tours, Guided
6-7,*228*
Walking Tours, Self-guided
74-75,102,108,110,113,118
Walnut Creek 47,169,*252*
Walnut Grove 217
Washington Square 74
Wawona 185
Western Railway Museum
56-57,*246*
Whale Watching 208-9,*243*
Wilder Ranch State Park
162-3,*233*
Wineries 99,100,107,147,
206-7
World War II 4,35,54,
95,188,199

Yosemite 26,77,184-5,
200-1,202-3,*254*
Yosemite Camera Walk
202-3,*248*
Yuba Arts Glass 16

Zellique Art Glass 16-17

The Perfect Gift

San Francisco & Beyond:

101 Affordable Excursions

The perfect gift for anyone living in or visiting northern California. Your friends and family will have fun with it year-round and enjoy it as a keepsake of their excursions. Show appreciation for co-workers, volunteers, clients or teachers with a copy. If you borrowed this book, reward yourself with "the Bay Area's best-loved guidebook!"

Mail this order form to: Travel for Less Press
209 Apollo Dr., # 5
Hercules, CA 94547

San Francisco and Beyond:
101 Affordable Excursions @ $10.95 each   = _____

Sales Tax: Calif. residents add $.90 per book   = _____

Postage, handling & packaging:
Add $2 per book ($5 maximum)   = _____

                                        Total   = _____

Please include a check or money order payable to Travel for Less Press.

Your name: _____

Your telephone #: _____

Ship to name and address:_____

_____

City,State,Zip: _____

Call (510) 741-8440 for phone orders
or for information on quantity discounts.

About the Author

Pamela P. Hegarty has published more than 250 northern California travel articles. She writes for *Good Housekeeping, Woman's Day, McCall's, San Francisco Focus, California Highways, Tours & Resorts, Golden State* and *Country Inns*. She is author of *Best Places to Kiss in Northern California* and *Best Places to Kiss in New England*. Her work has appeared in seven *Fodor's* guidebooks, including *National Parks of the West , California* and others focusing on our state. Her stories have appeared in the *San Jose Mercury News, Contra Costa Times, Santa Rosa Press Democrat, Stockton Record, Boston Herald, New York Newsday, San Francisco Examiner* and more.